LITERARY LODGINGS

Elaine Borish, an American living in London, was born in New York City. She holds degrees from Rutgers, Boston University, and Northeastern University and has taught at universities in New England. As a resident of old England, she has lectured in English and American literature at Morley College in London. She has published several books including *A Legacy of Names* as well as numerous articles in leading newspapers and magazines.

Elaine Borish

LITERARY LODGINGS

12/18/98

For Barbara!
With all our
best wishes
Your English Colleagues

Fidelio Press

Boulder • London

Published by
Fidelio Press
61 Pine Tree Lane
Boulder, Colorado 80304

Copyright © 1995 by Elaine Borish

Library of Congress Catalog Card Number: 95-60775

ISBN 0-9524881-0-8

Printing History

   1st Edition-- 1984
   Published by Constable and Company, London, England

   2nd Edition-- 1995

Printed in the United States of America.

Cover illustration and design by Allee Trendall

CONTENTS

LONDON

THAMES & CHILTERNS

THE SOUTH-EAST and SOUTH

THE WEST COUNTRY

WALES

THE MIDLANDS

ILLUSTRATIONS

Note: The following portraits are published by kind permission of the National Portrait Gallery, London: Arnold Bennett, Oscar Wilde, Rudyard Kipling, Rebecca West, H. G. Wells, T. S. Eliot, Vita Sackville-West, John Keats, Edward Lear, J.M. Barrie, Alfred Lord Tennyson, Virginia Woolf, Benjamin Disraeli, Siegfried Sassoon, Lewis Carroll, A. E. Housman, Nöel Coward, J. B. Priestley, Thomas De Quincey, John Galsworthy, Charles Dickens, Wilkie Collins, Beatrix Potter, and Dorothy L. Sayers.

The portrait of Mark Twain is published by courtesy of Mark Twain Home Foundation, Hannibal, Missouri.

To the wonderful person who shared the work
and the fun in the making of this book —
to my husband

PREFACE

People have always been fascinated with places associated with authors, and the literary pilgrimage has long been accepted as a good excuse for travel. What better way to worship at the shrine of a beloved or respected author than to visit the actual location which was once part of the writer's life and is perhaps reflected in the books?

A journey to the haunts of a favorite author can only deepen love and understanding and result in a thrilling emotional experience. Seeing the plaque that marks the house in which Charles Dickens was born, the landscape that inspired Wordsworth, or the writing-box used by Jane Austen—all of these give great pleasure and satisfaction to untold numbers.

But how these delights increase when the traveler is able to *stay* in the place where a favorite author once lived! When the traveler can dine and lodge in the very house in which the author once dined and lodged and acquire an intimacy not otherwise available, what ineffable joy may result!

Fortunately, writers also traveled and often wrote their immortal lines in inns or lodgings that continue to excite, sometimes only because of the literary connection. Or perhaps the home in which the writer once lived changed hands over the years to become a hotel. As a hotel guest, the literary pilgrim is able to revel in the author's own past surroundings.

Unfortunately, writers did not always oblige by selecting in their travels places destined to remain intact for future generations. They may have stayed in inns which have fallen victim to the ravages of time, or they may have stayed with friends, or taken furnished rooms to frustrate or deprive devoted followers.

Sometimes the hotel in question may have reverted to a private house—like the Lob's Wood Hotel in Surrey which was once the home of J. M. Barrie, its magical woods and nearby lake his Never-Never Land. Or like the King's Arms in Kenilworth where Sir Walter Scott stayed while collecting material for his novel, *Kenilworth,* but which recently ceased to offer lodgings and now functions merely as a pub.

Only buildings that once housed writers and exist today as hotels are included in this book. The rule for *Literary Lodgings* is that the hotel in Britain associated with an author must be alive, the author not.

Because the presence of certain former clients will nourish the prestige of hotels, hotels take pride in the association. Often they are so eager to be identified with a celebrity that they make inaccurate claims with a "Queen Elizabeth slept here" syndrome. Worse yet, they make research more difficult.

Although Jane Austen never journeyed north of the Trent, a charming little inn in Derbyshire boasts of her presence there. Simply because they are located on a river, several hotels elect Izaak Walton as a former guest. Claims for Dr. Johnson and Charlotte Brontë are numerous and difficult to substantiate. And so it goes on.

The visitor approaching the stately historic house of an author, or envisioning a grand architectural facade with columned portico and steps flanked by royal beasts, may well wonder precisely what lines were written between the lions. Even when the building under consideration is a country cottage or a big city hotel, questions arise: What were the circumstances which brought the writer to this place? When? How was the writer influenced by it? What books emanated there? What are the relevant facts in the particular period of the author's life? What is the hotel like today? Is it worth a visit?

Here is an invitation to pleasurable holidays. Satisfaction awaits the follower who adapts the words of the Biblical Ruth: for whither thou goest, I will go; and where thou hast lodged, I will lodge.

ARNOLD BENNETT

at

The Savoy
London WC2

In the facade a few windows burned here
and there, somehow mournfully. He knew
the exact number of guests staying in the
hotel that night; but their secrets, misfortunes, anxieties, hopes, despairs, tragedies,
he did not know. And he would have liked
to know every one of them.

—*Imperial Palace*

In a corner of North Staffordshire, in the valley of the River Trent,
lies a chain of six towns called "the Potteries": Tunstall, Burslem,
Hanley, Stoke-upon-Trent, Fenton, and Longton. This industrial
conglomeration, the only region in England named for the work
that is done there, was incorporated in 1910 as the city of Stoke-
on-Trent and known familiarly as Stoke. Bottle-shaped kilns once
blackened the area as they did their coal firing to produce pottery
and porcelain known by such names as Wedgwood, Spode, Royal
Doulton, and Copeland.

Enoch Arnold Bennett first saw the smoke of Stoke from Hanley
where he was born on 27 May 1867, the eldest of six children. But
he is associated with a house in Waterloo Road (Trafalgar Road in
his novels) in Burslem (Bursley) in which he grew up. At twenty-
one he managed to escape from the restrictions of his provincial

life and from his father's autocratic rule by obtaining work in London as a shorthand clerk for a firm of solicitors.

He dabbled in freelance journalism and won a writing competition which encouraged him to consider a change in career. He left the law firm in 1894 and went to work for *Woman* writing articles and reviews. A few years later, he became assistant editor and then editor of that weekly magazine, and at thirty-one he was ready to try to earn his living by writing fiction.

His first novel, *A Man from the North* (1890), is about a man who comes to London from the Potteries, works in a lawyer's office, writes articles, and tries to produce a novel. The autobiographical elements are recognizable but, unlike his fictional hero who failed in his ambition to become a writer, Arnold Bennett achieved success as an author upon publication of this book.

The great breakthrough came with his discovery that he could use the familiar background of his youth for fiction. *Anna of the Five Towns* was his first novel set in the Potteries. He recreated the region he knew, giving artistic order to the shapeless sprawl of towns. He made six equal five by eliminating Fenton and calling the area the Five Towns, a name that has caught on in a world he has immortalized. He captured the essence of life in the Potteries in such collections of short stories as *The Grim Smile of the Five Towns* and *The Matador of the Five Towns* and in such novels as *The Card*, *The Old Wives' Tale*, and the Clayhanger trilogy (*Clayhanger, Hilda Lessways*, and *These Twain*). He also captured triumphant success as a novelist.

A hard worker, he knew how to live well with the money he earned. After he had finished writing his first novel, he made his first trip abroad, to Belgium. He loved foreign travel and made a visit to Paris the following year. In later years, he fulfilled his dream of owning a yacht.

Paris had enormous appeal for him and, at the age of thirty-five, after publication of *Anna of the Five Towns*, he decided to live in the capital of modern realism. In Paris, in 1907, he married a Frenchwoman, Marguerite Soulie. He continued to plunge himself into his work, and the books he produced include *The Old Wives' Tale*, regarded as his masterpiece. When he returned to settle in

Arnold Bennett
(1867-1931) and
The Savoy Hotel,
London, on which
he based his novel,
Imperial Palace

England, where he bought a country house in Essex in 1913, his reputation was made.

These Twain (1916) was the last of the Potteries novels. He became active in the London theatre and wrote plays, sometimes in collaboration, and he wrote stage adaptations of his own works. He gradually spent more and more time in London, occasionally staying at the Savoy, and eventually left his country house. With a flat in London, he made the city his home as well as his subject.

Shortly after his marriage ended in 1921 by a deed of separation, he met and fell in love with Dorothy Cheston, an extremely attractive actress who was appearing in the Liverpool production of his play, *Body and Soul*. Marguerite refused to grant a divorce, but he was to spend his remaining years with Dorothy. His first and only child, a daughter, was born in 1926.

Despite his love for travel, Bennett was not a wise traveler. On his last visit to France, in December 1930, he drank tap water in his room and was reproached by Dorothy. In their Paris hotel restaurant, he drank carafe water and was reproached by the waiter. Back in London he forced himself to work on *Dream of Destiny* although he was feeling unwell. In February his illness was diagnosed as typhoid. As his condition worsened and he lay ill in a semi-conscious or semi-delirious state, straw was spread on the busy streets outside his flat over Baker Street station to diminish the noise of the traffic. The life of the man from the north ended on 26 March 1931.

Tributes flowed in from the anxious world which had watched. Even Virginia Woolf, who attacked him in *Mr. Bennett and Mrs. Brown* for being preoccupied with externals, wrote these moving words in her diary: "Arnold Bennett died last night, which leaves me sadder than I should have supposed. A lovable genuine man .... Some real understanding power, as well as a gigantic absorbing power .... Queer how one regrets the dispersal of anybody who seemed—as I say—genuine; who had direct contact with life—for he abused me; and I yet rather wished him to go on abusing me; and me abusing him."

He was a generous and beloved person. Somerset Maugham said, "It was impossible to know him without liking him." H.G.

Wells wrote that he "radiated and evoked affection to an unusual degree." Rebecca West declared, "London will not seem quite London without his flamboyant figure."

As a novelist he is well remembered, not only as a regional writer of the Potteries, but as a writer who could turn his pen to any place or subject. Two of his finest later novels take place in London—*Riceyman Steps* (1923) and *Imperial Palace* (1930).

Imperial Palace, his last and longest novel, immortalizes the Savoy in its detailed study of every aspect of the running of a great hotel. Bennett placed his fictional hotel next to St. James's Park rather than in the Strand alongside the Thames, and he always maintained that it was not the Savoy. Nevertheless, the Imperial Palace is indistinguishable from the Savoy.

Perhaps because of his own deprived and provincial background, perhaps because of his addiction to travel, Bennett was fascinated by hotels. He had used the luxury hotel theme in an early novel, *The Grand Babylon Hotel* (1902), and references to hotels appear throughout his novels. A character exclaims in *Hilda Lessways*, "Hotels! There'll be more money and more fun to be got out of Hotels soon than of any other kind of enterprise in the world!"

Bennett felt compelled to return to the intriguing subject in his final work. He wrote in his journal on 25 September 1929: "The big *hotel de luxe* is a very serious organization; it is in my opinion a unique subject for a serious novel; it is stuffed with human nature of extremely various kinds. The subject is characteristic of the age; it is as modern as the morning's milk; it is tremendous, and worthy of tremendous handling. I dare say it's beyond me."

In preparation for the novel he had lunch, in March 1927, with the publicity director of the Savoy, who gave him an abundance of ideas. He had frequent meetings with the managing director, George Reeves-Smith, to whom he dedicated his novel, "from one of the warmest of his admirers." The original manuscript is now among the hotel's private treasures.

Bennett stayed at the Savoy while accumulating the facts and minute details on the organization and running of a gigantic luxury hotel, the finest in the world. The officials co-operated with him in every way. In a letter of 15 September 1929 from the Savoy to his nephew he wrote: "I am now staying here. I am collecting hotel-material for my novel, and I never had such material. . . . Hard work collecting it; but everything is open to me and everybody at my disposition. I visited the laundry the other day. . . ."

Bennett takes the reader into laundries and kitchens and cellars. He calls one chapter "Bowels of the Hotel" and gives this view of the kitchens: "The kitchens of the Imperial Palace restaurant were on the same floor as the restaurant itself, and immediately adjoining it. You passed through an open door, hidden like a guilty secret from all the dining-tables, then up a very short corridor, and at one step you were in another and a different world: a super-heated world of steel glistening and dull, and bare wood, and food in mass raw and cooked, and bustle, and hurrying to and fro, and running to and fro, and calling and even raucous shouting in French and Italian: a world of frenzied industry. . . ."

With such outpouring of the details of hotel business, readers may expect to be bored. They are not. The details go on and on, but interest rarely wanes as Bennett goes behind the scenes and through the keyholes.

Out of a cast of eighty-five, there are three central characters: Evelyn Orcham, the talented managing directer who has made the Imperial Palace first among luxury hotels of the world; Violet Powler, who rises from a post in the laundry to head housekeeper; and Gracie Savott, wealthy daughter of millionaire financier, Sir Henry Savott, who schemes to negotiate a merger of the hotel. But the character of the hotel is central to the novel.

As for the plot, with a quarter of a million words in the novel, the action could be summarized in about a dozen: It is about the proposed merger by which Savott gets control of the "unique hotel." But Bennett communicates his fascination as he presents a study of humanity in the milieu of a hotel.

But what a hotel! The history of the Savoy begins in 1246 when Henry III presented to Queen Eleanor's Uncle Peter, Count of Savoy, a parcel of land between London and Westminster on which he built a splendid palace. It was eventually destroyed; but the site was destined to contain, some six hundred and fifty years later, another kind of dazzling palace—a great luxury hotel called the

Savoy. A gilt statue of Count Peter now has a prominent position over the span in the Strand courtyard entrance to the Savoy.

In the forecourt of the hotel is the famous Savoy Theatre, associated with Richard D'Oyly Carte, the impresario who inspired the Gilbert and Sullivan partnership and built the theatre as a home for their highly successful operettas. The Savoy Theatre, the first in the world to have electric lights, opened with *Patience* in October 1881. To keep the theatre entrance free from the clutter of waiting vehicles, the forecourt exists as the only thoroughfare in England in which traffic keeps to the right. Three years after being severely damaged by fire in 1990, the theatre was restored and reopened with a swimming pool on its roof.

Richard D'Oyly Carte saw the advantage of having a fashionable hotel adjacent to his theatre and began construction in 1884. Five years later, the seven-story, steel-framed building, which used concrete for the first time, was completed. Though only half the size it is now, perhaps its most startling feature was the existence of a huge number of bathrooms—seventy. (A recently-opened rival hotel boasted four bathrooms for its five hundred guests.)

The Savoy was the epitome of luxury. D'Oyly Carte secured the services of the best available people in the world to look after the cuisine and management—Auguste Escoffier and César Ritz. The hotel glittered with royalty and with society personalities. The legend had begun; the legend continues, even as the hotel passes its centenary.

Step through the revolving doors and you are in a jewelled city. The large pillared lobby with reception and service areas offers choices that lead to the famous Grill Room, or to the American Bar and Shopping Arcade, to the Drawing Room or lifts. Or straight ahead to the sumptuously-decorated Thames foyer with white piano contained within a gazebo—a divine setting for afternoon tea with musical accompaniment—and beyond it is the River Restaurant with a glorious view across the Thames.

Equally and predictably luxurious are the guest rooms with their individual and antique furnishings. Suites consisting of bedroom and sitting room overlook the River Thames, which adds a breathtaking view to impeccable service.

7

Always attentive to pleasing guests, the hotel has even made culinary history. Once, after a theatrical first night, the chef of the Savoy created for Arnold Bennett, a recherché dish known as Omelette Arnold Bennett, a large open omelette made with smoked haddock. So the well-known and well-liked novelist, one of the few non-opera singers to be commemorated by a special dish, is well-remembered at the Savoy; his name may be sought on the menu between the Soufflé Tetrazzini and Péche Melba (which also had their debuts here). And the distinguished Savoy, in turn, has the distinction of being the setting and subject of a novel by an equally distinguished author.

THE SAVOY
The Strand
London WC2R 0EU

Telephone: (0171) 836 4343   Fax: (0171) 240 6040

200 Rooms (55 single, 85 twin, 10 double, 48 suites) with individual and antique furnishings, the most desirable rooms having panoramic Thames River views.

The spacious lobby leads to the Thames Foyer where harp or piano music accompanies afternoon tea, the American Bar for a cacophony of cocktails, English drawing room for a peaceful retreat, coffee shop open noon to midnight, and two restaurants—the posh River Restaurant and the handsome and historic Savoy Grill Room.

In the street leading to the Savoy's entrance (the only street in London where traffic drives on the right) is the historic Savoy Theatre, rebuilt with an Arts Deco interior after a disastrous fire largely destroyed it in 1990.

A Fitness Gallery above the Savoy Theatre features a rooftop swimming pool, with daylight filtering down through the atrium.

Standing on a bend of the River Thames, the hotel offers superb views towards St. Paul's Cathedral in one direction and towards the Houses of Parliament in another. Nearby are Victoria Embankment Gardens with a green walk alongside the river. Also nearby is Covent Garden, and a short walk along the Strand leads into Trafalgar Square and the National Gallery.

Charing Cross is the nearest tube station and British Rail Main Line Station.

OSCAR WILDE

at

The Cadogan Hotel
London SW1

Each narrow cell in which we dwell
Is a foul and dark latrine,
And the fetid breath of living Death
Chokes up each grated screen,
And all, but Lust, is turned to Dust
In Humanity's machine.

--The Ballad of Reading Gaol

A negative literary tour of England might include the London street where Dryden was beaten up and left for dead, or the River Ouse where Virginia Woolf drowned herself, or the church of Framlingham in Suffolk where the poet Surrey lies buried having been beheaded after conviction on a charge of high treason, or the site of the jail in Bedford where John Bunyan was incarcerated. It could also include the Cadogan Hotel in London where Oscar Wilde was arrested.

The events leading to Oscar Wilde's popularity and fame as a writer are less complicated than the events leading to his arrest and imprisonment. From his prison cell in Reading Gaol he wrote, "The two great turning-points in my life were when my father sent me to Oxford, and when society sent me to prison."

The starting point of his life was 16 October 1854 in Dublin, where Oscar Fingal O'Flahertie Wills Wilde was born to parents with strong literary tastes which both he and his elder brother Willie inherited. He went to Trinity College, Dublin. Then came

10

Oscar Wilde (1854-1900) and The Cadogan Hotel, London, where he was arrested

Magdalen College, Oxford. After the long university career, he came to London in 1879.

In London he made a charming host noted for his witty sayings. He became famous as an epigrammatist and raconteur as well as an author of poems, fiction, and plays. In 1881, his book of poems was privately printed. In that year he tried also to secure the production of his play *Vera*. He was to write other unsuccessful plays before his career as a playwright was launched with *Lady Windermere's Fan* in 1892, followed by *Salome, A Woman of No Importance, An Ideal Husband, The Importance of Being Earnest*.

But he was lifted out of obscurity and thrust into the limelight by an accident, by Gilbert and Sullivan's *Patience* of 1881, which satirized the so-called aesthetic or pre-Raphaelite movement. Wilde was invited to America to give a lecture in January 1882, prior to the New York production, in a publicity scheme to show the public what the movement was all about and thereby increase interest in the operetta. It increased interest in him. People came to believe that the character of Reginald Bunthorne, the fleshly poet who walked down Piccadilly with a poppy or a lily in his medieval hand, was based on Wilde; and Wilde capitalized on that impression. "Anyone could have done that," he said. "The great and difficult thing was what I achieved—to make the whole world believe that I had done it."

Back from his successful American tour early in 1883, Wilde renewed his friendship with Constance Lloyd, whom he married the following year. He had a reasonably happy marriage and was on the threshold of a brilliant career.

He edited *Woman's World* from 1887 and became a writer of note, with many clever short stories and with the novel *The Picture of Dorian Gray* to his credit. He seemed to be fulfilling the prediction written in his own words in the year of his graduation from Oxford: "I'll be a poet, a writer, a dramatist. Somehow or other I'll be famous, and if not famous, I'll be notorious."

The year 1891 represents a peak in his literary career with his acceptance everywhere as a fine talent. But that was also a fateful year, for in 1891 he met Lord Alfred Douglas—'Bosie'— and the meeting led to the catastrophe of his life. Wilde, an established author and famous society personality, a married man with two children, was thirty-six when he was introduced to the twenty-year-old Oxford undergraduate with a flair for poetry. The love affair which was to develop between them led, inexorably, to Wilde's downfall.

Douglas was the third son of the eighth Marquis of Queensberry, the instigator of the Queensberry Rules of Boxing. The eccentric nobleman, vain, tyrannical, and subject to fits of fury, had abused his wife, neglected his family, and ignored his son's existence. Now he became aroused by the liaison between the two and launched a series of threats and attacks culminating in a message which he left for Wilde at his club. On the back of a visiting card were the words with the famous misspelling, "For Oscar Wilde posing as somdomite."

Wilde brought action for libel against the Marquis of Queensberry, assuring his solicitor that he was innocent of the charge. When Queensberry's counsel threatened to produce a number of youths to testify with incriminating evidence, Wilde's counsel decided to withdraw from the prosecution, and Queensberry was found not guilty.

Having been made to appear guilty by facts and information which came out as a result of the examination, Wilde was now liable to prosecution for offences. He was, after all, living outside the law, albeit an unjust or even a cruel law. Queensberry's agents rounded up witnesses by bribing them, or threatening them with prosecution and prison, and produced a collection of disreputable people with whom Wilde was alleged to have associated. With things stacked against him by such unscrupulous means, Wilde should have abandoned the action and gone abroad. By proceeding with it, he was doomed.

After the verdict, he was urged by friends to take the boat train across the Channel. But he did not flee. Overtaken by inertia or some inexplicable need to be a martyr, he went instead to the Cadogan Hotel. There he stayed, drinking and waiting for the inevitable to happen. A warrant of arrest was issued on 5 April 1895 at about five o'clock, and a few hours later came the fatal knock on his door.

After the trial, the judge summarized Wilde as "the center of a circle of extensive corruption of the most hideous kind among young men." (More hideous than murder, one wonders.) He was given the maximum sentence possible, of imprisonment for two years with hard labor. He was forty-one and to all intents and purposes, his life was over.

A character in *Lady Windermere's Fan* says, "Misfortunes one can endure—they come from outside, they are accidents. But to suffer for one's own faults—ah!—there is the sting of life." Wilde knew he brought his troubles on himself.

Prison conditions were harsh and inhumane, and his suffering and humiliation were increased by his being made a bankrupt by the vindictive Queensberry and by having his children legally taken from him. Released on 19 May 1897, he left for France.

An injury to the middle ear received in prison from a fall in his cell caused him continuous discomfort and pain. He submitted to surgery but never fully recovered from the operation which was performed in October 1900. He contracted cerebral meningitis and died in Paris on 30 November, six weeks after his forty-sixth birthday.

The Cadogan Hotel maintains the turret room which was his, the very lovely Room 118 with crystal chandelier, blue draperies over the windows and pink padded headboard over the bed. The curved window seat in the corner alcove overlooking Sloane Street and Cadogan Place is a comfortable spot for viewing the pretty London scene outside and for reviewing the tragic scene which took place inside. But in such a bright and cheerful environment, it is difficult to visualize the dark events:

Wilde, his face expressionless, is seated in an armchair by the fireplace smoking. His friends are seated at a table on which are half-empty glasses of hock. Arresting officers arrive and read out the charge of "committing acts of gross indecency with various male persons." Wilde leaves with the Scotland Yard detectives.

Fortunately, the Cadogan Hotel itself yields a positive report. The five-story, red-brick Victorian building, located in fashionable

Chelsea, is not much changed from the time it was built in the late nineteenth century.

The peaceful and elegant atmosphere which characterizes the entire ground floor begins in the small entrance area with paneled walls, oak reception desk and porter's desk, and old-fashioned cage lift next to the carpeted stairway. Ersatz Grinling Gibbons wood carvings of lions, floral garlands and bunches of fruit on the desks, pillars, and walls add interest to the decor as well as a touch of history. The lions are from the crest of Lord Cadogan.

Beyond the reception area, a cedar-paneled lounge is decorated in warm colors with comfortable settees and armchairs, a very friendly and inviting room. Through arches can be seen the impressively elegant dining room. On the walls of the bar are photographs of Oscar Wilde as well as Lillie Langtry, a reminder that the back half of the hotel was formerly her private residence. A restored Lillie Langtry Room represents a part of her home just as it was when she entertained such notables as the artist James McNeill Whistler and Oscar Wilde. Now used for conferences, it displays the deeds of transfer of her house to the hotel. All is successfully designed to give a tranquil turn- of-the-century feeling.

The feeling of contentment carries over to thoughts of Oscar Wilde. Here he can be remembered for the legacy of laughter and comedy which he left behind. He defies his own aphorism that "one can survive everything nowadays except death." The last word was his. Biographies, films, and plays continue to be written on his life and work; his plays are continually being performed, and his writing remains in print. His epigrams have become part of the language: "I can resist everything except temptation."

His best aphorisms are a mixture of fun and profundity: "Experience is the name all men give to their mistakes." Although axioms taken from his comedies are meant to be played for laughs, they also have serious application to life. A character in *Lady Windermere's Fan* says, "In this world there are only two tragedies. One is not getting what one wants and the other is getting it." Wilde wrote in *A Woman of No Importance,* 'The only difference between the saint and the sinner is that every saint has a past, and every sinner has a future." Perhaps it can be said that Oscar Wilde had both.

15

When the master of the instant riposte was asked by an American customs officer whether he had anything to declare, he replied, "Nothing. Nothing but my genius!" Indeed, his genius survives in the works he created which continue to amuse and entertain.

THE CADOGAN
75 Sloane Street
London SW1X 9SG

Telephone: (0171) 235 7141   Fax: (0171) 245-0994

Owned by Historic House Hotels Limited

65 bedrooms and 5 suites.

Two adjoining ground floor rooms, the Langtry Dining Room and the smaller Langtry Sitting Room, are suitable for meetings and private dining.

The menu of the excellent restaurant changes daily.

Opposite the hotel, in Cadogan Place, are gardens and tennis courts for the use of hotel guests.

Location: Near Knightsbridge Underground Station and several bus routes. Convenient for shopping in the desirable Knightsbridge area.

RUDYARD KIPLING

at

Brown's Hotel

London W1

At the bottom of the valley a little brook
had undermined its footbridge, and frothed
in the wreckage. But there stood great
woods on the slopes beyond—old, tall, and
brilliant, like unfaded tapestries against the
walls of a ruined house.
"All this within a hundred miles of
London," he said.

— An Habitation Enforced

Brown's Hotel is still the place one goes to for elegant old world atmosphere. In the pleasant surroundings of the lounge, tea at four o'clock is a most agreeable and traditional institution.

Throughout the hotel are oak-paneled walls hung with prints and paintings. Fireplaces, carpeting, and warm-colored fabrics contribute to the style and unhurried scene. Bedrooms are furnished and decorated traditionally, each with character of its own.

From its inception in 1837, the year when Queen Victoria began her reign, Brown's Hotel has shown concern for the care and comfort of clients. James Brown opened his hotel at 23 Dover Street in the select residential district of Mayfair. He was able gradually to expand his successful venture by acquiring three neighboring houses, numbers 22, 24, and 21. The four buildings together make up the Dover Street front as seen today.

Mr. and Mrs. Brown knew how to cater to the needs of the gentry. The proprietor's wife had been lady's maid to Lady Byron, and that connection with the poet's family is recalled by the present Byron Room.

The hotel was sold to James John Ford in 1859 and taken over by his son Henry, who managed the hotel for forty-six years beginning in 1882. Improvements continued to take place. Electric lighting came in 1884 followed by "fixed baths" in the following year. An expansion program in the late 1880s extended the hotel at the back to Albemarle Street. Finally, it was acquired by Trusthouse Forte in 1948. But the hotel has kept the original and simple name as well as the standards and traditions set in Brown's day.

From country gentry and wealthy American tourists to royalty—in fact and in fiction—Brown's Hotel in Mayfair was *the* place. Characters in a novel by Edith Wharton regularly alighted at Brown's, as did characters from real life such as Henry James. In more recent times, Agatha Christie used it as the setting for *At Bertram's Hotel*. A sampling from the list of visitors is impressive.

Alexander Graham Bell came in 1876 carrying his invention which, he explained to the owner's young son, could carry voices along wires. On the ground floor next to the Byron Room is the Graham Bell Room, from which the first telephone call in Britain was made. Theodore Roosevelt came in 1886, taking time out to marry Edith Kermit Carew; a copy of the marriage certificate hangs in the hotel. Upstairs, the Roosevelt Room contains a portrait of the twenty-sixth President of the United States. Mark Twain slept here. And an American honeymoon couple, Franklin and Eleanor Roosevelt, stayed in 1905. So frequently did the humorist S.J. Perelman return to the hotel, that he was prompted to write: "I have a deep affinity for Brown's. . .I am regarded as such a fixture here that even the hall porters ask me for directions!"

In what is now the Hellenic Suite, the exiled King George of Greece held court from 1924 until the monarchy was restored in 1935. And during World War II, the Dutch government in exile declared war on Japan in Room 36 of Brown's Hotel.

One attractive room, decorated with illustrations from the works of Rudyard Kipling and with his portrait over the mantelpiece, is named after the literary celebrity. The Kipling Room is part of the suite that Kipling always occupied during his frequent visits to the hotel.

Rudyard Kipling
(1865-1936) and
Brown's Hotel, Dover
Street, London, where
he spent his honeymoon

Rudyard Kipling was himself named for the place in England where his parents became engaged—the delightful village of Rudyard in Staffordshire on the edge of the Peak District National Park. The young married couple left England to live in India, where John Lockwood Kipling had secured a teaching position at the Fine Arts School in Bombay. Later that year, their first child, Rudyard, was born in Bombay on 30 December 1865.

It was normal practice for Anglo-Indian children to be sent home to England to be educated in the healthier climate of a country not ravaged by dangerous epidemic diseases. Thus, when Rudyard was six and his sister Alice three, the children were placed with an English family in Southsea on the Hampshire coast. Unfortunately, they were mistreated and miserable. Mrs. Holloway, or "Aunty Rosa" as she was called, apparently disliked Ruddy and subjected him to unkind treatment and frequent beatings. Only after five unhappy years in that foster home did his mother discover the horrendous conditions and extricate her child from the hateful environment. He was then sent to school, to the United Services College, in a resort town in Devon named Westward Ho! after the title of the popular novel by Charles Kingsley. The picture of odious school life was brilliantly told in a later work of fiction, *Stalky & Co*. The preface poem of that novel includes these stanzas:

Western wind and open surge
    Took us from our mothers;
Flung us on a naked shore
(Twelve bleak houses by the shore!
Seven summers by the shore!)
    'Mid two hundred brothers.

There we met with famous men
    Set in office o'er us;
And they beat on us with rods—
Faithfully with many rods—
Daily beat on us with rods,
    For the love they bore us.

But Rudyard left the school after five summers, not seven as stated in the poem. Unsuited to a military career for which the school prepared its inmates, he sailed for India in September 1882. His career as a writer flowered in Lahore where he was given his first employment as a journalist on the local newspaper. His father had taken up a new post as curator of the museum in Lahore, and Rudyard, not yet seventeen, was able to live happily with his family while reporting for the *Civil and Military Gazette*. The Indian stories he later wrote were to bring him immense fame, but he left India for good in 1889 and never returned except for a very short visit to his parents in 1891.

London was the place for making a literary reputation, and to London he went. He settled in Villiers Street and wrote. From those cheap lodgings in Charing Cross, the struggling writer became the successful author who frequented Brown's Hotel.

Kipling met an American literary agent and publisher, Wolcott Balestier. The relationship flourished and developed into a deep and intimate friendship. The two men even collaborated on the writing of a novel.

Kipling's two successful years in London brought him critical acclaim. Feeling the strain of overwork, he embarked in August on a recuperative journey which took him to South Africa, New Zealand, Australia, Ceylon and India. In Lahore, in December 1891, Kipling received word of the sudden death by typhoid of his dear friend. Distraught, Kipling returned to London and immediately announced his intention of marrying Wolcott's elder sister Caroline. It seemed to many that mutual love for the dead man was the only thing they had in common.

Henry James attended the wedding on 18 January 1892, perhaps reluctantly, for he wrote to his brother William that Carrie seemed "a hard, devoted, capable little person, whom I don't in the least understand his marrying. It's a union of which I don't forecast the future though I gave her away at the altar in a dreary little wedding." Nevertheless, it was a happy marriage, full of love and care and understanding.

The honeymoon night and wedding breakfast were set in Brown's Hotel. When the young couple left on the 26th, their hotel bill for £22 was presented, paid in full, by the owner as a wedding gift. To Brown's Hotel, Rudyard Kipling returned continually throughout life.

The Kiplings lived in Vermont, Carrie's American home, for the first four years of their marriage. But on holidays to England from Vermont, they stayed at Brown's. On finally leaving America and returning to England in 1895, they stayed with his parents in Tisbury and then in Rottingdean, but expeditions to London were set at Brown's Hotel. They partook of the London literary and social scene, and Brown's continued to be an essential way of life for the Kiplings even after they moved into their permanent home in the country.

In 1902 Kipling found the dream house—Bateman's—in which he lived for the rest of his life. The grey stone house with the date AD 1634 inscribed over the door, with its oak beams and staircase, has become a National Trust property and is open to the public. Its remote location in the small village of Burwash in East Sussex, some fifty miles from London, gave Kipling the privacy he longed for. He settled in, as did the American couple who settle in England in *An Habitation Enforced*. The poem which follows that short story, *The Recall*, begins with these two verses:

I am the land of their fathers,
    In me the virtue stays.
I will bring back my children
    After certain days.

Under their feet in the grasses
    My clinging magic runs.
They shall returns as strangers,
    They shall remain as sons.

Kipling found roots in the Sussex countryside, which became new subject matter for his writing. He used the surroundings of

Bateman's for such volumes as *Puck of Pook's Hill* and *Rewards and Fairies*.

But escape from the country was also necessary, and he escaped, inevitably, to Brown's. It was the place for deep emotional scenes and key events. The Kiplings spent most of the war years at the hotel, and he saw visitors there as well as at Bateman's. In those terrible war years he was to lose the second of his three children. Earlier, in 1899, their beloved daughter Josephine had died at the age of seven while the family were on a visit in New York. Now, his son John was reported missing in action. One visitor to Brown's at that time was his old friend Julia Catlin. When he escorted her to her car, Kipling said, "Down on your knees, Julia, and thank God you haven't a son." His son John died in the battle of Loos in October 1915, and the body was never recovered.

'Have you news of my boy Jack?'
Not this tide.
'When d'you think that he'll come back?'
Not with this wind blowing, and this tide.

'Has any one else had word of him?'
Not this tide.
For what is sunk will hardly swim,
Not with this wind blowing, and this tide.

He did much writing at the hotel and dictated an account of Canadian troops landing in Flanders. His cousin and friend Stanley Baldwin visited and wrote of breakfast with Kipling and a pleasant time at the hotel.

Indeed, Kipling spent so much time there that he was asked why they did not have their own place in London after the war instead of always being at Brown's. His answer, a reference to Carrie's compulsiveness as a housewife, was, "Mother couldn't run two houses."

A month after his seventieth birthday, while at Brown's Hotel, he had a violent hemorrhage and was rushed to Middlesex Hospital where he died four days later, on 17 January 1936.

23

BROWN'S HOTEL
Dover Street
London W1A 4SW

Telephone: (0171) 493-6020   Fax: (0171) 493 9381

Rooms: 165 with private bathrooms and air-conditioning, telephone, and television.

Meals: All meals and high tea available.

Good central location near Green Park and Green Park Underground Station.

EDITH WHARTON

*

at

The Charing Cross Hotel
London WC2

And the low wide bed, as rutted and worn as a high-road,
The bed with its soot sodden chintz, the grime of its brasses,
That has born the weight of fagged bodies, dust-stained
averted in sleep,
The hurried, the restless, the aimless—

--Terminus

"I think the full tide of human existence is at Charing Cross," Dr. Johnson remarked long before a great mainline railway and underground station with a vast railway hotel also marked the site. The name of Charing Cross derives from the stone cross, the last of twelve set up by a heartbroken Edward I in 1290 to mark the resting places of his beloved Queen Eleanor as her funeral cortege traveled slowly from Harby in Nottinghamshire where she died to Westminster Abbey where she was buried. A parliamentary decree of 1643 destroyed the monument, and it is actually an 1863 replica of the original cross that stands in the forecourt before the great Charing Cross Hotel. In more recent times, literary history was made when Edith Wharton stayed at the Charing Cross Hotel in 1909.

It is a fine railway hotel catering for tourists and businessmen who no doubt appreciate its superbly convenient situation in the Strand near Trafalgar Square. From the hotel can be seen the National Gallery and St. Martin in the Fields. The Houses of Parliament and Westminster Abbey, Covent Garden and

Whitehall—all are nearby. Theatres and restaurants are within walking distance of the hotel.

Shortly after the hotel was built in 1864, an annex of ninety bedrooms was added and connected to the main building by a footbridge across Villiers Street. A further structural change was necessitated when, during World War II, enemy bombardment on the night of 16 April 1941 damaged the hotel. Restored in 1951, the original mansard roof was replaced by a new and modern top story.

The large, efficient, and moderately-priced hotel has another literary connection in its Betjeman Restaurant, named for the poet. Sir John Betjeman indicated his fondness for the hotel and dined frequently at what he called a "most finely appointed hotel dining room." He singled out the grand staircase with its inviting "broad carpeted stairs" that make a pleasant climb to the first floor where the principal rooms are located—the Italian Renaissance-style restaurant with original corner columns, the lounge in similar style, and banqueting rooms.

It is most appropriate to think of the Charing Cross Hotel in connection with a literary guest of distinction, the remarkable Edith Wharton.

Born in aristocratic old New York City on 24 January 1862, Edith Newbold Jones became Edith Wharton when, at the spinsterish age of twenty-three, she married Edward (Teddy) Wharton, twelve years her senior. Within a few years, the marriage began to show signs of disintegration and Edith turned to writing, perhaps as an outlet.

Teddy Wharton was an ineffectual man with no vocation and no real interests. Edith was becoming a self-assured and forceful personality and was beginning to establish a reputation as a writer. Clearly, she had outgrown her non-intellectual husband, who was also showing symptoms of mental illness. His increasingly severe manic-depressive condition finally led to a divorce in 1913, after nearly thirty years of marriage.

Edith Wharton's first book was published in 1897 when she collaborated with her architect-friend, Ogden Codman, on a volume called *The Decoration of Houses*. Walter Berry, a distant cousin, helped her with the style and organization and remained her lifelong friend and mentor. Her understanding of the need for proportion and balance in architecture and her impeccable good taste came to the fore when she designed and built her home in Lenox, Massachusetts, in 1900. When Henry James came to stay at The Mount, as the country home of the Whartons was called, he described it in a letter as "a delicate French chateau mirrored in a Massachusetts pond."

Best known as a writer of novels and short stories, Edith had published the first of her eighty-six short stories in 1891. Walter Berry continued to encourage and advise her in the fiction she wrote.

Edith's circle of friends, invariably men, included Henry James. When they first met at a dinner party in Paris, the young Edith Wharton was overawed by the famous author and too timid to converse with him. Over a dozen years later, when he was living at Lamb House in Rye, their friendship developed into a warm and extremely close relationship that lasted until his death. She visited him often at Lamb House on her frequent trips to England and was also often entertained at the home of Howard Sturgis, Queen's Acre, in Windsor.

For someone who had no need to work, Edith Wharton made the difficult choice of becoming a writer. She applied discipline to her craft and wrote regularly each morning. *The Valley of Decision*, her first novel, appeared in 1902 when she was forty. She was still at work on a novel in 1937, at the time of her death on 11 August, and *The Buccaneers* was published posthumously.

In between came such novels as *The House of Mirth* (1905), *Ethan Frome* (1911), *The Reef* (1912), *The Custom of the Country* (1913), and *The Age of Innocence* (1920), for which she won the Pulitzer Prize.

In Europe, Edith found the sympathetic and literary people she needed. She had looked for a house in England and considered settling in the country Henry James had chosen for his home, but she felt dissatisfied and took up residence in France, reserving

England as a holiday place. Rye and Windsor were her two main retreats on her frequent visits to England for a good time.

In June 1909, Edith Wharton took a holiday in London with William Morton Fullerton, and they stayed at the Charing Cross Hotel. The story of Fullerton is the story of the single true love of her life.

She originally met Fullerton, an American journalist who was based in Paris as a correspondent for the London *Times*, at her home in Lenox in 1907. She had returned to The Mount from an exciting tour abroad which had included a round of parties, dinners and gay Paris life, as well as a motoring expedition through France in which she was joined by Henry James. Fullerton was now on a visit to America, and his friend Henry James arranged the meeting at Lenox. Fullerton was an extremely attractive, sensual man with a long and involved history of becoming entangled with the women he captivated.

He captivated Edith. She was forty-five and he, forty-two. Magical feelings were mutually kindled and, after he left, Edith began to keep a private journal addressed to him, but not intended for his eyes. In the diary, she expressed the longing to be to Fullerton "like a touch of wings brushing by you in the darkness, or like the scent of an invisible garden that one passes by on an unknown road." She also moved forward the date of her projected return to France and left in December.

Naturally, their friendship resumed in Paris. In the year 1908, she continued to write and to lead a remarkably busy social life. But she found time to be alone with him—some hours in the country, a quiet lunch, a gallery exhibition. She was simply, and discreetly, in love. Henry James came over, his last time in France, and the three enjoyed a good time together.

Her love for Fullerton deepened. By the spring of 1908, her conflicts over morality and adultery and her puritanical concern for order in society seemed resolved. Their friendship was fused into a passionate, physical union.

Her writing went well. A fourth volume of short stories was published in September 1908, *The Hermit and the Wild Woman*, followed in October by *A Motor-Flight Through France*. Her first

Edith Wharton
(1862-1937) and
The Charing Cross
Hotel, London,
where she stayed
with her lover,
William Morton
Fullerton

collection of poems, *Artemis to Actaeon*, appeared in April 1909, and at least ten of the poems in that volume were based on her relationship with Fullerton. Edith Wharton often used incidents, people, and places she knew in her writing.

On 3 June 1909, she and Fullerton crossed the Channel to Folkestone, where they spent the night. In London the next day, they took Suite 92, two bedrooms and a sitting room, at the Charing Cross Hotel. Henry James joined them there for dinner, and they spent a gay evening with dim red lights, champagne, and good conversation. After James left, the two had a passionate night. Fullerton was scheduled to leave for America in the morning to visit his parents.

In the morning, alone after he had gone, Edith sat propped up in bed writing, as was her wont. But this time she did not write fiction. She wrote a fifty-two-line poem. *Terminus* is the name of the erotic poem which she composed that morning about the night before. The title cleverly suggests a station hotel as well as a temporary end to their relationship. It begins with amazing candor:

Wonderful was the long secret night you gave me, my Lover,
Palm to palm, breast to breast in the gloom. The faint red
    lamp
Flushing with magical shadows the common-place room of the
    inn,
With its dull impersonal furniture, kindled a mystic flame
In the heart of the swinging mirror. . . .

That afternoon, she and James drove to Queen's Acre where she stayed for ten days before going back to London and another social whirl. When Fullerton returned from America, they spent another night in London, then went for a motor tour with Henry James in her chauffeur-driven car before the pair returned to Paris. James was sixty-six and exhausted.

The *Terminus* incident is fictionalized at the Terminus Hotel in Paris in *The Reef* (1912). In that novel, Sophy Viner and George Darrow consummate their passion in a Paris station hotel near the Gare du Nord, during a spring rain (it had rained in London), in a room that is reminiscent of the one at the Charing Cross Hotel: ". . .the grimy carpet and wall-paper, the black marble mantelpiece, the clock with a gilt allegory under a dusty bell, the high-bolstered brown-counterpaned bed, the framed card of printed rules under the electric light switch, and the door of communication with the next room."

Paradoxically, the writer who worked assiduously to preserve her privacy, who guarded it even in her autobiography, left bits of her private life scattered throughout the novel. But who could know the significance of the fictional account? Or the truth of the poem?

If the tone of the novel is different, and somewhat seedier, that is because the Edith Wharton of 1912 looked back with distaste. The affair that began in the autumn of 1907 ended in the summer of 1910. His three-year span of attention to a love relationship was almost over. Her impossible situation caused her to become disenchanted. Perhaps with Teddy's own adulterous adventures now revealed, she felt obliged to measure them both by the same moral standards. In any event, the affair petered out. He ceased to be the man of her dreams but remained the attractive man she had loved and who had loved her in return.

After The Mount was sold in 1911, and after her divorce, France became the permanent home of Edith Wharton. From Paris, she moved to the Pavillon Colombe, just twelve miles north of the city, and later she had a winter home at Hyéres on the French Riviera. During World War I, she ran missions for refugees, for which she was awarded the Legion of Honor.

She returned to the United States only once, in 1923, when she was awarded an honorary doctorate from Yale University—the first woman to be so honored. This was a singularly appropriate tribute to the writer who frequently dealt with the intricacies of the lives of women who are victims in a world made for men. Her illumination of those issues and her intense psychological probing continue to be appropriate.

THE CHARING CROSS HOTEL
The Strand
London WC2N 5HX

Telephone: (0171) 839-7282   Fax: (0171) 839 3933

Member of Mount Charlotte Hotel Group with toll free reservation number in the U.S.A.: 1 800 44 UTELL

All 218 bedrooms have private bathrooms and are comfortably furnished; each has a television set, radio, and tea/coffee making facilities.

The Betjeman Carving Restaurant serves throughout the day.

There are four bars and a residents' lounge.

Located at Charing Cross Underground Station and Charing Cross Main Line British Rail Station, the hotel is in the heart of theatreland with easy access to restaurants and major tourist attractions such as the National Gallery.

E.M. FORSTER

at

The Kingsley Hotel
London WC1

And even more curious was the drawing-
room, which attempted to rival the solid
comfort of a Bloomsbury boarding-house.
Was this really Italy?

—*A Room With a View*

The Kingsley Hotel in Bloomsbury is an unpretentious, unimpos-
ing, moderately-priced hotel located very near the British Museum.
The red-brick building with turrets at each end was built at the turn
of the century. The year of its inception, 1900, is inscribed on the
facade high above the front door. A reception hall with pillars and
two crystal chandeliers leads to a large and comfortable lounge for
residents on the left. With its fireplace and stuffed chairs and sofas,
the room is the epitome of "solid comfort."

A lift makes the ascent to six upper floors with a total of 145
bedrooms. But before the addition of a wing in 1926, the front
section of the original hotel consisted of only a hundred rooms.

Opposite the lounge is the plush Bloomsbury Bar and the
Thackeray Room, used for conferences and named for the author
of *Vanity Fair*. The hotel itself was named for another writer,
Charles Kingsley, remembered for such works as *Westward Ho!*
and *The Water-Babies*. But apparent literary interest stops short of
honoring the author who actually lived in this pleasant hotel.

Long before E.M. Forster wrote his well-known novels, long
before he became part of the Bloomsbury group of artists and
intellectuals, he came to the Kingsley Hotel. In fact, he and his
mother took up residence at the hotel while seeking a place to live.

The story begins, however, with the birth of Edward Morgan Forster on 1 January 1879 and the death of his father twenty-two months later. He was brought up in a world of women and adored the over-protective mother who dominated him throughout her life. Alice Clara Forster moved with four-year-old Morgan to a house near Stevenage in Hertfordshire called Rooksnest, the prototype for the house which gave his fourth novel its title, *Howards End.* Already he was coming into contact with places and incidents which were to be adapted as elements in his novels.

They were forced to leave that beloved house when he was fourteen, and the boy entered the detested Tonbridge School. His hatred for it is expressed when he described it as Sawston School in *The Longest Journey.*

After leaving Cambridge, with no career in mind, he decided to embark on the almost obligatory grand tour of Europe. Fortunately, a private income allowed him to seek personal fulfillment without the immediate need to take on a permanent profession. With his mother, he left England in October 1901. Notes he made in Italy of people, places, and events became the bases for several early novels. San Gimignano, for instance, was the Monteriano of *Where Angels Fear to Tread.*

On their return to England a year later, mother and son settled into the newly-built Kingsley Hotel while trying to form definite plans. The Kingsley Hotel had the advantage of proxmimity to the Working Men's College in Great Ormond Street where Forster taught a weekly class in Latin.

The following spring, with no prospect yet of regular employment, son and mother went on another tour of the Continent. But this time, he went on a Greek cruise while she stayed in Florence for a holiday of her own. He joined her after the tour of Greece was over. In Florence, they attended a performance of Donizetti's opera, *Lucia di Lammermoor,* with the soprano Tetrazzini singing the leading role. The event later made its way into *Where Angels Fear to Tread* as an effective little scene.

The two travelers returned to England in August 1903 and again stayed at the Kingsley while searching for a place to live. In the spring of 1904, they took a flat in South Kensington and exchanged

E. M. Forster (1879-1970) (in Indian cosume), and the Kingsley Hotel, London, where he lodged with his mother

it after some months for a house in Weybridge—their home for the next twenty years. They moved in 1924 to Abinger Hammer in Surrey, their home until Alice Forster's death.

It might be said that Forster bloomed in Bloomsbury, for it was during his stay at the Kingsley Hotel that he began to contribute essays and stories to the *Independent Review* and wrote parts of his early Italian novels. When he checked into the hotel, his luggage contained the inspiration provided by his visits to Europe. He began the writing of *A Room With A View*, but *Where Angels Fear to Tread* was published first, in 1905. This successful novel was followed by *The Longest Journey* (1907), *A Room With a View* (1908), *Howards End* (1910), and, after a long hiatus, *A Passage to India* (1924).

His links with Bloomsbury are further emphasized by his affiliation with the Bloomsbury circle of friends with Cambridge or family ties. He reviewed Virginia Woolf's first novel of 1915, *The Voyage Out*, with unbounded admiration. He later praised *To the Lighthouse* and thought it her best novel. Although they remained good friends until her death, Virginia Woolf frequently criticized his works in print. In one article, she discussed the failure of Forster's work to reconcile realism with vision because of a too-literal rendition of too much observation. In a review of his series of lectures published as *Aspects of the Novel*, she differed with him on the concept of "Life."

Aspects of the Novel emanated from the distinguished series of Clark Lectures which Trinity College, Cambridge, invited Forster to deliver in 1927, thus re-establishing his Cambridge connection. The success of the eight lectures led to their publication and to his being offered a three-year fellowship at King's College.

Forster had a long life and a varied career which included reviewing and editing as well as the writing of short stories, important books of criticism and essays, two biographies, and travel books. During World War I, he served with the International Red Cross in Alexandria as a searcher, which involved the gathering of information about missing soldiers. The literary yield of the years spent in Egypt were *Alexandria: A History and a Guide* and *Pharos and Pharillon*, a collection of essays.

His travels took him to India in 1912 and again in 1921 as private secretary to the Maharaja of Dewas. *The Hill of Devi*, about his experiences in Dewas, proclaimed his two visits to be "the great opportunity of my life." It was after his second trip to India that the novel generally accepted as his masterpiece appeared in 1924— *A Passage to India*. (There was to be a third visit to India in October 1945 for a conference of writers.)

Forster's myriad activities included serving as president of the National Council for Civil Liberties and broadcasting for the BBC. After the death of his mother in 1945, King's College elected him to an Honorary Fellowship and gave him rooms at the college, where he lived for the last twenty-five years of his life.

He collaborated with Ralph Vaughan Williams on a pageant and wrote the libretto for Benjamin Britten's opera, *Billy Budd*. And he did continue to create fiction during the apparent periods of silence. He remained an active writer until nearly the end, which came on 6 June 1970. And after the end, came the posthumous works: *Maurice*, the novel about homosexual love, was begun in 1913 and published in 1971. A collection of short stories with the chilling choice of title for a posthumous volume, *The Life to Come*, appeared in 1972.

Despite Forster's immense versatility, his reputation rests primarily on his novels. In the early years of his development as a novelist, the fame that this gentle person never sought, sought him—and found him writing at the Kingsley Hotel in Bloomsbury.

THE KINGSLEY HOTEL
Bloomsbury Way
London WC1A 2SD

Telephone: (0171) 242 5881   Fax: (0171) 831 0225
U.S.A. Toll Free: 1 800 847 4358 or 1 800 44 UTELL

145 bedrooms, each with private bathroom, television with channel for in-house movies, and tea and coffee making facilities.

The Kingsley Restaurant on the ground floor offers a choice of carvery or a la carte menus.

Traditional English Bar and comfortable lounge.

Location: Near the British Museum and close to Bloomsbury Square and Oxford Street.

W. S. GILBERT

at

The Mansion House at Grims Dyke

Middlesex

London

The song of birds
In ivied towers;
The rippling play
Of waterway;
The lowing herds;
The breath of flowers;
The languid loves
Of turtle doves—
These simple joys are all at hand
Upon thy shores, O Lazyland!

--Utopia Limited

The name of Gilbert is inevitably and irrevocably linked with that
of Sullivan. The extraordinary Gilbert-and-Sullivan team created
supreme and lasting light operas. Sullivan's entrancing music is
absolutely right for the lyrics which can hardly be recalled without
the accompanying melody. Yet the lyrics written by W. S. Gilbert
are characterized by such wit, brilliance, power, and precision that
he ought to be acknowledged as a first-rate poet in his own right.
When Utopia—unlimited—is established, it will present a world
in which ". . .Literary Merit meets with proper recognition—As
Literary Merit does in England!"

Before they met, Arthur Sullivan was a promising composer and
William Schwenk Gilbert was a prominent dramatist. The pair
were introduced in 1870 when they collaborated on an unsuccessful operetta called *Thespis* and then parted company. Later, Richard

D'Oyly Carte, convinced that they were a perfect partnership, and wanting to establish an English comic opera tradition in a theatre of his own, brought about the joint production of *Trial by Jury* in 1875. This huge success was followed by *The Sorcerer, HMS Pinafore, The Pirates of Penzance* . . . a total of thirteen operas which found a home at the Savoy Theatre and gave the partners fame and fortune.

It was a magical combination—professionally—but they were never friends. They were dissimilar in background and personality and quarrelled often, sometimes bitterly. Sullivan's music was appreciated by royalty, and he was knighted in 1883. Many bemoaned the waste of his musical talent which stooped to supply background for Gilbert's lyrics. And Sullivan himself, up to his death in 1900, no doubt remained convinced that he was unfaithful to his musical calling.

Gilbert was merely "the man who writes words for Sullivan," and his words were often attacked. One newspaper was offended by the gibes in *Iolanthe*. Notables such as Charles Lutwidge Dodgson (Lewis Carroll, the author of *Alice in Wonderland*) found it despicable that Gilbert made clergymen seem ridiculous. He objected also to Gilbert's use of profanity: "I never use a big, big D——."

Nevertheless, Gilbert acquired enormous popularity as he expressed the foibles of the Victorian age in ingenious lyrics that entertained a large and appreciative audience. The matchless wit of his words continues to amuse vast numbers of people who listen to the still-relevant eccentricities of lawyers, artists, soldiers, politicians, lovers, kings, people—themselves.

> If this young man expresses himself
> in terms too deep for *me*,
> Why, what a very singularly deep young man
> this deep young man must be!

As for pretenders and bores, he

... has got them on his list;
They really won't be missed.

Who can forget his chorus of police in the *Pirates of Penzance* who sing heroically and repeatedly about going forward into danger, "to glory, though they die in combat gory," but who have to be pushed out, for they *don't* go! Or the First Lord of the Admiralty who polished up the handle of the big front door so carefullee that now he is the Ruler of the Queen's Navee? He could go beyond satire. A good piece of poetry with beautiful imagery is the love song of Strephon and Phyllis:

All in all since that fond meeting,
When, in joy, I woke to find
Mine the heart within thee beating,
Mine the love that heart enshrined!
Thou the stream and I the willow
Thou the sculptor, I the clay,
Thou the ocean, I the billow,
Thou the sunrise, I the day!

Well rewarded for his literary contribution, Gilbert was able to purchase a beautiful home at the edge of London with the proceeds from the vastly successful productions. He acquired Grims Dyke in 1890, and it remained his home for the last twenty years of his life. He and his wife were happy in the large estate built by the eminent Victorian architect, Norman Shaw. In the heart of Harrow's Weald, formerly the hunting ground of royalty, the Gilberts gave fancy dress dinners, balls, and lavish garden parties. He enjoyed dancing and the company of children, and indulged in a favorite pastime of photography. He loved his home with its well-kept and extensive grounds, which included a lake.

At Grims Dyke, with its seemingly limitless utopian possibilities, *Utopia Limited* was written. This penultimate opera of the Gilbert and Sullivan partnership opened at the Savoy Theatre in 1893. The team parted after their next, and last, opera in 1896, the unsuccessful *The Grand Duke*. Gilbert, at home, continued to write

41

plays. But although both tried, neither Gilbert nor Sullivan achieved any real success on his own. Gilbert lived the life of a country squire and was knighted, finally, in 1907.

On a sunny day in the year 1911, on the 29th of May, two local girls, guests of the Gilberts, were swimming in the lake in the grounds. One called for help, and Gilbert, ignoring his doctor's instructions to avoid cold water, swam to her rescue. She was safely returned to a manageable depth, but the effort was too much for his heart. "I would like to die upon a summer day in my own garden," Gilbert had once said. His wish was fulfilled. His ashes lie buried in the parish churchyard in Stanmore, not far from Grims Dyke.

He was seventy-five, the last survivor of the successful trium-virate. Sullivan had died at the age of fifty-eight and D'Oyle Carte in 1901 at fifty-six. One cannot help recalling the Yeoman's words:

> What kind of plaint have I,
> Who perish in July?
> I might have had to die,
> Perchance, in June!

Today, his spirit is very much alive and well and singing at his former home in the rural setting of North London, now a hotel known as the Mansion House at Grim's Dyke. Although it has lost much of its original acreage (but not the lake with its tragic history), it is still a country home turned hotel. And it is a friendly place, particularly on Sunday evenings when Gilbert and Sullivan soirées are held with the English Heritage Singers performing in full Edwardian costume. In addition, a summer season of Savoy operas attracts thousands of followers from all over the world.

One enters the foyer, with its plaque of W. S. Gilbert, from a long driveway nearly opposite a pub with the curious name, The Case Is Altered. In the reception hall, it becomes obvious that character, and characters, have been retained. The oak-paneled Yeoman Room restaurant has always been the dining room of the house. The adjoining Patience Bar was the library. The Iolanthe Hall has the original ceiling, minsrels' gallery, and carved marble fireplace. (How was the Azalea Room permitted to intrude?) The

The Mansion
House at Grims
Dyke, former
home of
W. S. Gilbert
(1836-1911)

house has nine bedrooms, and the Gilbert Suite is traditionally furnished with a four-poster bed. A newly-built wing offers an additional forty bedrooms.

And there in the Iolanthe Hall, on Sunday evenings, guests join in the singing of the words of W. S. Gilbert—clever, entertaining, witty words which will never be forgotten. What! Never? Well, hardly ever!

The MANSION HOUSE at GRIMS DYKE
Old Redding
Harrow Weald
Middlesex
London HA3 6SH

Telephone: (0181) 954 4227   Fax: (0181) 954 4560

47 bedrooms include the Gilbert Suite and Gold Room with four poster beds; the ensuite accommodations are supplied with television, radio, hairdryer, and tea/coffee making facilities.

Four meeting rooms are available for a variety of functions.

The Music Room Restaurant serves traditional English food.

Located in 110 acres of woodlands just ten miles from London's West End, the hotel is a short taxi drive from Stanmore Underground Station (Jubilee Line).

MARK TWAIN

at

The Langham Hotel
London W1

We have a luxuriously ample suite of apart-
ments on the third floor, our bedroom looking straight up Portland Place, our parlour
having a noble array of great windows
looking out upon both streets (Portland
Place and the crook that joins it onto Regent
Street).

—Letter to Rev. Joseph H. Twichell, 1873

Samuel Langhorne Clemens took his pseudonym from the river
call of the Mississippi. "Mark twain" meant two fathoms or twelve
feet—safe water. So intrigued was he with the great River, that he
had even apprenticed himself as a pilot in order to learn about it.
But he eventually found his own safe water in journalism.

For someone who claimed to abhor all travel, Mark Twain
certainly did a lot of it. From the time of his birth in the remote
settlement of Florida, Missouri, on 30 November 1835, he seems
never to have stayed in one place for very long. When he was four,
the family moved to Hannibal, a town on the Mississippi River and
the place of recollected youth of his two great novels, *Tom Sawyer*
and *Huckleberry Finn*.

As a young man he left his home town, traveling east and
stopping at various places before arriving in New York in 1853.
Then back to St. Louis. Then on to San Francisco. He lectured there
and elsewhere before leaving again for New York in order to
embark in June 1867 on a trip around the world. A commission

45

from the San Francisco *Alta California* to write travel letters enabled him to go to France, Italy, Greece, Turkey, Palestine.

His first trip abroad did not include England, but the journey was a crucial one. His irreverent letters became enormously popular and were published in 1869 as his first famous book, *The Innocents Abroad*. Also on that cruise, he met Charles Langdon, whose sister Olivia he was to marry in February 1870. With Livy, he settled as editor of the Buffalo *Express* before eventually becoming established in Hartford. A son, born in November 1870, died at eighteen months. Susy, his favorite, was born in March 1872; and Clara, the only one of his children to survive him, in April 1874. Jean, the youngest died after an epileptic seizure in 1909.

So successful was *The Innocents Abroad*, that *Roughing It*, about the West, soon followed. Now a respected man of letters, he made his first trip to England in 1872 to protect his copyright interests and to lecture, but primarily to gather material for a satirical travel book he was planning to write on England. He stayed for three months but never wrote the book.

His reception was enthusiastic, and he expressed surprise at the great ovation extended by his host country: "I did not know I was a lion." Twain returned the warm English welcome by confessing, "I would rather live in England than America—which is treason." As for the English countryside, he exclaimed: "Rural England is too absolutely beautiful to be left out of doors."

He simply adored England. Perhaps that is why he could not write the projected travel book. It may be true that he was too busy with banquets, speeches, and social diversions, but as a genuine Anglophile, Twain maintained that he liked the English too much to satirize them in a book.

He turned instead to another book. Within the three months spent in London, he produced his share—he collaborated with Dudley Warner—of *The Gilded Age*, an angry novel about business corruption after the American Civil War. Twain dated his preface to the English edition 11 December 1873 from the Langham Hotel, London, and left for home.

Mark Twain
(1835-1910) and
the Langham Hilton,
to which he kept
returning

While the novel he did write in England achieved only limited recognition, the notes he sent home for the book he did not write indicate strong potential success, as evidenced by this excerpt about an expatriate:

> There was once an American thief who fled his country and took refuge in England. He dressed himself after the fashion of the Londoners, and taught his tongue the peculiarities of the London pronunciation and did his best in all ways to pass himself for a native. But he did two fatal things: he stopped at the Langham Hotel, and the first trip he took was to visit Stratford-on-Avon and the grave of Shakespeare. These things betrayed his nationality.

The passage evinces his great gift of comic exaggeration as well as the Langham's popularity with Americans.

Twain's return to England in May 1873, this time with the family, was sheer triumph. With Livy and young Susy, he spent a few weeks in London, returning to the same hotel. "His rooms at the Langham were like a court," writes his biographer, Albert B. Paine. He was indeed treated royally, and the social whirl was arduous. To escape for a much-needed rest, the family went on to York and Edinburgh, Glasgow and Ireland, before returning to London. But Livy was homesick, tired, and pregnant. Twain took her and Susy home in October and returned to England alone almost immediately, staying until January for a triumphal tour as a lecturer and literary celebrity.

Again he stayed at the Langham. In a letter of November 19, from Parlor 113, he muses on the scene from his window: "Out here on Langham Place that old 'semi-detached' tooth-pick of a steeple stands up just as short & ugly as ever. . . that very same Punch & Judy man has arrived with a tap or two of his drum. . . . the man taking off his hat humbly & beseechingly to people in various Langham Hotel windows."

By the time the family were back in England in the summer of 1879, Twain's veneration for England had somehow dissipated.

His humanitarian side objected to the social divisions that existed in the mother country and caused him to modify his cordial feelings toward England.

He did not go abroad during the decade of the 1880s. At home in America, he produced the classic *Life on the Mississippi* (1883) and his great masterpiece, *Huckleberry Finn* (1884)—as well as two anti-England books. *The Prince and the Pauper* (1882) was concerned with justice while *A Connecticut Yankee in King Arthur's Court* (1889) criticized nobility and expressed a dream for the end of monarchy and aristocracy.

He was in London when he received word of Susy's death on 18 August 1896. Livy and Clara had rushed back to be with her in her illness but were in mid-Atlantic when the cable arrived to say that Susy, aged twenty-four, had died of meningitis. Twain later wrote, "It is one of the mysteries of our nature that a man, all unprepared, can receive a thunder-stroke like that and live." Afterwards, they lived largely abroad, in England or the Continent.

From 23 Tedworth Square in Chelsea, he wrote his last travel volume, *Following the Equator* (1897). Then they settled into the Dollis Hill house in North London, which they closed in September 1900 to return home. Awaiting the sailing date at Brown's Hotel gave him the opportunity to poke fun at Brown's: "The rooms are as interesting as the Tower of London, but older I think. Older and dearer. The lift was a gift of William the Conqueror...."

He stayed again at Brown's when he returned to England for a final triumphal trip to receive a Doctor of Letters degree from Oxford in June 1907. "It is unlikely," he said, "that when I go away I shall ever see England again...." He had spent more than eleven years of his life abroad. Olivia Clemens had died in Florence three years earlier. He was to die three years later, on 21 April 1910. But it all began when he was lionized in London at the Langham Hotel.

The fashionable Langham Hotel, just opposite the BBC and across the road from All Souls' Church (with its 'semi-detached' tooth-pick of a steeple), was first launched in 1865. Opened by the Prince of Wales (later King Edward VII), it could boast of the royalty and literati who frequented the hotel in its heyday— Oscar Wilde and Arnold Bennett, Dvorak and Toscanini. Sir Arthur

Conan Doyle referred to the Langham in several of his Sherlock Holmes stories, including "A Scandal in Bohemia" and "The Sign of the Four." When Mrs. Wallis Simpson was a guest during the abdication crisis, the tint of scandal confirmed its mythical status.

The hotel served as a first aid post during World War II but, badly damaged during a 1940 air raid, was forced to close its doors. It later became part of the BBC properties. In 1986, the building was purchased for the purpose of returning it to its former function as a select hotel and has only recently been restored with painstaking care to the recreation of details of Victorian architecture.

Opened by Hilton International Hotels in March 1991, the shrine to America's great novelist is again ready to receive writers and worshipping fans. Long a favorite of many other Americans, with a list of distinguished guests including Henry Wadsworth Longfellow, Bret Harte, and Ellen Glasgow, it is well placed to continue to attract writers of merit.

THE LANGHAM HILTON HOTEL
1 Portland Place
London W1N 3AA

Telephone: (0171) 636-1000   Fax: (0171) 323-2340

410 guest rooms and suites, decorated in French provincial style, have white marble bathrooms and are equipped with international direct dial telephone, remote control television, individually controlled air conditioning, mini-bar, writing desk, hairdryer, and trouser press.

24 hour room service is available.

The main restaurant, nostalgically called "Memories of the Empire," offers dishes from India, Thailand, and China as well as English fare.

Tsar's Russian theme restaurant specializes in vodkas and caviares served with blinis and cream.

The Chukka Bar offers savory dishes and cheeses.

Additional features are the grand ballroom, conference rooms, exercise room with sauna and solarium, and hair salon.

The Palm Court, evoking the spirit of Victorian London when grand people patronized the grand hotel, provides traditional afternoon tea.

THAMES & CHILTERNS

THOMAS GRAY

at

Burnham Beeches Moat House
Burnham
Buckinghamshire

Far from the madding crowd's ignoble strife,
Their sober wishes never learned to stray;
Along the cool sequestered vale of life
They kept the noiseless tenor of their way.

--Elegy Written in a Country Churchyard

Thomas Gray's childhood home in London was full of ignoble strife and he was placed far from it when a maternal uncle, Robert Antrobus, who lived at Burnham in Buckinghamshire, took him in.

Born on 26 November 1716, Thomas Gray was the fifth of twelve children and the only one to survive infancy. His long-suffering mother had to contend with the unfortunate marriage she had made. His father had fits of temper and moods of fury when he would attack his wife. Robert Antrobus, an assistant master at Eton College, arranged for the boy of nine to enter the college; and thus the young Thomas escaped from the stifling home atmosphere into a landscape of beauty in the Thames Valley.

Thomas Gray enjoyed the beauties, the poetry, the traditions, and the history which surrounded him. During those happy years at Eton, he formed intimate friendships with Richard West, Thomas

Ashton and Horace Walpole. He appreciated the accessibility of nearby Windsor Castle as well as the statue in the school yard of Eton's founder, King Henry VI, and paid homage in the poem published in 1742, "Ode on a Distant Prospect of Eton College":

Ye distant spires, ye antique towers,
  That crown the watery glade,
Where grateful Science still adores
  Her Henry's holy shade;
And ye, that from the stately brow
Of Windsor's heights the expanse below
  Of grove, of lawn, of mead survey,
Whose turf, whose shade, whose flowers among
Wanders the hoary Thames along
  His silver-winding way.

School holidays were spent at his uncle's house at Burnham, situated in an area famous for the forest of glorious beeches which continue to give the area a unique appeal. A letter Gray wrote to Horace Walpole in August 1736 from the house in Burnham describes the scenery all around:

I have at the distance of half a mile thro' a green
Lane, a Forest (the vulgar call it a Common) all my
own; at least as good as so, for I spy no human thing
in it but myself; it is a little Chaos of Mountains &
Precipices. . .such hills as people, who love their
Necks as well as I do, may venture to climb, & Crags,
that give the eye as much pleasure, as if they were
more dangerous: both Vale & Hill is cover'd over
with most venerable Beeches, & other very reverend
Vegetables, that like most ancient People, are always
dreaming out their old Stories to the Winds.

The "venerable beeches" are still there in the forest known as Burnham Beeches to give pleasure to walkers and nature lovers;

and literary pilgrims may easily visualize young Thomas walking in those woods, Virgil in hand.

The house itself gives the appearance of a grand and spacious country estate set in exquisite and extensive grounds. The view of the light green house with white trim from the curving driveway is impressive and inviting.

The original early Georgian house known to Thomas Gray consisted of the central portion with bays on each side of the front door. Extensions were added on at each end in the nineteenth century. In 1966 the historic house was converted into a hotel and enlarged in 1973 with a new wing at the back to contain fifty-four bedrooms. A further refurbishment increased the number of guest bedrooms to eighty and included a spacious indoor swimming pool and leisure club.

Just inside, a friendly bar to the right of the entrance area is the place for a drink before dinner in the attractive restaurant just to the left. The handsomely-decorated restaurant is enhanced by a framed copy of Gray's famous *Elegy* and by a painting of the author on the wall opposite.

Indeed, the high standard of comfort belies the discomfort felt by young Thomas, as expressed again in a letter of August 1736 to Horace Walpole from this house. He complained that his uncle's dogs "...take up every chair in the house, so I'm forced to stand at this present writing, & tho' the Gout forbids him galloping after 'em in the field, yet he continues still to regale his Ears & Nose with their comfortable Noise and Stink." (Thomas Gray was never fond of animals.)

After Eton, Gray continued his studies at Cambridge, where he eventually became a university professor. He lived the life of a scholarly recluse but returned frequently to the area he knew from his Eton days. A search into the Buckinghamshire haunts of the poet from the beginning of his creative life in Burnham to his death in Cambridge must necessarily include the nearby Buckinghamshire village of Stoke Poges.

When his father died in 1741, his widowed mother decided to live with her sister and moved to Stoke Poges. Gray made many visits there and did much writing, including his well-known *Elegy*.

Thomas Gray
(1716-1771) and
Burnham Beeches Hotel

His mother died in 1753 and is buried in the Stoke Poges churchyard. His words, inscribed on the tombstone of his devoted and adored mother, describe her as "the careful tender mother of many children, one of whom alone had the misfortune to survive her."

Thomas Gray died on 30 July 1771 at the age of fifty-five and is buried by the side of his mother. A monument pays tribute to the creator of one of the best-known poems in the English language who lies among the "unhonour'd Dead" where "the curfew tolls the knell of parting day."

BURNHAM BEECHES MOAT HOUSE
Grove Road
Burnham
Buckinghamshire SL1 8DP

Telephone: (01628) 603333　　　　Fax: (01628) 603994

Eighty guest rooms include two suites and two four-poster bedrooms, all with private bath and shower, traditional furnishings, and trouser press.

The Burnham Room and the Georgian Room are used for private functions. There is also a Ballroom and a new conference suite with Gray's Bar and a terrace overlooking the grounds.

Further amenities include tennis courts, croquet lawn, and putting green within ten acres of parkland and an indoor leisure complex with swimming pool, spa bath, solarium, sauna and mini gym.

Conveniently located near London's Heathrow Airport and only twenty odd miles from central London.

REBECCA WEST AND H.G. WELLS

at

Monkey Island Hotel
Bray-on-Thames
Maidenhead
Berkshire SL6 2EE

This was the Monkey Island Inn. The third
Duke of Marlborough had built it for a
"folly," and perching there with nothing but
a line of walnut trees and a fringe of lawn
between it and the fast full shining Thames
it had a grace and silliness that belonged to
the eighteenth century.

--The Return of the Soldier

After a brief career as an actress, Cicely Isabel Fairfield began
another career as a journalist, changing her name to Rebecca West
in tribute to the strong heroine of Ibsen's play *Rosmersholm*. Early
in her new profession as a writer, she contributed to the feminist
weekly *The Freewoman* a provocative review of the most recent
novel of H. G. Wells. The world-famous author wanted to meet the
fiery young critic who referred to him as "the old maid among
novelists" and invited her to lunch at his home in Essex where he
lived with his wife and two sons.

The year was 1912. Rebecca West was twenty and H.G. Wells
was in his mid-forties, twenty-six years her senior. He could boast
a long Don Juanish catalogue of mistresses but had no intention of
ever leaving the wife who understood and tolerated his sexual
infidelities and kept a stable home as background for his turbulent
life. He was at the pinnacle of his reputation as a writer, having

pioneered English science fiction with such works as *The Time Machine* and *The War of the Worlds* and having produced social comedies of lower middle class English life with such novels as *Kipps, Tono-Bungay,* and *The History of Mr. Polly.*

After a particularly painful love affair, he had turned to studies of the relationships between men and women in his fiction. The neophyte reviewer's critical remarks on *Marriage,* his latest novel dealing with the idea of freedom between the sexes, aroused his interest, and the fateful invitation was issued.

Wells wrote of this first meeting, "I had never met anything quite like her before, and I doubt if there ever was anything like her before. Or ever will be again." She reported, "I found him one of the most interesting men I have ever met. He talked straight on from 1.15 til 6.30 with immense vitality and a kind of hunger for ideas." Thus began the friendship that was to develop into an intense ten-year love affair. When she saw him again at his London house in Hampstead shortly after the initial meeting on 27 September 1912, their mutual attraction was electric enough to culminate in a kiss. Yet, a year elapsed before the liaison began in earnest.

The inexperienced young Rebecca was ready to proceed with a great adventure, but the more worldly older man, succumbing to pressure from his current mistress, was reluctant to become involved. Rebecca wrote pleading letters to him, but he resisted her intelligence, beauty, and courage and responded only to her published articles.

Her review of his next novel of 1913—"infinitely nobler than Mr. Wells's last book"—commended only the first chapter: "The first thirteen pages of *The Passionate Friends* stand among the most beautiful achievements of Mr. Wells's art of elucidating emotion . . . .But for the rest," she concluded, "the book rubs on one's nerves." The author of *The Passionate Friends* was now finally and irresistibly intrigued by the passionate feminist. By the autumn of 1913, they were lovers. By the end of the year, she was pregnant.

Despite her outspoken feminist stance, despite his attacks on sexual hypocrisy, they were secretive about her predicament. She went to the remote seaside town of Hunstanton in Norfolk and remained secluded until the birth of her son Anthony on 4 August 1914. The complex relationship of single mother and married man continued for a tempestuous decade filled with assumed names and roles, remote residences, and secluded retreats. With emotions as widespread as elation and anguish, it was a union in which demands, complaints, jealousies, and altercations gradually became the norm.

Their shared life, albeit troublesome, did yield productive writing and happy times together in the succession of homes in which she lived and on holidays. In particular, their frequent excursions to Monkey Island Inn on the River Thames near Bray are to be singled out as times of complete contentment. Wells had known and loved the place since boyhood, when, as a schoolboy at Bromley, he often visited his uncle who lived nearby. Rebecca too adored the Monkey Island Inn, and it became their own very special place, the place in which she and Wells were most happy. Wells alluded to it in a letter as one of those times of perfection.

So enamored was she of the idyllic island that for her first novel, published in 1917, Rebecca West seized upon it and described exactly the enchanting site where she and Wells found rapture. *The Return of the Soldier* deals with the amnesia of a shell-shocked soldier which causes him to forget his wife and ten years of an apparently happy marriage. However, he remembers vividly his former love of some fifteen years earlier, when he fell in love with "the daughter of the man who keeps the inn on Monkey Island at Bray on the Thames." The innkeeper's daughter recalls that "quiet kind people, schoolmasters who fished, men who wrote books, married couples who still loved solitude, used to come and stay in the bright little inn." One might add that the author came with Wells and both were enraptured.

The novel plays with some images and facts from actual life. Uncle Ambrose lives nearby, as did Well's own uncle, and the inn is presented as seen from the end of the path leading from Uncle Ambrose's gates:

> In front were the dark green glassy waters of an
> unvisited backwater; and beyond them a bright lawn

59

set with many walnut trees and a few great chestnuts, well lit with their candles, and to the left of that a low white house with a green dome rising in its middle and a veranda whose roof of hammered iron had gone verdigris colour with age and the Thames weather.This was the Monkey Island Inn.

The fictional couple have a silly quarrel over someone named Bert Wells (the first initial of H.G. Wells's name stood for Herbert) and are parted. The psychoanalytic doctor who treats the soldier's amnesia Rebecca West mischievously portrays as Wells: "a little man with winking blue eyes, a flushed and crumpled forehead, a little grey moustache that gave him the profile of an amiable cat, and a lively taste in spotted ties."

The Return of the Soldier was well received and soon went into a second printing. *The Judge* followed in 1922, and her reputation as a novelist became established. But the union with Wells was deteriorating. After a decade of emotions ranging from euphoria and bliss to anguish and despair, its demise came in 1923. It took seven years before she finally found peace in a happy marriage to Henry Maxwell Andrews, a Scottish investment banker.

Rebecca West never stopped writing. Her literary output is great and greatly respected. Many consider her finest literary achievement to be *Black Lamb and Grey Falcon* (1941). She wrote her most popular work, *The Fountain Overflows* (1957), at the age of sixty-five and *The Birds Fall Down* (1966) at seventy-four.

She died in 1983, aged ninety, and several volumes were published posthumously. There are to her credit eleven books of fiction, ten non-fiction, and torrents of journalism. But the great honor of her life came in 1959 with another change of name when she was created a Dame Commander of the British Empire and became Dame Rebecca West.

Before it was a hotel, the Monkey Island Inn, built in 1744, was a fishing lodge and pavilion of the third Duke of Marlborough. Today his name is invoked in the recently-built extension of 1970, the Marlborough Room, with its walls appropriately decorated with battle scenes illustrating episodes from the life of the Duke.

Dame Rebecca West (1892-1983)
and H. G. Wells (1866-1946)
enjoyed rapturous escapes at the
Monkey Island Hotel,
Bray-on-Thames, near Maidenhead

The Marlborough Room, a Regency style restaurant, adjoins the River Room, a setting that is highly suitable for conferences or large receptions. Large areas of glazing on three sides allow for superb views upstream of the River Thames. Another very attractive setting for conferences is the Wedgwood Room. With its octagonal shape, open fireplace, and plasterwork ceiling depicting classical figures and mermaids, it must present a challenge for business people to concentrate on the meeting in progress.

But the *piece de resistance*, the central masterwork which relates to the name of the hotel, is the painted domed ceiling of the Monkey Room. Although some believe the origin of the name Monkey Island to be derived from Monk's Eyot when the monks of Burnham owned the island, it is questionable whether there ever were monks at Burnham, and the name may therefore more accurately be ascribed to the simian decoration of the Duke's lodge. The artist Clermont had an obsession with monkeys and, probably given free choice of subject, depicted them dressed in contemporary fashion in several river scenes. In that historic room, it is fashionable now to have afternoon tea or drinks.

Twenty-seven bedrooms or suites have grand views of the extensive gardens or of "the dark green glassy waters of an unvisited backwater." It may have been an obscure site at a previous time, but its convenient location was bound to transform Monkey Island into a popular haven. It is within easy reach of Heathrow Airport, and London is a mere thirty miles away. About a mile and a half downstream is Windsor with its royal castle, and half a mile upstream is the village of Bray with its thirteenth-century parish church, approached through an attractive little fifteenth-century gatehouse. Rebecca West's fictional couple stood at the island's end watching "the sunset smouldering behind the elms and Bray church-tower."

Access to the island was by water until a suspension footbridge installed in 1956 eliminated the need to ring a bell and wait for someone to row over and fetch the visitor. Ordinary punts were kept at the ready for ferrying supplies, while punts with cushions were available for visitors. When the bell sounded in *The Return of the Soldier*, the inkeeper's daughter "would get into a four-foot punt that was used as a ferry and bring it over very slowly. . . ." Today guests park their cars on the other side of the island before crossing the wood-planked, metal-sided bridge to reach the beautiful lawn shaded by huge walnut trees. A stone-paved path leads to the Monkey Island Hotel.

Returning to Old Mill Lane after pleasantly indulging at the inn, the happy traveler might be relieved to know that any undulating feeling is due to architectural design, for the bridge does in fact sway a bit, making it a matter of libration, not libation.

MONKEY ISLAND HOTEL
Bray-on-Thames
Maidenhead
Berkshire SL6 2EE

Telephone: (01628) 23400   Fax: (01628) 784732

Rooms: 27 guest rooms and suites, all with private bath, television, telephone, mini bar, tea/coffee making facilities, and room service,

Leisure facilities: Fishing from the island is permitted for residents only, who bring their own tackle.

Location: British Rail Maidenhead Station, three miles away, is thirty minutes from London's Paddington Station.

HENRY JAMES

at

The Randolph Hotel
Oxford
Oxfordshire

Oxford is the same old Oxford still. . . . We
spent a large portion of yesterday strolling
from college to college and from garden to
garden and the pleasure was great.

—Letter to his parents from the Randolph Hotel,
4 June 1872

Like typical tourists today, Henry James made Oxford a stop on his
itinerary. But Henry James was no ordinary traveler. In the first
year of his life—he was born in New York City on 15 April
1843—the James family went abroad and young Henry learned
to walk and talk in England. He returned several times with his
restless family to the European scene and kept returning continually to travel, to study, and, ultimately, to live in England.

In 1869 he made his first adult trip abroad and spent eleven
weeks in England before going on to the Continent. He was to call
it his "passionate pilgrimage." In England, he went in search of
castles, ruins, or sites with literary associations. He visited such
places as Malvern, Leamington, Tintern Abbey, Worcester,
Tewkesbury, Salisbury, and Winchester. Oxford was a particular
favorite. In a letter of 26 April to his brother William, he called it
an "incomparable town" and went on to describe an evening walk
he made to Christ Church to deliver a letter: "It was a perfect
evening and in the interminable British twilight the beauty of the
whole place came forth with magical power. . . ." He was invited
to dine at several of the college halls, and he especially enjoyed

various college gardens. He wrote of the gardens, "They are places to lie down on the grass in forever, in the happy belief that the world is all an English garden and time a fine old English afternoon."

So overwhelmed was he with his visit to Oxford that a letter he wrote from Venice to William the following September contains this initial reaction: "I personally prefer Oxford; it told me deeper and richer things than any I have learned here." Another letter from Venice to a friend expresses his love for the mother country: "The more I see of the Continent, the more I value England."

Although a cautious spender, he did not deny himself the comforts of a good first-class hotel when on his travels. In Oxford, he put up at the best—the Randolph Hotel.

The Randolph Hotel, built in 1864, was quite new when Henry James stayed there. The dark brick, Victorian Gothic-style edifice, now a four-star hotel owned by Trusthouse Forte, is still the best and most luxurious in Oxford. Located in the heart of the city just opposite the Ashmolean Museum, it is ideally situated for visiting and "strolling from college to college." (The hotel was named after the museum's benefactor, Dr. Francis Randolph.) In the rich and relaxing lounge are served those delicious cream teas for which the Cotswolds area is known.

No wonder Henry James returned to the Randolph when he returned to Oxford in the summer of 1872. On that occasion he was acting as escort for his sister Alice who was making her grand tour with Aunt Kate, part of the James household. The group went from Liverpool, where the ship docked, to Chester, where they stayed at the Queen Hotel. Years later, Lambert Strether of *The Ambassadors* stayed at this hotel in Chester.

Henry James wrote home from Oxford of their progress. The threesome had traveled to Derbyshire ("scenery. . .strangely raw and vacuous"), Lichfield ("truly divine Cathedral"), Warwick and Leamington ("most lovely"), before reaching Oxford. While "doing" Oxford, they made a detour to nearby Blenheim Palace: "It is all more lordly and lovely even than when I saw it before."

The group went on to London, then to the Continent—France, Switzerland, and Italy. At the end of the tour, after seeing Alice and Aunt Kate safely ensconced on board their ship in Liverpool for the return voyage, James stayed on in Europe to test his determination to become a financially independent writer.

About two years later, at the age of thirty-one, he began to prove himself. He had earlier tried his hand at writing with some success. He had produced travel pieces, stories, and a longer work of fiction which appeared in the *Atlantic Monthly* in 1871; *Watch and Ward*, an indication of the greatness to come, was revised and published years later in book form.

In 1875 he published a volume of his collected short stories about Americans abroad called *A Passionate Pilgrim and Other Tales*. In the title story, the characters wander through Oxford and give the author an opportunity to describe his beloved city with its "hoary college walls" and "antique stillness." That year also saw the appearance of a book of travel articles, *Transatlantic Sketches*, and the novel *Roderick Hudson*—an auspicious start for the author of such masterful novels as *Washington Square*, *The Portrait of a Lady*, *The Spoils of Poynton*, *The Turn of the Screw*, *The Wings of the Dove*, and *The Golden Bowl*.

The year 1875 also marked the start of his life as an expatriate. He wrote in a letter from London that November: "I take possession of the old world—I inhale it—I appropriate it!"

He was eventually to appropriate Lamb House in Rye, the house with which he is generally associated and in which he lived from 1898 until his death in 1916. But he was lionized in London before he retired to Rye. He felt comfortable and content with London and delighted in its connections with Dickens, Thackeray, Defoe, Dr. Johnson. For nine years he resided in Bolton Street in Mayfair, a short street with Green Park at one end and Curzon Street, where Becky Sharp lived, at the other. It pleased him to think of his immediate neighborhood as belonging to the character created by Thackeray. Early in 1886 he left the small, dark rooms of his Mayfair quarters and installed himself in a bright, large, fourth-floor flat with a view, in De Vere Gardens, Kensington.

He became a well-known literary figure, particularly after the success of *Daisy Miller* in 1878, and was much in demand socially. During the middle years, as he called this period of his life, he wrote

Henry James
(1843-1916) stayed
at the newly-built
Randolph Hotel
when he made his
first visit to England
and Oxford

such mature novels as *The Bostonians, The Aspern Papers, The Lesson of the Master,* and *The Princess Casamassima.*

His books were warmly praised by the critics but not purchased in substantial quantities by the public; although he was a critical success, he was not a great financial success. In the 1890s, the respected author, the cosmopolitan artist, ventured into the theatre in the search for a more lucrative outlet. He hoped that a drama of his would overtake the London stage, but he experienced the most devastating failure of his life.

On the opening night of his play *Guy Domville,* 5 January 1895, the nervous author attended a performance of Oscar Wilde's *An Ideal Husband* in an attempt to make the tense hours pass quickly. As he listened to the laughter of an audience that was being given the frivolous entertainment it wanted, he must have had a premonition of the fate that awaited his own serious play with its unhappy ending.

Guy Domville was an instant disaster. As the play was drawing to a conclusion, George Alexander delivered the line, "I'm the last, my lord, of the Domvilles" and a voice from the gallery loudly responded, "It's a bloody good thing y'are." The audience howled and hooted, and general chaos reigned at the end of the play. When actor-manager George Alexander came out to restore order, adding at the end of his brief speech of apology that the company would try to do better in the future, another voice shouted, " 'Taint your fault guv'nor, it's a rotten play." The sensitive author fled from the scene of his humiliating failure.

He was given some encouragement in several decent reviews; particularly kind was the critic for the *Saturday Review*, George Bernard Shaw. But a career as a dramatist was essentially over for Henry James. This is especially ironic when we consider that Henry James, who spent his life considering the ironies of life, has written scores of fictional works that have been adapted into successful and effective productions for stage, cinema, television, and even opera.

Needing to get away from the fiasco, James traveled to Ireland, then returned briefly to London before again escaping to the Osborne Hotel in Torquay, Devonshire. Although Torquay was simply too far from London, his positive response to it made him feel the advantages of a country retreat and gave him the idea which led to the purchase of his dream house in Rye.

Henry James left London for the Sussex country retreat which derives its name from Mayor James Lamb who built it in 1723. Now owned by the National Trust, Lamb House is open to visitors, who come in droves to see the home of the legendary master. In his own time, guests came in droves to see Henry James. He was hospitable to a partial rollcall of such names as Edmund Gosse, H.G. Wells, Joseph Conrad, Stephen Crane, Ford Madox Ford, George Gissing, G.K. Chesterton, Rudyard Kipling, Max Beerbohm, and Edith Wharton.

From Rye, he did not travel so much as he did in his younger London years, but the inveterate traveler did continue to go out in search of interesting sites, people, and ideas. One of his obsessive ideas found expression in *The Jolly Corner*. That tale concerns an American expatriate who, after a period of thirty years abroad, returns to New York in search of himself, the self that might have been had he remained at home. It is a haunting and frightening autobiographical idea, a journey into the self. But for Henry James there was no alternative. He had to fulfill his destiny as a writer living in Europe.

In all of his travels, Oxford ranks high. In his decision to reside in England, Oxford again ranks high, for Henry James had written of it, "The whole place gives me a deeper sense of English life than anything yet."

THE RANDOLPH HOTEL
Beaumont Street
Oxford
Oxfordshire OX1 2LN

Telephone: (01865) 247481   Fax: (01865) 791678

Rooms: 109 guest bedrooms and eight suites, which vary in size and decor, have private bathroom, television, radio, telephone, hairdryer, and trouser press. The Balliol and Trinity suites, named for two of the nearby colleges, were designed for complete luxury.

Dining: The Spires Restaurant offers tempting cuisine and seasonal specialities, while a coffee shop offers informal meals.

Public Rooms: The Chapters Cocktail Bar is for evening drinks; also available for private banquets or business meetings are five function rooms and a Ballroom.

Lounge: Afternoon tea is served in this splendid setting which was featured in the film, *Shadowlands*.

Location: In the city center on Georgian Beaumont Street within walking distance of the colleges and just opposite the Ashmolean Museum.

Transportation: One hour from London with easy motorway access via the M40. Or by British Rail from Paddington.

THE SOUTH AND SOUTH-EAST

JANE AUSTEN

at

The Royal Victoria and Bull Hotel
Dartford
Kent

> They were three days on their journey. . . .
> They reached town by three o'clock the
> third day, glad to be released, after such a
> journey, from the confinement of a carriage,
> and ready to enjoy all the luxury of a good
> fire.
>
> —*Sense and Sensibility*

In the Middle Ages, when Dartford was Darentford, huge numbers of pilgrims forded the River Darent at this convenient stopping place on their first night out from London. Through the apple and cherry orchards of Kent they continued, on the so-called Pilgrim's Way, to their destination—Canterbury Cathedral. Thomas à Becket was murdered in the cathedral in 1170, and his martyrdom and canonization gave rise to the most popular pilgrimage in Britain. Countless numbers rode out to the shrine, "the hooly blisful martir for to seke" (as Chaucer says in *The Canterbury Tales*).

Few pilgrims visit Dartford today. A place that is normally and understandably avoided by tourists, modern Dartford is an industrial town with a landscape that includes factories and smoking chimneys and with a population that accounts for urban sprawl and commuters. But at least one old world feature exists to make the short journey from London worthwhile—the Royal Victoria and Bull.

Formerly known as The Bull, the name of this important old coaching inn was changed after the accession of Queen Victoria, who visited it on several occasions. Once a number of inns stood in the main street, and this majestic inn is not to be confused with a smaller one (no longer in existence) nearly opposite called the Bull and George. The use of the word "Bull" is ancient; one theory is that its derivation is ecclesiastical and originates from the bulla or seal given by a priory to a place which housed its visitors.

That Jane Austen, like those ancient Canterbury pilgrims, spent the first night out at Dartford after a visit to her brother's family in Kent, that she spent it in a unique and pleasant hotel, would seem to be reason enough to revive the tourist industry of Dartford.

Jane Austen's life appears to be geographically restricted. She was born on 16 December 1775 in the village of Steventon in Hampshire where she spent the first twenty-six years of life. Then, with her father's retirement, the family moved to Bath where she lived for the next five years. In 1806, the year after her father's death, her widowed mother moved to Southampton with her daughters before finally settling in Chawton in Hampshire in 1809. There Jane remained for the last eight years of her life, except for the final days. She was taken to Winchester to be given medical care when her health failed. Death came on 18 July 1817, and she is buried in Winchester Cathedral, where a memorial inscription pays tribute:

> The benevolence of her heart, the sweetness of her temper, and the extraordinary endowments of her mind obtained the regard of all who knew her and the warmest love of her intimate connections.

Significantly, it refers to Jane Austen the beloved human being, not to Jane Austen the beloved author whose books have brought joy to so many.

Silhouette of
Jane Austen (1775-1817)
and The Royal Victoria
and Bull, Dartford,
an old coaching inn
where she stayed on
journeys to Kent
to visit her brother

Although she never traveled abroad, Jane Austen, like the characters in her novels, did a great deal of traveling to English places, particularly to holiday resorts in the south such as Sidmouth, Lyme Regis, and Charmouth. Concerned with accuracy, Jane was not tempted to write about areas outside the realm of her experience. Her novels dealt only with the places she knew and with the people she knew to inhabit them. So naturalistic is her writing, and so strongly is the reality felt by readers, that when Tennyson was being shown the site where the Duke of Monmouth landed in Lyme Regis, he impatiently responded to his friend: "Don't talk to me of Monmouth. Show me the exact spot where Louisa Musgrave fell!"

Jane Austen visited London frequently to see a favorite brother, Henry, and both she and her elder sister Cassandra made journeys to Kent to visit their brother Edward.

Edward had been adopted (like Frank Churchill in *Emma*) by a distant cousin, Thomas Knight. Mr. and Mrs. Knight had no children of their own and no heir to their fortune. After Thomas Knight died in 1794, Edward took over the fine eighteenth-century Palladian mansion known as Godmersham Park and later the name of Knight as well. The house lies in the beautiful valley of the Stour only eight miles from Canterbury. Between 1794 and 1813, Jane was often at Godmersham enjoying the country-house society and the life of leisure of the more affluent branch of the Austen family. Both sisters enjoyed the spacious mansion filled with loving children and the superb setting with garden and deer park.

Conditions of travel were arduous, and an inn to break the journey was essential. Jane passed through Dartford many times on her way to or from Godmersham. She stayed in Dartford on a number of occasions in the nineteen-year period when she was making journeys into East Kent, sometimes arranging to take advantage of the good inn in Dartford. In a letter of 17 January 1809 she expresses the intention to sleep at Dartford: "There certainly does seem no convenient resting place on the other road."

It seems likely, therefore, that she would choose the best inn in Dartford—the old Bull (which later became the Royal Victoria and Bull). But there is confusion over the profusion of Dartford inns.

An oft-quoted letter of 24 October 1798, written when she and her mother were returning to Steventon (having left Cassandra behind to help care for the children of Edward and Elizabeth), is headed from the Bull and George—the inn across the road. Even then conversation about the weather took precedence: "We had one heavy shower on leaving Sittingbourne, but afterwards the clouds cleared away and we had a very bright *chrystal* afternoon."

She went on to describe an unsettling incident in which her luggage was sent off in error: "After we had been here a quarter of an hour it was discovered that my writing and dressing boxes had been by accident put into a chaise which was just packing off as we came in, and were driven away towards Gravesend on their way to the West Indies." A man on horseback was speedily sent out to retrieve the boxes.

David Waldron Smithers, an authority on Jane Austen in Kent, offers the plausible explanation that the favored inn, the Bull, had no rooms available on that particular occasion, and so they had to put up over the road. Other letters refer to the Bull, as in this extract from a letter of June 1808: "At Dartford, which we reached within the two hours and three-quarters, we went to the Bull, the same inn at which we breakfasted in that said journey, and on the present occasion had about the same bad butter. At half-past ten we were again off. . . and by six o'clock were at Godmersham."

Nowadays the butter is better at the old Bull, which remains the best hotel in Dartford. This old coaching inn retains its medieval gallery which overlooks the courtyard, in which stands an authentic nineteenth-century coach. The courtyard, now covered over by a glass roof, is a superb example of one of the few surviving galleried inn courtyards in the land.

The visitor might well pause for reflection in the courtyard, with its long history which dates back to about 1450. The reason for the author's presence at this establishment—her visits to Kent—had a definite influence on her writing. The experiences of these journeys provided her with knowledge of people, of society, of the interactions of family groups, as well as of activities of great houses. The insights are there to be treasured in her novels.

Sense and Sensibility, her first book, was written in 1798 and revised and published in 1811. She was by then journeying into Kent, and the book contains many references to travel. *Pride and Prejudice* and *Northanger Abbey* belong also to the first period of great creativity. She paid her last visit to Kent in 1813, the year in which she completed *Mansfield Park. Emma* was completed in 1815 and *Persuasion* in 1816.

Although her output was small, although so little is known of her, the feeling of closeness to Jane Austen and her six novels is intensified in the presence of such associations in the Kentish setting from which her genius flowed. Even today, a pilgrimage to Kent with a stop at the Royal Victoria and Bull in Dartford can open vistas into her world.

THE ROYAL VICTORIA AND BULL HOTEL
1 High Street
Dartford
Kent DA1 1DU

Telephone: (01322) 224415   Fax: (01322) 289474

Eighteen bedrooms, five with private bathrooms, are equipped with television, radio, telephone, and tea-making facilities. One guest bedroom located on the gallery level overlooks the courtyard where drinks are served until 11 p.m.

Dartford is only fifteen miles from central London, and trains leave for the capital from the town center every fifteen minutes.

T.S. ELIOT

at

The Cliftonville Hotel
Cliftonville
Margate
Kent

"On Margate Sands.
I can connect
Nothing with nothing. . ."

--The Waste Land

In the summer of 1921, when Thomas Stearns Eliot was concerned
with his health and needed to get away from his stressful life as
bank clerk, poet, and literary critic, he came to the holiday resort
of Margate for a rest cure and stayed for three weeks at the
Albemarle. The hotel has undergone many changes since then, not
the least of which is its name. Called the Norfolk for a while, it is
now known as the Cliftonville Hotel. Under any name, it is the
scene at which Eliot was able to recuperate and to write a significant portion of his great poem, *The Waste Land.*

Born in 1888 in St. Louis, Missouri, T. S. Eliot spent happy
holiday times in East Gloucester on the New England coast of
Massachusetts, where the Eliots were an established and cultured
family. He later enrolled at Harvard and was expected to have
an academic career in the philosophy department. But after
nearly a year of study at Oxford, he decided not to return to take
the examinations for his Harvard doctorate. He would leave his
American life and prospects behind to make a new life for himself
in England as a poet. His birth as a poet may be said to have begun

in the year 1915 when "The Love Song of J. Alfred Prufrock" was published.

The year 1915 was also that of his precipitous marriage to the very attractive and vivacious Vivien Haigh-Wood. They were both twenty-six when they began their unhappy life together. She had a very excitable nature, and he was very soon to learn of the chronic illness which afflicted her, a nervous condition marked by excess physical energy, erratic behavior, and frequent nervous collapses. Because of her steadily deteriorating health, there was hardly a time when Vivien was not a problem. Her health—both physical and mental—remained fragile up to the time of her death in a mental home in 1947.

Aghast at news of the marriage, his disapproving parents discontinued his allowance, thereby adding financial hardship to all the other problems of the mismatched couple. Eliot took a teaching position at a grammar school in High Wycombe and soon transferred to a school closer to home at Highgate. But he felt unsuited to the work and resigned. After leaving the teaching profession, he joined Lloyds Bank in March 1917.

Eliot seemed to enjoy his work as a bank clerk, although it took up much of his time and caused great anxiety. He also did editorial work, gave lectures, and reviewed books for several periodicals. He was introduced to members of the Bloomsbury circle and developed a close friendship with Virginia Woolf in particular. He published a volume of criticism and several collections of verse, which included such poems as "Gerontion," "The Hippopotamus," and "Sweeney Among the Nightingales." But he spoke of an eager desire to get started on a long poem and had just begun to work on it when the writing was curtailed by a visit from his family.

He had not seen his mother for six years, not since his visit to America to confront his parents with the news of his marriage and determination to settle in England. His father had since died, and his mother, now seventy-seven years of age, arrived in England in June 1921 together with his sister and brother. Although Eliot tried to keep his wife out of the way in the country, as was his frequent practice, his energetic mother did manage to meet Vivien. The visit

T. S. Eliot (1888-1965) wrote much of *The Waste Land* while recuperating in Margate at the Albemarle, now the Cliftonville Hotel

was a strain for Eliot, and by the time the family left at the end of August, he was in a state of exhaustion and anxiety, suffering from feelings of failure and depression. A specialist ordered a complete and immediate rest cure. On October 12, he was given a three-month leave of absence from the bank for a condition diagnosed as nervous breakdown and left for Margate.

Vivien accompanied him to the seaside resort. On October 22, he moved into the Albemarle Hotel, staying in the "white room" for the first week and in a more modest room for the next two weeks. Before Vivien returned to London to allow him to convalesce on his own, she wrote in a letter that Eliot was improving. Actually, he was well enough to start working on *The Waste Land* and completed a substantial portion of his long poem at the Albemarle, including the "Fire Sermon" section. When he left Margate on 12 November, he attached to the manuscript the hotel bill, which came to £16.

While at Margate, he considered what to do next about his condition and decided to secure further treatment at a sanitorium in Lausanne. From London, he traveled to Paris and Lausanne, where he completed the final sections of *The Waste Land*. Hints appear in it of his visits to the places of rehabilitation—Lausanne ("By the waters of Leman I sat down and wept") and the Kentish seaside ("On Margate Sands/I can connect/Nothing with nothing").

The year of publication of *The Waste Land* makes 1922 a major year for English literature. The indisputable masterpiece, larger and more ambitious than anything Eliot had written up to that time, has had enormous influence on future writers. Its subject is the decline of Western civilization, and its style is rich with complex allusions.

Eliot's use of Margate is a reminder of his presence in the seaside town which became a background for his comments on the theme of nullity. The River Thames of the present is contrasted with the river in the Elizabethan past, and the Thames-daughters speak in succession against this background. The poem might have been written even if he had not gone to Margate, but it would certainly have been written differently.

When Eliot returned to London in January, his malaise, alas, also returned. Nevertheless, one can appreciate the immediate and efficacious effect of Margate, and of the Albemarle Hotel in particular, on the well-being of the poet.

Miles of safe and magnificent sands have long made Margate a prime seaside resort to which people flocked for health cures. Formerly a small fishing town, Margate was destined to develop as a fashionable watering place in the mid-eighteenth century with the advent of the bathing machine and the belief in the curative effects of sea water and air.

In Margate the first bathing machines were used. Invented by Benjamin Beale, these horse-drawn huts carried the bather into the sea in a cubicle with hoods which could be lowered to give a modicum of privacy to the bather preparing for a dip into the sea. Once immersed and splashing about in the water, the bather must have doffed his modesty as well. In any case, the bathing machine gave Margate the lead over other fashionable spa towns.

Sea water was alleged to have restorative powers. It could cure a variety of ailments from asthma and arthritis to consumption and cancer. But surely, it must have been its promise to renew sexual prowess and vitality that played a large part in the success of this fashionable form of medical therapy. People flocked to sea resorts to partake of the salubrious waters, and spas developed to provide pleasurable activities to seekers of health and fun. As sea bathing was done in the early morning, elegant spas offered entertainment for the rest of the day in a variety of pastimes—card games, libraries, dancing, theatre. Watering places like Margate have had their heyday, and evidence of bygone days is still to be seen.

A walk from one end of Margate to the other will reveal the old Sea-Bathing Infirmary of 1792 at one end and the Jubilee Clock down by the harbor. Cecil Square, built in 1769, provided a large assembly hall with rooms for tea, cards, and dining.

Margate always had the reputation for gay and gaudy times. Thomas Gray spoke of it disparagingly as "Bartholomew Fair by the seaside." His description might be more apt today. Located on the Thames estuary within easy access of London, Margate has become a lively place with a huge Dreamland amusement park, a long promenade with a pier and lido, and an assortment of entertainments and floral gardens. Indeed, the changes that have come about in more recent times, have altered the character and appearance of Margate.

The seaboard town was allowed to sprawl without plan, and rows of bungalows spill over into the countryside. Unattractive shopfronts have desecrated the facades of Georgian houses in the streets running down to the sea. Hawley Square is somewhat desolate, and its elegant Theatre Royal is now a bingo parlor. And the Albemarle Hotel where Eliot stayed while he wrote a large segment of *The Waste Land* has become Butlin's Cliftonville Hotel. Just as Eliot contrasted the rich and meaningful associations of the Thames of the past with those of his own time, so the Margate of Eliot's day may be contrasted with the setting that exists today.

Located in the center of hoteldom, the Cliftonville is one of a large group of Butlin's Hotels designed to assure the guest of a typical English family holiday. Its character must have changed dramatically since Eliot stayed in the white room, content to write an innovative poem full of allusions gathered from his mind and imagination. The scene in the reception area—large groups of noisy holiday makers checking in, children shouting and running about, slot machines and game machines everywhere—would obviate the need to rely on the imagination. The hotel is nevertheless worth a visit for lovers of T. S. Eliot, as it is the venue in which an important literary work was created.

The influence and popularity of the poet of *The Waste Land* continues to be felt even after his death in 1965. His plays are occasionally revived—*Murder in the Cathedral, The Family Reunion, The Cocktail Party, The Confidential Clerk*—but one recent theatre piece has achieved mass popularity and insured his posthumous fame.

In May 1981, the musical play *Cats* opened in London with music by Andrew Lloyd Webber, based on Eliot's "Old Possum's Book of Practical Cats" of 1939. The light verse inspired by his favorite household pets will make Eliot's name known to the millions who find his poetry too abstruse and his plays too deep to dip into, perhaps even the very people who inadvertently follow his trail when they dip into Margate waters in search of recreation on Margate sands.

THE CLIFTONVILLE HOTEL
Eastern Esplanade
Cliftonville
Margate
Kent CT9 2LE

Telephone: (01843) 221444   Fax: (01843) 227073

Part of the middle-class, family-oriented Butlin's holiday group of hotels, the Cliftonville is designed for mass appeal. Its size is vast with about 260 rooms.

VITA SACKVILLE-WEST

at

The George Hotel
Cranbrook
Kent

... fruit-growing Kent, hop-growing Kent,
Kent unreached by the tentacles of London.

—Family History

Born on 9 March 1892 at Knole, a vast fifteenth-century house in
the Kentish countryside near Sevenoaks, Vita Sackville-West came
from a noble ancestry with a strong literary tradition. Queen
Elizabeth I had bestowed the great house, with its fairy-tale turrets
and towers and an estimated 365 rooms and fifty-two staircases,
on her cousin, Sir Thomas Sackville, who was also Vita's illustrious
ancestor. His literary achievements include *The Mirror for Magis-
trates* (1563) and *Gorboduc* (1561), the first English tragedy. His
grandson, the third Earl of Dorset, was a friend and patron of poets,
while the fifth Earl of Dorset wrote poetry and translated *Le Cid*
into English. The sixth Earl, a patron of poets, filled the rooms
of Knole with such notables as John Dryden, Alexander Pope,
Matthew Prior, and Thomas Shadwell and himself wrote poetry
and ballads. Vita followed the great literary tradition.

Vita thoroughly enjoyed the ancestral history and the romance
of the great house, which represented a rich heritage. Among the
portraits on the walls were the third Duke of Dorset painted by
Gainsborough and the fourth Earl of Dorset by Van Dyke. She had
a keen interest in the family and events associated with Knole and
studied its background assiduously. A deep and genuine passion
for her girlhood home exacerbated her resentment that she could

not, as a female, inherit Knole. "If only I had been Dada's son, instead of his daughter," she lamented.

With the death of her father in 1928, the great ancestral house went to her uncle Charlie and then to her cousin Eddy, who could not love Knole as she did. In a letter to her husband she wrote, "there is some sort of umbilical cord that ties me to Knole." Now in the hands of the National Trust, Knole is open to the public, its treasures on display for all to view.

Vita met Harold Nicolson in 1910 when she was eighteen, and they were married in 1913. Two sons were born to the well-suited couple—Ben in 1914 and Nigel in 1917. Vita and Harold remained completely devoted to each other, despite homosexual inclinations in each of them.

Vita had met Violet Keppel when she was twelve and formed an exciting friendship with the girl who was two years younger than herself. The girls shared much in common including a dominant mother and a fantasy life in a great house. In April 1918 Violet discovered Vita's duality, and they embarked on a passionate love affair that became for Vita a great romantic adventure which included an elopement to Paris. Other women were to enter Vita's sexual life, while Harold, of course, had his male attachments.

Perhaps the most notable of Vita's female alliances was Virginia Woolf. They met for the first time in December 1922 and were mutually fascinated. Vita wrote *Seducers in Equador* for the Hogarth Press, which was owned by Virginia and Leonard Woolf, and dedicated the short novel to Virginia. Virginia Woolf more than returned the compliment with *Orlando*, which Nigel Nicolson called "the longest and most charming love-letter in literature."

The eponymous hero of that novel is a young man, recognizable as Vita, living in the Elizabethan era in a great house, recognizable as Knole. Orlando passes through three centuries, changing sex, and ending up on the date of publication—ll October 1928. Full of unmistakable symbols as well as private references, the novel bequeathed Knole finally to Vita. It was, as Harold pointed out to Vita, "a book in which you and Knole are identified for ever."

Despite sexual complications, Vita and Harold remained completely in love with one another and remarkably well matched.

They endured unhappy separations caused by his career in diplomacy, wrote to each other every day when they were apart, shared confidences, were loving parents, and each exhibited total concern for the well being of the other. The two talented people enjoyed a happy and successful union.

Harold was sensitive and encouraging in Vita's career as a writer, which was launched with publication of her first book of poems in 1917. Ten years later, she won the coveted Hawthornden Prize for her long poem, *The Land*. Her first novel, *Heritage* (1919), established her reputation as a writer of fiction. But the three novels written around the time of the discovery and move to Sissinghurst—*The Edwardians* (1930), *All Passion Spent* (1931), and *Family History* (1932)—are her best known and finest.

The Nicolsons had been living quite happily in the Kentish Weald at Long Barn, a cottage they purchased in 1915. But when their peace was threatened by the prospect of a large poultry farm which would take over the neighboring property, they decided to look for another place.

Cheated out of Knole, Vita found consolation and complete satisfaction when she found Sissinghurst, a ruined sixteenth-century castle in Kent which also had family associations. "Fell flat in love with it," she wrote in her diary after first seeing it on 4 April 1930. She was to remain in love with Sissinghurst for the rest of her life, until her death on 2 June 1962.

She and Harold were excited by the romantic wreck and the many possibilities they saw for its regeneration. They envisioned an ideal home and were elated when their offer was accepted on 6 May. Others were less impressed with the derelict property in seven acres of waste land. Their son Nigel Nicolson, thirteen when he first set eyes on the estate, records his initial impression in *Portrait of a Marriage*: "It was the battered relic of an Elizabethan house in which not a single room was habitable."

Immediately upon becoming owners of Sissinghurst, the happy couple set about instituting plans for its restoration. On the weekend following the purchase, Vita and Harold went to the George Hotel in the nearby village of Cranbrook and stayed at that convenient base while they embarked on the repair and renovation

Vita Sackville-West
(1892-1962) and
The George Hotel,
Cranbrook, where she
and Harold Nicholson
stayed during renovations
at nearby Sissinghurst

87

of their new acquisition. From the George Hotel, they could easily get to Sissinghurst to tread in the mud and debris and dig with their own hands, working and making decisions for the rebuilding of the ruin. They returned frequently throughout the summer, sleeping at the George; and their dreams of shaping Sissinghurst into a perfect family home began to be realized. Not until September were they able to spend the night on camp beds in an upper room of the great brick tower of the castle. Full residence was not possible for a further two years.

In a state of euphoria after the purchase of Sissinghurst, Vita finished up proofs of *The Edwardians* and immediately immersed herself in the writing of a new novel, *All Passion Spent*. The following year saw publication of *Family History*.

In *Family History*, Vita Sackville-West describes a castle in the country which is in fact Sissinghurst. The heroine of the novel expresses the author's own feelings of excitement at seeing it for the first time:

> The lane widened, and the fan of light showed up
> a group of oast-houses beside a great tiled barn; then
> it swung round on a long, low range of buildings with
> a pointed arch between two gables. . . .The hard winter
> starlight revealed an untidy courtyard, enclosed by
> ruined walls, and opposite, an arrowy tower springing
> up to a lovely height with glinting windows.

Vita's creative energy was at the same time being applied to the reclamation of Sissinghurst.

The high rose-brick tower with its two octagonal turrets was the first part of the estate to be completed. Vita selected the tower room on the first floor as her own library and writing retreat. It was to be for the next thirty-two years the private citadel of what she called "Sleeping Beauty's castle." She herself painted the corner cupboard of that special room green, as it is today. Together, Vita and Harold succeeded in creating a magnificent home with exquisite gardens, which remain, over fifty years later, among the most famous in England.

Sissinghurst is now owned and maintained by the National Trust. Open to the public, it reveals to visitors the writing sanctuary of V. Sackville-West, the author whose literary career included travel books, short stories, history, and biography, as well as poetry and novels—a total of some fifty volumes. A visit to Sissinghurst is extremely worthwhile, as is an excursion to the place so intimately connected with the creative life of Sissinghurst—the George in Cranbrook.

Cranbrook, one of the most attractive small towns of Kent, is characterized primarily by the white weatherboarded houses and shops which line its streets. Weatherboarding—its name reveals its purpose—is the fixing of horizontal, overlapping wooden boards on a timber-framed wall to give extra warmth and protection and help keep out the damp.

Also weatherboarded is the splendid octagonal windmill which overlooks the town as it rises from its position at the eastern end of Stone Street to a height of nearly seventy-five feet.

Among other landmarks of note is the enormous medieval parish church. Called the Cathedral of the Weald, it features sixteenth-century glass, intriguing gargoyles, and American connections with memorial tablets to Dr. Comfort Starr and John and Samuel Eddye who emigrated to New England in the early seventeenth century. In addition there is the seven-sided Providence Chapel of 1828, the sixteenth-century Cranbrook School, and a museum.

Where the High Street turns the corner into the narrower Stone Street, the tile-hung and weatherboarded George Hotel, with its typically wealden architecture, extends along Stone Street. The George boasts that it has been in continuous operation for over five hundred years. Indeed, its structure dates to the fifteenth century. Inside, Tudor beams continue to support, and the great open hearth of what was once the kitchen remains in the dining room. A magnificent oak staircase leads to the upstairs bedrooms.

In one of those heavily beamed bedrooms, Queen Elizabeth once slept when she visited the town in 1573. The prosperity produced in the fourteenth century by the flourishing cloth trade, made Cranbrook important enough for a royal visit. The Queen was entertained at the George and presented with a silver-gilt cup. It must have been heavy, for she rested in one of the beamed bedrooms of the inn, making it another of those ubiquitous places claiming that "Queen Elizabeth slept here."

Apart from the immediate goal of visiting the historic George and the nearby Sissinghurst Castle home of Vita Sackville-West, two other literary treats await: the Bull in the tiny village of Sissinghurst, where Vita and Harold Nicolson also occasionally stayed; and the nearby village of Rolvenden in which lived Frances Hodgson Burnett, author of *Little Lord Fauntleroy* and *The Secret Garden*.

THE GEORGE HOTEL
Stone Street
Cranbrook
Kent TN17 3HE

Telephone: (01580) 713348   Fax: (01580) 715532

With eight guest rooms having private bathrooms, the George has recently undergone restoration and continues to recall its past glory as a focal point of the town.

Situated in the center of Cranbrook, the capital of the Weald, the George is a good base for the enticements of this old-fashioned market town as well as the surrounding countryside.

SIR ARTHUR CONAN DOYLE

at

Undershaw Hotel
Hindhead
Surrey

...he had settled in modest comfort into the
old house of Cosford upon the eastern slope
of the Hindhead hill.

--Sir Nigel

To follow in the footsteps of Sherlock Holmes, aficionados often
seek out the fictional premises at 221B Baker Street. Letters still
pour into that non-existent Baker Street address. But anyone
wishing to follow in the footsteps of the creator of the world's most
acclaimed detective can go to the actual abode of Arthur Conan
Doyle at Hindhead in Surrey.

"Home of the late Sir Arthur Conan Doyle" are the words
on the sign outside the Undershaw Hotel. Accompanying those
words is a silhouette of the famous detective, complete with pipe,
magnifying glass, and deerstalker cap. The facts relating to how
Undershaw came to be Conan Doyle's home are elementary.

Born in Edinburgh in 1859, Arthur Conan Doyle went to
Edinburgh University where he received medical training as well
as basic training for the stories he was later to write. He was
influenced by a certain Dr. Joseph Bell, a fascinating lecturer who
used an intriguing method of deductive reasoning to diagnose
cases. Eventually, Conan Doyle set up a medical practice in
Southsea on the Hampshire coast. There, in 1885, the struggling
young doctor married Louise Hawkins, whose dying brother he had
been treating.

Even in those early days, he tried his hand at writing. Literary success came with his brilliant idea of using a detective who could rely on logic and science to reconstruct a crime, a detective whose methods were reminiscent of those of Dr. Bell. As Sherrinford Holmes evolved to become Sherlock Holmes, as his friend Dr. James Watson became Dr. John H. Watson, and as *A Tangled Skein* became *A Study in Scarlet,* Arthur Conan Doyle became the creator of one of the most celebrated characters in English literature.

Although not financially successful at first, a literary career was launched. By 1891, Conan Doyle decided to give up his medical practice and devote himself entirely to writing.

Louise was diagnosed, in 1893, as having tuberculosis and given only a few months to live. She remained in a delicate state of health for the next thirteen years. To prolong her life, the couple went to live in Switzerland. Meanwhile, he continued to write and to travel and even managed to go on an American speaking tour.

The return to England, which they both longed for, was made possible by the writer Grant Allen, himself a victim of tuberculosis. Allen believed in the therapeutic qualities of Surrey as a safe place for sufferers of the disease. Doyle investigated. He wrote that the place would be suitable for her recuperation "because its height, its dryness, its sandy soil, its fir-trees, and its shelter from all bitter winds present the conditions which all agree to be best."

He decided to have a house built at Hindhead and hired a Southsea architect and old friend to build a "considerable mansion" to his own specifications. The ambitious plan indicated a considerable change in his financial position compared with the early years in Southsea, when he polished up the brass plate on his own front door. The desire to return to England was fulfilled. In October 1897, he and Louise were able to move into Undershaw, as the house was named in a reference to its position below or under a *shaw*, the Old English word for a small wood or thicket.

Undershaw was a large and comfortable house, and Conan Doyle continued to work, write and give readings. In addition to his literary labors, he took advantage of available country sports and enjoyed the open air and the fields. He also laid out a tennis court in the grounds.

Undershaw Hotel, Hindhead, "a considerable mansion" built to Sir Arthur Conan Doyle's (1859-1930) own specifications and his home for many years

Here, in his study, he resurrected Sherlock Holmes. Earlier, he had arranged for the demise of his hero in *The Final Problem* when, together with the evil Professor Moriarty, Holmes is killed as he disappears over the edge into the Reichenbach Falls in Switzerland. Having achieved literary fame and financial success, Conan Doyle had tired of the immortal figure who had taken over his life. He wanted to get on with other works. "I am weary of his name," he wrote in a letter to his mother, the "Ma'am" as the formidable lady was addressed.

But the public complained. At Undershaw Conan Doyle did much of the writing of *The Hound of the Baskervilles* with Sherlock Holmes back as the detective-hero. Chronologically, however, that story is set before the death of Sherlock Holmes. Perhaps one reason for the knighthood of Sir Arthur in 1902 was gratitude for the return of the popular detective. The public lamented and the author relented. In 1903, in *The Adventure of the Empty House*, Holmes returned alive and well and living at 221B Baker Street with the explanation, not that he had survived the fall into the chasm, but that he never fell at all. He had climbed to safety on the other side of the cliff, unbeknown to Watson.

Conan Doyle's historical novel *Sir Nigel*, also written at Undershaw, shows an easy familiarity with the Surrey scene as young Nigel journeys along the Pilgrims' Way to Dover: "To their left was a hilly country, a land of rolling heaths and woods, broken here and there into open spaces round the occasional farmhouse of a franklin. Hackhurst Down, Dunley Hill, and Ranmore Common swelled and sank, each merging into the other. But on the right, after passing the village of Shere and the old church of Gomshall, the whole south country lay like a map at their feet."

After Louise died in 1906, he married Jean Leckie whom he had met earlier, in 1897, and whom he deeply loved. But he had remained true to his chivalrous standards and loyal to his invalid wife. Just a year after the death of Louise, he married Jean and moved to a new home at Crowborough in Sussex, where he remained until his death on 11 July 1930, at the age of seventy-one. Undershaw was sold.

The Undershaw Hotel is located forty-two miles south of London within easy reach of two busy roads (the A3 from London and the A287 from Haslemere, two miles to the east). But trees and shrubbery surround it so effectively that neither sight nor sound of traffic is disturbing. The south side of the hotel overlooks the Nutcombe Valley to the hills of the South Downs, and the beautiful view is enhanced in the springtime when framed by rhododendrons, ablaze in color. The wrought iron gate through which the red-brick hotel may be approached incorporates the name "Undershaw" and the initials "ACD."

Inside is further evidence of the Arthur Conan Doyle connection. In the hall is the great stained-glass window with heraldic shields of the Doyle family. Somehow, he had forgotten to include the arms of his mother's ancestors. To placate the angry Ma'am, that coat of arms was quickly installed in the window over the main staircase.

Brass finger plates on the doors incorporate his monogram. Door handles need only be gently pushed, not twisted or turned, his own specification to make door opening easy for Louise, whose hands were crippled by arthritis. Shallow stairs also made movement easier for her arthritic limbs. Spacious and well-lit rooms include the study where he wrote much of his material.

It is all there. To remember Sir Arthur Conan Doyle, forget Baker Street. Go to the place where the famous Baskerville hound first bayed—go to Undershaw.

UNDERSHAW HOTEL
Portsmouth Road
Hindhead
Surrey GU26 6AH

Telephone: (01428) 604039   Fax: (01428) 604205

Rooms: Main rooms have en suite baths. Rooms are individually furnished and most face south overlooking the Nutcombe Valley and nearly four acres of lovely hotel gardens.

Doyles Restaurant: The dining room, with seating for thirty, is the very one used by Sir Arthur Conan Doyle himself. An imaginative menu uncovers culinary mysteries with its emphasis on English dishes such as Lymswold fritters with blackcurrent sauce or rack of lamb marinated with mint.

Location: Sixteen miles south of Guildford on the A3 road and 42 miles south of London. Access to Gatwick and Heathrow airports within one hour by car.

JOHN KEATS

at

The Burford Bridge Hotel
Dorking
Surrey

O thou wouldst joy to live in such a place.

--Endymion

Would John Keats have finished his long *Endymion* if he had not secluded himself in a hotel at the foot of Box Hill? Probably. But although the answer may remain forever uncertain, what is certain is the fact that he went there with the explicit purpose of completing *Endymion* and proving himself as a poet.

He started the long classical legend of Endymion and the Moon-goddess around October 1816, having chosen this haunting story to be a test of his poetic ability. He dated the poem 16 December and left it unfinished. But this successful beginning, together with the success of his earlier first volume of poems, led to a turning point. He made the final and irrevocable decision to end his career in medicine and to devote himself to poetry.

He had always had an intense interest in language and poetry. When he was eight, his father died as the result of a fall from his horse, and when he was not quite fifteen, his mother died of tuberculosis. John, born on 31 October 1795, the eldest of the four Keats children, was withdrawn from school by his guardian and apprenticed to a surgeon and apothecary. The orphan had to be able to earn a living.

His apprenticeship over, he entered Guy's Hospital for a six-month term which would qualify him to practice. He completed the course, passed the examination in July 1816, and needed only to wait for his twenty-first birthday before he could legally set up his own practice. In the interim, he could prepare for his profession. But instead of gaining further experience at Guy's, he went to the fashionable seaside resort of Margate, where he could be free to write.

Weeks passed and so did his birthday, but he took no action toward establishing a professional opening. Success with such poems as *On First Looking into Chapman's Homer, I Stood Tiptoe*, and *Sleep and Poetry* helped to seal his fate. Before long, he was inextricably involved with *Endymion*.

Progress on the projected four books of that four-thousand-line poem went slowly, and he digressed from time to time to other poems. In the spring of 1817, he went to the Isle of Wight and worked on Book Two; and in the autumn, feeling that a change of scene would be beneficial to the creative process, he accepted an invitation to go to Oxford to write Book Three. He still had another book to go, and his rate of writing slowed down considerably. He had hoped to have it finished by autumn, but winter was now fast approaching. At the start of the poem, he expressed the hope,

> O may no wintry season, bare and hoary
> See it half finished; but let Autumn bold,
> With universal tinge of sober gold,
> Be all about me when I make an end.

Only one solution was possible. He needed to get away again, as he wrote in a letter to his friend Benjamin Bailey, "to change the Scene—change the Air and give me a spur to wind up my Poem, of which there are wanting 500 Lines."

So, about a year after he first started *Endymion*, he found a quiet retreat a mere twenty miles from London to which he escaped to complete the long poem. The Fox and Hounds, as the inn was then called, was situated in Surrey about one mile north of Dorking, between that village and Leatherhead. He arrived at the old coaching inn on 22 November 1817. From then, events proceeded with fairy-tale success toward a happy conclusion.

John Keats
(1795-1821) and
The Burford Bridge
Hotel, under
Boxhill, where
he completed
his long poem
Endymion

The low white building now stands in a garden of two acres, amidst beautiful scenery. About fifty feet behind it is the hill which takes its name from the box trees which grow on it. Box Hill rises steeply to a height of almost five hundred feet. In fact, only box and yew trees can keep hold in the steep western slopes near Burford Bridge. Before the hotel, spreads the Mickleham Valley with its little River Mole, a weed-choked river spanned by the three arches of the stone Burford Bridge and described by the poet Alexander Pope as "the sullen Mole, that hides his diving flood." It tends to disappear in dry seasons and flow underground.

Keats stayed in a small back room overlooking the stable yard. The bedroom window gives a view of lawn with fine old trees, a beech and a cedar. How he must have admired the scene which, with a large garden at the back, with a hermit's grotto or summer-house, made him feel at once comfortably at home and free from worry. He must have been excited also by the fact that his room was next to one that had been occupied by his boyhood hero, Admiral Nelson. Nelson stayed here when he took his last farewell of Lady Hamilton before the Battle of Trafalgar.

From a path behind the inn, Keats climbed Box Hill. He could slip through the garden gate near the hermitage to walk up the hill through the box and yew trees to look down into the peaceful valley. Exhilarated by the natural scenery, he climbed up the hill the first night and returned with a flow of inspired lines. Extremely happy in his quiet new environment, he wrote in a letter: "I like this place very much. There is Hill & Dale and a little River—I went up Box Hill this Evening after the Moon—you 'a seen the Moon—came down—and wrote some lines."

And these are the lines he wrote:

> The moon put forth a little diamond peak,
> No bigger than an unobserved star,
> Or tiny point of fairy scimitar;
> Bright signal that she only stooped to tie
> Her silver sandals, ere deliciously
> She bowed into the heavens her timid head.

Like his hero Endymion, faced with failure and immersed in troubles, he had entered the cave of quietude and emerged renewed. Lines from *Endymion* describe the autumnal beauty of Box Hill:

> Where shall our dwelling be? Under the brow
> Of some steep mossy hill, where ivy dun
> Would hide us up, although spring leaves were none;
> And where dark yew trees, as we rustle through,
> Will drop their scarlet berry cups of dew?
> O thou wouldst joy to live in such a place.

Keats joyed to live in this place. He continued to write. Confining himself to his small room for most of the day, he wrote an average of eighty to eighty-five lines a day. *Endymion*, with its familiar first line, "A thing of beauty is a joy for ever," was soon finished. The place and date—Burford Bridge, 28 November 1817—were appended to the draft of Book Four. In a state of elation following completion of this large work which he had chosen to prove his ability, he stayed on for another week. Before he left Burford Bridge, he produced a very moving lyric, "In a drear-nighted December." He emerged as a true poet. He was twenty-two.

The sensuous delights, the music, so melodious and rhythmically satisfying, the richness of imagery—these qualities make Keats one of the greatest of English poets. *Hyperion, The Eve of St. Agnes*, the great odes—*Ode to Psyche, Ode to a Nightingale, Ode on a Grecian Urn, To Autumn*—so full of emotional intensity, sensation, and artistry, have found a permanent place in literature and in the hearts of an appreciative public.

But his was to be a tragically short life. As his literary power ascended, his health and happiness descended. One of his brothers emigrated to the United States. Another died young of tuberculosis. Keats, too, contracted the fatal disease. The illness caused a self-imposed separation from his beloved Fanny Brawne and made marriage impossible. It sent him to Italy in search of a more beneficial climate, but he died in Rome on 23 February 1821. He was twenty-five.

The Box Hill experience must be remembered as a peak period of happiness in his life. Now modernized and given a straighforward name, the Burford Bridge Hotel, a rambling building with forty-eight bedrooms, offers informal public rooms and high standards of comfort throughout.

The hotel still nestles near the River Mole under the steep side of Box Hill, now preserved by the National Trust, and it is still a popular place for walks and picnics—as it was for Jane Austen, who selected Box Hill as the setting for an excursion in *Emma*, which ended so disastrously when the heroine was unkind to Miss Bates.

A visitor to this hotel may very well write a postcard home using Keats's own words, "I like this place very much."

BURFORD BRIDGE HOTEL
Burford Bridge
Dorking
Surrey RH5 6BX

Telephone: (01306) 884561   Fax: (01306) 880386

Rooms: 48 guest bedrooms of this Trusthouse Forte hotel include two suites; most rooms have bench windows or balconies overlooking gardens and all have private bathrooms, television, radio, telephone, and tea- and coffee-making facilities. Robes, hairdryers, and trouser press provided.

Restaurant: Views of garden; patio for alfresco summertime meals.

Tithe Barn: An attractive sixteenth-century setting, complete with minstrel gallery and timbered walls, for banquets, weddings, and special occasions.

EDWARD LEAR

at

Oatlands Park Hotel
Weybridge
Surrey

How pleasant to know Mr. Lear!
Who has written such volumes of stuff!
Some think him ill-tempered and queer,
But a few think him pleasant enough.

—Self-Portrait in *Nonsense Songs and Stories* (1895)

The pleasant enough master of the nonsense rhyme was born on 12 May 1812 in the district of London known as Highgate. He was an unattractive child with poor vision and poor health, who suffered also from epilepsy. The youngest of a large family of twenty-one children, he was rejected by his overburdened mother and placed in the care of his sister Ann when he was four and she was twenty-five. Ann looked after him with great concern and affection for the rest of her life, making an excellent surrogate mother until her death in 1861 at the age of seventy.

Edward lear began to earn a living from his drawings when he was fifteen, but it was as an ornithological artist that he achieved a reputation for accuracy and for beauty of design and execution. His first regular employment came when the Zoological Society hired him to make drawings of the parrots at the Regent's Park Zoo. It was also due to his profession as an artist that he became, inadvertently, a popular and professional nonsense writer.

In 1832, the Earl of Derby, impressed with Lear's work at the Zoo, invited him to the ancient and great family estate of Knowsley Hall near Liverpool to make illustrations of his unique collection of animals and birds. During the years spent at Knowsley, Lear earned the lifelong patronage and friendship of the noble family, who gave its name to the well-known horse race. More importantly, Lear's career as writer dates from that same period; he amused the children of the house with his silly rhymes, and the nonsense he made up for them was eventually published. The results of four years of work were printed in a private edition in 1846, *Gleanings from the Menagerie and Aviary at Knowsley Hall;* but that same year also saw the publication of Lear's *A Book of Nonsense,* a volume which brought him the lasting fame that eluded him as an artist.

A second edition of his *Book of Nonsense* appeared ten years later, and Lear offered to sell the copyright for one hundred pounds. But his publishers were unwilling to take the risk. When a third edition of two thousand copies followed in 1861 and sold out immediately, the publishers changed their minds; but Lear shrewdly, he thought, raised the price. Not appreciating its potential and value, he sold the copyright for a mere £125, the total profit realized for a book that went into nearly thirty editions in his own lifetime.

The theme of the loss of happiness is prevalent in the first *Book of Nonsense* and in others which followed. His Owl and Pussy-Cat seek contentment in a faraway land where they dine on mince and slices of quince with a runcible spoon and dance by the light of the moon. Other characters escape to the great Gromboolian plain or to the hills of the Chankly Bore, full of a haunting mystery.

Like his characters, Lear sought escape. His poor state of health plagued him throughout life, although he lived to be seventy-six. In particular, he suffered from chronic asthma and bronchitis, exacerbated by the English climate. Escape to warmer weather, at least in the winter time, could only be advantageous. Moreover, he reasoned, southern climes could provide him with exotic scenes to paint. Unaware that nonsense was his metier, he made the conscious decision to earn his livelihood as a landscape painter. Painting landscapes would also conserve his poor vision which was strained by the minute details required in drawing birds and animals.

He left for Italy in July 1837 and was henceforth to live a peripatetic life. He returned frequently to England at intervals, but largely spent his life abroad where he continued to draw or paint and to write. His journeys became professional searches for the picturesque which would yield landscapes that he could sell. He was willing to endure discomforts to obtain a sketch he wanted. Italy, Corfu, Albania, Greece, Corsica, Malta, Egypt, Palestine, Crete—these became his terrain for the rich supply of subject matter.

In addition to excursions into picturesque scenes and countries, he took occasional excursions into writing. He published over half a dozen travel books, with illustrations enhanced by his own accounts of the tour. He kept journals in which he recorded his own observations as well as such things as architectural details. Indeed, his first two volumes of *Illustrated Excursions in Italy,* published in 1846, so appealed to Queen Victoria, that she asked him in that same year to give her drawing lessons.

In London in 1849, he took rooms in Stratford Place suitable for use as living quarters and studio. Years later, in 1857, he lived at 30 Seymour Street, an address that now belongs to the Portman Court Hotel. But inevitably his health would fail and he would flee to the continent, where he continued to suffer from other physical ailments.

Back in England in 1860, he was determined to establish himself as an oil painter. From Holman Hunt, the pre-Raphaelite painter, he had learned that the elements to be included in the composition of a landscape could be found in England; it was not essential to be at the actual source. Thus, when he needed cedar trees for the large canvas he was planning, he was delighted to find the Oatlands Park Hotel with grounds in which stood cedar trees, which are still there today. He expected to work through the winter, and the Oatlands Park Hotel sounded like a good winter residence. He referred to its dry soil, which did not adversely affect his asthma or "roomatizsim." Its ideal location, less than twenty miles from central London, made it an accessible place where friends could easily join him. In September 1860 he settled in.

A royal palace had stood on the site which was now a residence for another king—King Lear, as Millais called him. Henry VIII built a palace here for his new queen, Anne of Cleves, who probably never actually lived there. Elizabeth I, however, was a frequent visitor to the imposing palace standing in nine acres, and it was a favorite residence of James I. The fourth son of Charles I was born there, and a cedar tree which still stands was supposedly planted to commemorate the event.

The palace was eventually demolished and a house erected on the site where the hotel now stands. Of that mansion with its formal gardens and shell grotto, only prints remain which can be seen in the lounge area. Rebuilt after a fire in 1794, the new house went through several changes of ownership until it was purchased in 1856, remodelled, enlarged with a new west wing, and converted into the Oatlands Park Hotel.

Since Lear's stay, the hotel has been further enlarged by a dining room extension in 1927 and a ballroom in 1930. Restored and refurbished in recent years, it functions as a large country hotel, with all sorts of sports from tennis and golf to clay pigeon shooting, and with ten acres of grounds offering superb views all around and down to the River Thames.

In the calm atmosphere of a lovely Sunday afternoon, it could give the impression of a well-kept Hollywood set design with the scenario showing residents seated in the large and comfortable lounge, perhaps having had a slow morning stroll about the grounds or having had a long morning sit, with face to sun. Perhaps they now sip a glass of sherry in the bright Atrium Lounge. Then, gradually, they get up to go into the dining room for the next tranquil activity, Sunday lunch in the Broadwater Restaurant.

In a letter dated 30 September 1860 to his very dear friend Chichester Fortescue, whom he often playfully addressed as 40sque, Lear described the hotel as, "a large & sumptuously commodious place . . .with nice broad terrace walks, & a wonderfully lovely view over the river Temms & the surroundiant landskip. . . I have a large light bedroom delightful to behold & wanting for nought."

Edward Lear (1812-1888)
stayed at the Oatlands Park
Hotel, Weybridge, to paint
a large landscape

While there, he made a nonsense drawing labelled "Lear feeding 'unfortunate birds' at Oatlands Park Hotel, Weybridge." Meanwhile he also wrote rhymes and decided to offer a new volume for publication.

Lear left the hotel for London at the end of January. But he returned again for a few days after his beloved sister Ann died on 11 March. As for the painting of "The Cedars," it was finished by the middle of May. He needed funds to cover expenses including those incurred by his stay at the Oatlands Park Hotel, but the painting was not immediately salable. It was finally purchased by Lady Ashburton in December 1867 for a fraction of the asking price.

Edward Lear's desire to become a respected and sought-after painter blinded him to his ability and popularity as a writer of nonsense. In his letters and in his diary, he hardly alludes to the poems. Yet his landscapes, a constant struggle, nearly died with the man, while his nonsense, so full of originality and subtleties, brought him immortality.

Other "volumes of stuff" are *Nonsense Songs, Stories, Botany and Alphabets* (1871) and *More Nonsense* (1872). *Laughable Lyrics* appeared in 1877, the fourth and last nonsense book to be published in his lifetime.

Based on the limerick form, his verses were adapted and perfected in his inimitable style:

> There was an Old Person of Bangor,
> Whose face was distorted with anger,
> He tore off his boots, and subsisted on roots,
> That borascible person of Bangor.

And:

> There was an Old Person of Philoe,
> Whose conduct was scroobious and wily;
> He rushed up a Palm, when the weather was calm,
> And observed all the ruins of Philoe.

His playfulness with words is evident. Sometimes he coins words which sound absolutely right and become part of the Lear vocabulary. In later works, he refers to the scroobious manners of the old person of Grange and invents a Scroobious Snake for his nonsense alphabet.

The nonsense becomes a vehicle for expressing deep feelings with an emotional quality that is true to life. His people are in contact with or exploited by the "they"—that gossiping, interfering, unsympathetic, ubiquitous world of anonymous people we all recognize. His characters—the Jumblies, the Dong with the Luminous Nose, the Pobble—all have human feelings. Though they may seem unlikely, though they may have extraordinary experiences, the reader accepts and believes. Humor arises from the incongruities. And when "runcible" and "ombliferous" definitely and perfectly modify the nouns they describe and sound so right, children of all ages are delighted.

But many of the poems are simply not *nice* and contain mean or vicious incidents under the amusing tone. Some characters become the unfortunate victims of blunders (the Old Man of Peru is baked by mistake), some are subjected to violence (the Old Person of Buda is smashed with a hammer). There is unhappiness, cruelty, drowning, even suicide (the Old Person of Tartary divided his jugular artery), and one wonders whether the many examples of unwarranted death in those delightful rhymes are altogether suitable for children. If one persists in trying to apply sense to nonsense, one could conclude that they pierce through protective armor.

> There was an Old Man of Cape Horn,
> Who wished he had never been born;
> So he sat on a chair, till he died of despair,
> That dolorous Man of Cape Horn.

Lear moved away from sheer nonsense and moved away from England, simply unable to tolerate its damp climate. Like his characters, he was always on the go. The Owl and the Pussy-Cat travel, as does Mr. Daddy Long-legs, who sails with Mr. Floppy

Fly to the great Gromboolian plain. The Jumblies went to sea in a sieve. The Yonghy-Bonghy-Bo travels

> With a sad primaeval motion
> Towards the sunset isles of Boshen.

When Edward Lear left England in August 1880, he was never to see his homeland again. He died on 29 January 1888 at San Remo on the Italian Riviera.

OATLANDS PARK HOTEL
Oatlands Drive
Weybridge
Surrey KT13 9HBE

Telephone: (01932) 847242   Fax: (01932) 842252

Rooms: 144 bedrooms, most with private bathrooms, all with telephone, television, in-house movies, radio, and tea- and coffee-making facilities.

The Broadwater Restaurant offers a la carte and table d'hote menus.

The bright and cheerful galleried Atrium Lounge, accented by red carpteting and complementary red cornice design, features a glazed dome.

CONRAD AIKEN

at

Jeake's House

Rye

East Sussex

We have bought Jeake's House in Rye, in
the same block that James, Henry lived
in. . .with beams and panels and studios
and views and a hotelful of bedrooms.

—Letter, January 13, 1924

Conrad Aiken is arguably the least publicized, most underrated
American writer of the twentieth century. Nevertheless, he had
produced during his lifetime a total of some fifty books including
thirty-five volumes of poetry, five novels, a memoir, and collections of stories, essays, and criticism.

He was born in Savannah, Georgia, in 1889, and he died there
in 1973. But he was removed from his childhood home and taken
to live with relatives in New England when the tragedy of his life
occurred. In 1901, his father killed his mother in a jealous rage, then
shot himself. The young boy of eleven found the slain bodies of
his parents, and, as he was to write in a later autobiography,
"finding them dead, found himself possessed of them forever."

When Aiken entered Harvard University, he met T.S. Eliot and
began a friendship which continued through the years when both
were living in England. He also met a Radcliffe student, Jessie
McDonald, whom he married shortly after leaving Harvard. After
the birth of two children, he decided to move with his family to
England. Living expenses would be lower, he reasoned, and his
children could receive an English education. He arrived in London

with his family in 1921 and moved to a rented cottage in the Sussex town of Winchelsea the following spring.

Aiken loved the English countryside and indulged in treks across the Sussex landscape, frequently making the two-and-a-half mile walk between Winchelsea and Rye. The two ancient hill towns face each other across the inlet known as Romney Marsh and rise from flat land which was once covered by the sea.

When the ancient sea town of Rye was designated a royal borough in 1289, it already had the distinctive title of Ancient Town with the status of a Cinque Port. Its rivers silted up, the town has been left stranded inland nearly three miles from the English Channel, no longer a port. "Where now the sheep graze, mermaids were at play," wrote Aiken.

Crowning the hilltop of Rye, the impressively large Church of St. Mary looks down on a medieval picture, a complex cluster of red-roofed houses and intriguing streets. Within fourteenth-century walls are cobbled lanes and half-timbered houses, many dating from the fifteenth century, which give the town its enormously appealing character. Here in Rye, Aiken found just the house he wanted. Although Jeake's House was in nearly derelict condition, he fell in love with it from the moment he spotted it for sale in January 1924.

Jeake's House was built in the seventeenth century as a storehouse for wool by Samuel Jeake II, who lived with his family at Hartshorn House, on the opposite side of the street. The tall storehouse had five floors, including attic and cellar, with a single room on each level. A plaque on the outside records with exactitude the placing of the foundation stone—at noon on June 13, 1689—and gives a horoscope of the aspects of the heavenly bodies at that time, indicating Samuel Jeake's strong interest in astrology. The signs must have been auspicious, for complicated structural changes over the years have led, finally, to its enlargement and existence as a guest house of great character.

The history of Jeake's House is intertwined with its neighbor on the right, Quaker House. As early as 1704, the Quakers had a burial ground and a meeting house which they sold in 1753 to the Baptists, who rebuilt it as a chapel. The storehouse itself became a school in

1853, and changes continued to be made until the Baptists moved away in 1909. The building was then converted into a dwelling. Further changes were instituted as the house gradually evolved into its present form. Now the galleried former chapel is the dining room where breakfast is served to hotel guests, and the former baptistry is below a trapdoor in the dining room. The attic room over the chapel, once used for drying wool, became Conrad Aiken's study when he purchased the property in 1924. He wrote of its superb view "from the great window of the great room, overlooking the Salts and the castle and the sea."

The flat area known as the Salts lies below the imposing fourteenth-century Landgate, the proper entry into town from the north and the only remaining original gate of the three which once guarded the town. Camber Castle, which Aiken could also see from his study, was built during the reign of Henry VIII as a defense against the French. The little fortress, now a mile inland, squats on the marsh between Rye and Winchelsea.

For Conrad Aiken, Jeake's House was simply irresistible. The property was situated on steep and cobbled Mermaid Street—still one of the most famous and delightfully picturesque streets any-where—just opposite the medieval, black-timbered Mermaid Inn; and around the corner was Lamb House, the attractive home of Henry James.

Aiken was to own Jeake's House, a crucial place of residence, from 1924 to 1947. The impulsive purchase was nevertheless accompanied with some misgivings due to the condition of the property. A letter dated 13 January informs a friend of the acquisition:

> The plaster is falling off the ceilings. The wallpapers hang in mouldy festoons from the walls. Rodents put ancient grizzled snouts out of holes in the floors. The whole house ticks like a clock factory with the hidden feverish activities of the Death Watch Beetle. The small garden is a haunted wood of black weeds and savage hollyhocks: one leafless tree hangs weeping

over the ruin. And creepers have closed all the windows, unopened for three centuries.

He must have exaggerated the horrendous state of neglect just as he exaggerated the age of the house, which actually dates only to 1689. Although he expressed wonder and doubt at his rash act ("I don't know why we did it. . . we bought it without minds"), he never wavered in his love for the house. Aiken's strong attraction must have been motivated in no small part by its location. Easy access to London (a two-hour train ride) as well as its antiquity and beauty made Rye a place that attracted writers and artists and gave it less stringent restrictions than prevailed in the usual small town.

There were fifteen pubs in Rye, and Aiken knew them all. His favorite was the nearest—the Ship Inn. Located near the bottom of Mermaid Street, the Ship was run by an old Sussex character whose talk and brew delighted him.

Pubs and old buildings worth exploring are everywhere. The church, largely rebuilt after the town was devastated by a French raid in 1377, features flying buttresses on the outside and a stained-glass window by Sir Edward Burne-Jones on the inside. Ypres Tower, built in 1249 as a defence against the French, is now a worthwhile museum of local history, with an elevated terrace for a good view all around and down to the River Rother.

Two cobbled streets running out of Church Square are particularly rich in splendid old buildings—Watchbell Street, named for the alarm bell that warned when French were sighted in the Channel, and Mermaid Street, with the well-known Mermaid Inn of 1420. A coaching inn in the eighteenth century and a haunt of smugglers, the Mermaid is an architectural gem with oak-beamed interior, oak paneling, and maze of twisting corridors.

Another gem is the fifteenth-century Hartshorn House, with three overhanging and distinctive gables. Known as "The Old Hospital" for having served as a hospital during the Napoleonic Wars, it had been the home of the Samuel Jeake family, given as dowry when the prosperous merchant (who built the wool storehouse opposite) married Elizabeth Hartshorn.

Conrad Aiken
(1889-1973) purchased
Jeake's House, Rye,
in the countryside
he loved

The Old Grammar School, named Peacock's School for the man who founded it in 1636, the former apothecary's shop with its lovely curved and bow windows, and the butcher's shop with its brass fittings—all may be singled out for special attention on the High Street. Fifteenth-century Flushing Inn in Market Street features a sixteenth-century wall painting in the dining room, while the Town Hall, with its arcaded ground floor, dates to 1743.

Literary connections too are abundant in Rye. A sign on a building in Lion Street announces that John Fletcher, the Elizabethan dramatist and collaborator with Beaumont, was born in 1579 in Fletcher's House, now tearooms. In more recent times, the novelist Rumer Godden resided near the top of Mermaid Street at Number 4; and Radclyffe Hall, whose *Well of Loneliness* created a sensation in 1928, lived at Number 4 High Street.

But the most popular literary figure is Henry James, who lived from 1899 to 1914 in eighteenth-century Lamb House. Afterwards, the novelist E.F. Benson, author of the *Mapp and Lucia* stories which are set in Rye, also resided in that superb Georgian house, now in the care of the National Trust. In the surrounding area lived contemporaries of James—H.G. Wells, Stephen Crane, Joseph Conrad and Ford Madox Ford. But those in search of literary roots need go no further than Jeake's House. Among the many writers who arrived during Conrad Aiken's residence are E.F. Benson, Malcolm Lowry, Radclyffe Hall, Julian Huxley, and T.S. Eliot.

Indeed, Rye was an altogether happy choice for Aiken. In Rye his third child was born, but harmonious family life did not thrive at Jeake's House. On one of his regular jaunts across the ocean to obtain writing assignments or meet with his publishers, he met the woman who was to become his second wife. In Boston in the autumn of 1926, Clarissa Lorenz interviewed him for a feature story for the Boston *Evening Transcript*, and the couple were married in February 1930. He returned to Rye with Clarissa, who eventually wrote an autobiography focusing on the ten years of her life with Aiken; she gives her impression of Jeake's House:

> A dark passageway led to the kitchen, the only win-
> dow over the sink looking out on the garden, a jungle

of weeds. No heating unit in the L-shaped dining room adjacent, or in the rooms above except a wee potbellied stove in Conrad's spacious study. Leaded windowpanes, buckled floorboards, one bathroom for eleven rooms. How had Jessie managed?

Aiken was obsessed with Jeake's House and expressed terror at the thought of losing it. He cherished everything about it, even the Virginia ivy which covered the entire facade. Clarissa complained that the ivy was loosening the bricks and allowing dampness to seep into the house, thereby aggravating her painful arthritis. But he adamantly refused to have it removed and went into a fury when it was cut down in his absence.

Aiken wrote with remarkable concentration during the prolific years at Jeake's. From his spacious study on the second floor, he had an inspiring view beyond the inlet to the Channel. Even when carpenters invaded the house in 1930 for noisy refurbishment, he was able to continue writing at the dining room table. Alas, these were also years of marital disharmony. Creativity may have flourished, but his second marriage did not. When it ended in divorce in 1937, Mary Hoover became the third of Aiken's wives to settle into Jeake's House.

Art continued to flow as Mary, a promising young artist, painted while he wrote. Among the works Aiken produced during his years in Rye are short stories which have become classics: "Mr. Arcularus," "Spider, Spider," and "Silent Snow, Secret Snow." In between short stories he wrote novels: *Blue Voyage* (1927), *Great Circle* (1933), *King Coffin* (1935), *A Heart for the Gods of Mexico* (1939), and *Conversation* (1930). Poetry, he wrote throughout his lifetime. And volumes of criticism.

Rye played a major role in his writing. *Ushant*, an important third-person autobiography in a stream-of-consciousness mode, appeared in 1952 but was begun in Rye. Its punning title is the Anglicized version of the Ile d'Ouessant, a rocky barrier reef at the head of the English Channel with a lighthouse signifying the approach to England. Aiken could peer towards it from the window of his upper-story study "which looked out to sea, past the castle on the marsh." He surely also felt the influence of his home when, as a correspondent for the *New Yorker,* he wrote the "London Letters" under the pseudonym of Samuel Jeake, Jr.

Aiken earned his living almost entirely by writing, but despite his success, money was scarce. His attempt to make ends meet, especially during the Depression years, introduces an ironic note to Jeake's. He accepted paying guests, including the writer Malcolm Lowry. By operating as a bed-and-breakfast hotel today, Jeake's House is continuing a tradition established in the writer's time. The irony is compounded by Aiken's prophetic description of Jeake's House as having "a hotelful of bedrooms."

The advent of war forced Aiken to leave England in September 1939 (because he was an alien living in a defense zone). He had completed all his novels, most of his short stories, and much of his poetry and criticism by the time he left. Aiken returned after the war to prevent Jeake's House from being requisitioned for the homeless and described in a letter the scene he found:

> Rye is relatively undamaged, but looking pitifully shabby and down at heel. The Mermaid a ruin, and Lamb House windowless and boarded up, and the small garden studio gone, and here and there groups of houses vanished.

Although Jeake's House survived with "tenacious dignity," postwar conditions and poverty necessitated the practical decision to sell the beloved home. Throughout the fifties, the Aikens stayed in a New York apartment, they lived in Washington when he served as poetry consultant at the Library of Congress, and they were in Cape Cod. Finally, in 1960, he completed the circle that began in Georgia when a patron and businessman bought the house adjoining Aiken's childhood home in Savannah and gave him right of occupancy for his lifetime.

He is well remembered at Jeake's, where Bedroom Number 3 on the upper floor was Conrad Aiken's bedroom. The window of this oak- beamed and cheerfully-decorated room overlooks gables and rooftops and a section of the cobbled street below. A resident gazing down at the pretty street scene will probably see a camera-laden tourist gazing up at the pretty historic house, or pedestrians struggling up the hill.

The Aiken Suite, formerly Conrad Aiken's study, consists of two bedrooms and bathroom. The larger bedroom is supported by oak beams and features a fourposter bed. Its large picture window opens out onto the scene that Aiken so often wrote about. Adorned with curtains and embellished with full-length cushioned window seat, it teasingly invites day-long contemplation over the extensive view of "the Salts and the castle and the sea. . . ."

The study might also temptingly suggest listening for the sounds of the typewriter ticking away, just as Aiken himself listened when, he declared, the ghost of Samuel Jeake came at night and used the machine, making clacking noises as keys pressed down on pages that were blank in the morning. But to indulge in such flights of fancy is to risk missing what Rye itself has to offer.

Guests descend the stairs into the friendly environment of the galleried dining room to begin the day's activities with a hearty English breakfast. The enthusiastic owners would undoubtedly oblige if they were requested to substitute Aiken's own standard breakfast, which consisted of tea, toast, and a one-minute boiled egg in a silver cup. They are there to answer questions and make helpful suggestions to insure an enjoyable visit.

Jeake's House offers a perfect opportunity to explore a literary mecca in an area of great charm and antiquity just seventy miles southeast of London.

JEAKE'S HOUSE
Mermaid Street
Rye
East Sussex TN31 7ET

Telephone: (01797) 222828   Fax: (01797) 222623

Open: All year

A family-owned hotel with twelve bedrooms, most with private bathrooms, furnished with antiques and gifted with views over the rooftops of Rye or over the marsh out to sea. The comfortable rooms are supplied with hot drinks trays and with television.

Breakfast, with a choice of traditional or vegetarian, is served in the attractive eighteenth-century galleried dining room.

Good central location.

J. M. BARRIE

at

The Royal Albion Hotel
Brighton
Sussex

"Hotel is quiet just now but the stars will no
doubt come in a rush for the week-end. . . .
Now to dress for our fashionable meal."

—Letter, 17 March 1920

The small and poor fishing village of Brightelmstone, located on
the southern coast of England, was transformed into a large and
stylish seaside resort after Dr. Richard Russell published his thesis
in 1750 on the meritorious effects of sea water. He had been
prescribing to his patients the sea-water cure with such enormous
success that he moved his practice to Brighton in 1754, and people
came in droves to partake of the new pastime of sea bathing.
Salubrious sea water, it was proclaimed, could cure a range of
diseases from asthma to tuberculosis. Indeed, Brightelmstone sea
water—both for bathing in *and* for drinking— was bottled and sold
in London to those who could not get to Brighton, much as today
tins of Cape Cod air are sold, presumably for those who cannot
leave their sweltering cities.

Fashionable visitors have been strongly attracted to Brighton
over the years. The historian Edward Gibbon came in 1781, just
after publication of his third volume of *Decline and Fall of the
Roman Empire*. Charles Dickens stayed on several occasions and
wrote *Bleak House* and *Dombey and Son* here. Thackeray visited
and included a description of "brisk, gay, and gaudy" Brighton in
his *Vanity Fair*. Among the artists are such notables as Sir Joshua
Reynolds, John Constable, and J.M.W. Turner.

121

But it was the arrival of the Prince of Wales in 1783 that brightened the character of Brighton and changed it irrevocably. From his very first visit, the Prince (later King George IV) was enchanted with the town and returned regularly. The villa that he required for his Regency revels was designed to accommodate and reflect his brilliant social life. It was the architect John Nash who, when the Prince a stately pleasure-dome decreed, brought about the realization of an oriental fantasy. The English imagination, captivated by Eastern splendors, now had its own splendid rendition in the minarets and pinnacles and onion-shaped domes of the fantastic Royal Pavilion.

Queen Victoria, however, did not find it suitable to her need for privacy, and the Royal Pavilion was sold to the town in 1850. The elegant eccentricities of the entire estate have been a delightful center for the public ever since.

To cater further to the needs of the pleasure-seeking public are the large and distinctive hotels which line the seafront, adding Victorian flavor to the character of Brighton and making the watering place a standard by which other seaside resorts are measured and some are named.

In an enviable position overlooking the English Channel and the Palace Pier, stands the Royal Albion Hotel. The hotel was built in 1826 on the site of Russell House, the former home of Dr. Richard Russell. In its day, Russell House was the largest house in town and had a garden extending down to the beach. The hotel which replaced it is on the seafront road, midway between the Conference Centre and the marina, on the junction of the main road to London, the A23.

To the Royal Albion came J.M. Barrie. Like so many others who preceded him, he too found fun in Brighton and became a regular visitor.

Born in Scotland in 1860, Barrie received his earliest education from his mother who encouraged him to write stories before he went to school. After graduating from Edinburgh University in 1882, he worked as a journalist, leaving for London in 1885 to pursue his writing career. Success came in 1888 with his first successful book, *Auld Licht Idylls,* a collection of sketches of

J. M. Barrie (1860-1937)
was a regular visitor to
The Royal Albion Hotel,
Brighton

Scottish life. There followed a variety of publications. *A Window in Thrums* (1889) was based on his birthplace of Kirriemuir. *The Little Minister* (1891) was a sentimental novel which he later dramatized to enormous theatrical success. *Margaret Ogilvy* was a deeply moving story and a loving tribute to his mother. The novel *Sentimental Tommy* (1896) was followed in 1900 by a sequel, *Tommy and Grizel*.

Barrie enjoyed even greater success as a playwright. In the theatre, his reputation as a dramatist became established in 1902 with *Quality Street* and *The Admirable Crichton*. Two years later, the vastly appealing *Peter Pan* guaranteed his immortality. The story of Peter Pan emanated from the games he played with the young sons of Arthur and Sylvia Llewelyn Davies. His own marriage to the actress Mary Ansell had been a failure, ending in divorce in 1909. He adopted the five Davies boys after the death of their parents and acquired the family he never had. In later years, he employed Lady Cynthia Asquith as his secretary and acquired a second surrogate family. The Asquiths frequently joined him on his jaunts to Brighton.

Theatrical success continued with such well-known plays as *What Every Woman Knows* (1908), *The Twelve-Pound Look* (1910), *Dear Brutus* (1917), and *Mary Rose* (1920). Barrie was a box office sensation who simply dominated London theatre. His final play, however, *The Boy David* (1936), was an unfortunate fiasco and reveals an unhappy episode with J.M. Barrie at a hotel in Edinburgh.

Barrie, at seventy-seven, was at the Caledonian Hotel awaiting rehearsals for *The Boy David* when he became ill. He remained too unwell to attend rehearsals or the opening on 21 November 1936 of the play which he believed to be his finest work, but which ran in London for only fifty-five performances. The strange Biblical drama was in fact the greatest failure of his career. Some months later, on 19 June 1937, Barrie died. The luxury Caledonian Hotel in Edinburgh may be cited for its role in the life of J.M. Barrie, but happier memories may be gleaned from his earlier holidays at the hotel in Brighton where he produced much of his writing.

As early as January 1917, Barrie was at the Brighton seaside, where he wrote his one-act play, *The Old Lady Shows Her Medals*. His letters are filled with references to Brighton and specifically mention the Royal Albion, as in this excerpt from a letter to Mrs. E.V. Lucas dated 27 February 1921: "I have been twice to Brighton for a few days. . . . No place is quite so like itself as Brighton, especially at the Royal Albion, but the air maketh amends."

A regular visitor, Barrie came for relaxation and for writing. He was there frequently in the 1930s playing midget golf and skee-ball on the pier—and writing. A letter from the Royal Albion in March 1930 marvels at the glorious weather—"as warm and sunny as July"—and complains that "they are re-building Brighton outside the hotel's door. However," he quickly adds, "I have got in some three hours' work."

He was at the Royal Albion with the Asquiths in 1931. At the age of seventy-one, he had gone for the express purpose of writing. The hotel evoked in him feelings of nostalgia which enabled him to turn to the Scotland of his youth for the story that was to be his last work of fiction, *Farewell, Miss Julie Logan*.

His creative efforts benefited, as did his well-being. He again reveals himself at the seaside invigorated by its healthful effects in a letter of September 1932: "I am at Brighton for a few days and so much better that I walk on the windy side of the pier while the 1,000 other visitors are on the sheltered side."

It was Brighton again in August 1934, when he wanted to be within easy reach of Peacehaven, where Cynthia Asquith was convalescing from a serious illness. When she was sufficiently recovered, he took the Asquith family on a Mediterranean cruise.

Barrie's pleasurable visits to Brighton were enhanced by a colorful character who owned the hotel, Harry Preston. Barrie would often emerge from his work to be greeted by his host with offers of champagne and cigars. Nowadays under the management of the Park Hotels Group, it is still a pleasing spot for visitors who might find, as did Barrie, the muse as well as amusement.

Built in 1826, the Royal Albion Hotel replaced Russell House, the home of the doctor who popularized Brighton by proclaiming the magical properties of sea water. The Royal Albion is a popular retreat for a clientele seeking the magical offerings of a seafront hotel.

The large lemon-colored building with contrasting white window frames, pilasters, and trimmings, carries the attractive yellow-and-white scheme into the interior, where, past the reception desk, is a lounge area in which a pot of morning coffee or afternoon tea may be enjoyed. The large lounge just beyond has a commanding view of the sea, as has the restaurant.

The current brochure points with pride to the hotel's history of intrigues and scandals involving the Prince of Wales, who stayed incognito. It ought also to single out J.M. Barrie and his accomplishments during visits to the Royal Albion.

THE ROYAL ALBION
35 Old Steine
Brighton
Sussex BN1 1NT

Telephone/Fax: (01273) 329202

Member of Park Hotels Group

One hundred and fifteen bedrooms (including two suites) on the upper four stories have private bathrooms and are comfortably outfitted with tea- and coffee-making equipment and with television.

A variety of function rooms makes it possible to cater for about 150 guests, a boon for conference facilites, for which Brighton is well known.

The restaurant, offering an a la carte menu, overlooks the sea. And the Mariners Bar is an attractive venue for a pre-prandial drink.

WILLIAM MAKEPEACE THACKERAY

at

The Old Ship Hotel
Brighton
Sussex

> Our young bride and bridegroom had
> chosen Brighton as the place where they
> would pass the first few days after their
> marriage; and having engaged apartments at
> the Ship Inn, enjoyed themselves there in
> great comfort and quietude.

—Vanity Fair

"The oldest hotel in Brighton" started life in the sixteenth century
as the small Ship Tavern with an entrance in Ship Street. Its original
and simple name was modified in 1650 to differentiate it from the
New Ship which was built opposite. The Old Ship was rebuilt and
enlarged several times, so that it now occupies the entire frontage
facing the sea between Ship Street and Black Lion Street. A
distinguished history has accompanied the hotel throughout the
centuries.

A succession of owners included the colorful Nicholas
Tettersell. As captain of a trading vessel, he played his part in
helping King Charles II flee to France after his defeat in the Battle
of Worcester. A copy of a painting by W. van de Velde of the rescue
ship, renamed the *Royal Escape*, hangs in the Tettersell Bar of the
Old Ship Hotel.

In the mid-eighteenth century, when Dr. Richard Russell
"invented" and popularized sea bathing, fashionable crowds
flocked to Brighton. So successful was the sea-water cure which
he prescribed to patients that the poor fishing village of

Brighthelmstone was transformed into a popular and fashionable watering place. A character in Jane Austen's *Pride and Prejudice* echoed the sentiments of the throng by suggesting that "a visit to Brighton comprised every possibility of earthly happiness."

The *New Brighton Guide* of 1796 singled out the Old Ship as a place "where the richer visitors resort." The hotel really came into its own when Brighton became the stylish sea resort selected by the Prince Regent (later to become King George IV) who wanted a villa for his own brilliant social life. He built the oriental fantasy known as the Royal Pavilion, which has become a splendid center for the public and a symbol and cynosure of Brighton. The sensational eccentricities of the exotic palace are still there to be viewed and enjoyed.

The rich and famous arrived to partake of the delights of the resort. Grand social events took place at the Old Ship, such as the Prince Regent's Ball in 1809. On 9 December 1831 Niccolò Paganini gave a dazzling violin recital, and a plaque in the Ballroom commemorates the event. In the literary world, Charles Dickens stayed there in 1841. And William Makepeace Thackeray stayed there in the 1840s while writing parts of *Vanity Fair*, in which he included a description of "brisk, gay and gaudy" Brighton.

Renovated in 1895, and with a new east wing completed in 1964, the Old Ship Hotel offers splendid views of the popular resort on the English Channel. The huge Victorian white-elephant relic of a bygone era contains the elegant Regency Room and the Ballroom, which was completed in 1767.

Of the 156 bedrooms, Room 242 has been designated the Thackeray Room. Simply but pleasantly furnished, its only relevant feature is a plaque on the wall outlining the facts of Thackeray's visit to the hotel and calling attention to his fondness for Brighton. He was "born in Calcutta in 1811. . ." it begins, and expansion on the bare biographical facts would seem to provide material for many novels.

The novelist's mother, Anne Becher, distraught over the loss of her beloved Lieutenant Henry Carmichael-Smyth, was sent to India in the hope that she would recover from a match deemed unsuitable by her family. The scheme worked, for in Calcutta she met and married Richmond Thackeray who had a good position in the service of the East India Company. They became the parents of an only child, William Makepeace Thackeray. Then, one day, Richmond Thackeray invited a new acquaintance home for dinner. What a shocking and painful scene must have ensued when Captain Henry Carmichael-Smyth walked in. The young lovers had been deceived. She was told that her beloved had died suddenly of a fever. He in turn had been presented with his own unopened letters to her (actually intercepted by a disapproving family), returned as proof of her decision to break the engagement. The deception practiced by Anne's family ignored future possibilities, for the young man had been promoted and his prospects were more promising. But nothing could now be done, and the captain resumed his duties.

When Richmond Thackeray died in 1815 of a fever, Anne agreed to marry the captain after a decent eighteen-month interval of mourning. Her young son was sent home to England, as was customary with most Anglo-Indian children, for the advantages of climate and schooling. Thackeray never returned to India but he and his stepfather were destined to become good friends. Indeed, Thackeray later used the retired Major Carmichael-Smyth as the prototype for his Colonel Newcome.

In England, the young Thackeray attended school in several places before going to Trinity College, Cambridge. But he left after his second year without taking a degree. Unsure of a career, he tried law, he studied art for a while, then he found his way into journalism.

Thackeray, who loved writing and was always busy with his craft, began to earn his living by contributing free-lance articles to a wide variety of magazines and newspapers such as the prestigious *Morning Chronicle* and *Punch*. Determined to succeed as a writer, he worked hard to establish himself.

In Paris, where he had gone to study art, he met and married Isabella Shawe. Two children were born, but the second died in infancy. After the birth of a third daughter in 1840, Isabella, who had been severely depressed, succumbed to mental illness.

Thackeray, busy and preoccupied with his work, failed to recognize the symptoms of his wife's worsening condition. As she continued to sink, he remained determined to rise to the ranks of great writers. In 1845 he started to write *Vanity Fair*. This was the year in which his wife, whose mental state had been steadily deteriorating, had to be removed from the family. She was never to recover from her incurable illness (although she outlived him by thirty-six years) and he buried himself in his work.

The first number of *Vanity Fair*, which was being published in monthly installments, appeared in January 1847, and the last in July 1848. With publication of his novel in volume form on 18 July 1848, coincidentally his thirty-seventh birthday, Thackeray was established as one of the leading novelists of the day.

Much of the novel was written when he was living in London at a variety of addresses, but the first numbers were written when he was living at the Old Ship in Brighton, where he sought seclusion (in the autumn of 1846) in order to work on his novel.

He met Miss Kate Perry, daughter of the former editor of the *Morning Chronicle*, who was staying in Brighton with her brother, and formed a close and lasting friendship with her. Miss Perry gives this recollection of how the famous title first came to Thackeray: "He told me. . . that, after ransacking his brain for a name for his novel, it came upon him unawares, in the middle of the night, as if a voice had whispered, 'Vanity Fair.' He said, 'I jumped out of bed, and ran three times round my room, uttering as I went, *Vanity Fair, Vanity Fair, Vanity Fair*'."

He was delighted with this title because it gave him a focus, a fair of vanities as a corrupting place, and he described early nineteenth-century society in authentic detail.

The book was a great success and he received the adulation of society. Destined to live a bachelor life, he was caught up in a social whirl; he sought fashionable company and places, ate and drank too much, and was frequently ill. He visited Brighton often, both for the society it offered and for recuperative purposes, and he started his next novel, *Pendennis,* in Brighton. *Henry Esmond, The Newcomes*, and other novels followed. He gave lecture tours and visited America.

William Makepeace
Thackeray (1811-1863)
(drawing by Daniel
Maclise) and the
Old Ship, Brighton,
where he completed the
first numbers of
Vanity Fair

Thackeray is associated with a number of houses in London, which are marked by the familiar blue plaques. He was fifty-three when he died on 24 December 1863, less than two years after moving into his new home in Palace Green (now the Israeli Embassy). A bust to his memory is in Westminster Abbey. But Thackerayans will surely want to visit the place where his peregrinations took him for relaxation and artistic creation. The Old Ship in Brighton is where Thackeray found conditions auspicious for producing a novel of the highest quality.

THE OLD SHIP
King's Road
Brighton
East Sussex BN1 1NR

Telephone: (01273) 329001   Fax: (01273) 820718

Rooms: 156, each with private bathroom, color television, radio, telephone, and courtesy tray. Many have views over the sea front and the two piers.

Location: On the sea front , just a short walk to shopping areas and the Lanes and a ten-minute walk from the railway station. From London's Victoria Station, the journey by rail takes an hour.

CAPTAIN FREDERICK MARRYAT

at

Chewton Glen Hotel
New Milton
Hampshire

He felt happy, as people do who have no
cares, from the fine weather—the deep
green of the verdure chequered by the
flowers in bloom, and the majestic scenery
which met his eye on every side.

—*The Children of the New Forest*

The case of Captain Frederick Marryat at Chewton Glen may be thought of as that of a minor novelist at a major hotel. The exquisite country-house hotel is situated on the edge of the New Forest between Southampton and Bournemouth and is only two miles from the sea. It is located a mere hundred miles from London, but the guest is immeasurably further removed from the cares and concerns of ordinary life.

The origins of the hamlet of Chewton go back to Norman times, but the present house, known as Chewton Glen, was built in the early eighteenth century in classic Palladian style. A new central section was added a century later, and further renovations were made this century, including the addition of a new bedroom wing when the house became a hotel in 1962. Duplex suites in the former coach house now provide additional bedrooms, bringing the total to over fifty, a substantial increase from the original eight.

Most of the coach house suites have a sitting room and outdoor private patio downstairs; upstairs are a balcony with view over extensive fields, a luxury bathroom, and a bedroom built in between original beams. Every effort was exerted to retain the

133

original beams, walls, rafters, even the bolts, of the old coach house. One suite has kept the vaulted ceiling intact, a ceiling high enough to permit passage of coaches and horses through the natural entrance between the rafters. With consistent good taste, the horse troughs and baskets which once held hay (and now hold flowers) have been preserved to enhance a lovely setting.

Luxuriously furnished throughout, and ideally situated in one of the richest areas of England, the hotel has won a succession of awards both for its fine restaurant and for continuing high standards of service.

The hotel is a perfect center for exploring the former royal hunting preserve of William the Conqueror. The New Forest still offers "majestic scenery. . .on every side" with wild ponies and deer, stretches of heath, thatched Tudor cottages, quaint old churches, and footpaths among ancient oaks and beeches. But why would anyone want to leave a perfect country home set in thirty acres of parkland, a home which offers every comfort from superb French cuisine to heated outdoor swimming pool?

In 1837 George Marryat bought the house, and indentures showing the purchase of the property are displayed in the sun lounge. The house remained Marryat property until 1855. During the 1840s the owner's brother, Captain Frederick Marryat, was a frequent visitor.

Born in London in 1792, Frederick Marryat made a successful and active career for himself in the Royal Navy. His *Code of Signals for the Merchant Service* was published in 1817. He was engaged in the Napoleonic wars and was at St. Helena when Napoleon died in 1821. A man of many talents, he made a drawing of Napoleon on his deathbed, which is now exhibited at the National Maritime Museum in Greenwich. Another sketch, a version of Napoleon's head alone, is in the Victoria and Albert Museum. In command of many vessels, with many diverse duties, he hunted smugglers in the English Channel and served in the Burmese War of 1824-26.

Marryat's experiences and adventures became the background for his literary work. Having made a name for himself as a distinguished naval man, he proceeded to make a name for himself as an author. His first novel, *Frank Mildmay*, was published in 1829.

Chewton Glen Hotel,
New Milton, where Captain
Frederick Marryat (1792-1848),
author of *Mr. Midshipman Easy*,
frequently stayed with his
brother

A year later, at thirty-eight, Marryat retired from the navy and sailed out into literary waters. The publication of *Peter Simple* in 1834 made him famous. *Jacob Faithful* (1834), *Mr. Midshipman Easy* (1836), and *Masterman Ready* (1841) are other familiar titles. Altogether, he completed about seventeen works of fiction as well as other books, essays, and pieces of journalism.

Eventually, Marryat settled in at Langham in a corner of Norfolk, where his attempts at farming had disastrous financial results. But he continued to write from his Langham home and from a variety of places—London, Brighton, America.

He is generally seen as a life-at-sea novelist in the tradition of Smollett. He influenced Robert Louis Stevenson, particularly in the writing of such works as *Treasure Island* and *The Master of Ballantrae,* and he greatly impressed Joseph Conrad, who called him "the enslaver of youth." Indeed, critics often refer to Marryat as Conrad's precursor in sea fiction.

Visits to Chewton Glen and the New Forest undoubtedly gave Marryat the background material for his final and perhaps most popular novel, *The Children of the New Forest.* The book was published in 1847, a year before his death. Logically, he must have derived inspiration for Arnwood, home of the Royalist family in the novel, from its actual prototype, Arnewood, owned by friends of George Marryat. That thatched house, called Cavalier Cottage and situated in the nearby village of Sway, gives the onlooker a view of another existing literary link.

The Chewton Glen Hotel keeps alive the memory of Captain Marryat's presence in the house. Names of his books and characters, not numbers, identify guest rooms. Memorable meals are served in the splendid Marryat Room. In the Marryat Bar hangs a framed letter with his signature. And from the bar, an imbiber might order a mint julep to honor Marryat as "the first Englishman to write about this famous American drink," as cited by the United Kingdom Bartenders' Guild.

Afternoon tea may be taken in the friendly atmosphere of the main lounge with its upholstered chairs and couches and polished tables. There the fire extends its warmth on chilly days, and there on view are old prints based on sketches made by Marryat.

If, despite the extensive comforts, the visitor wishes to venture out to explore this part of southern England, excursions to nearby villages can be rationalized as homage to the naval writer. The seafaring town of Lymington has Georgian houses and shops along streets which wind their way down toward a colorful harbor. The historic village of Buckler's Hard contains an interesting Maritime Museum and the Master Builder's House (now a hotel) in which lived Master Shipbuilder Henry Adams.

Virginia Woolf pays tribute to Marryat in her book, *The Captain's Death Bed and Other Essays*. The title essay gives a brief account of Marryat's accomplishments in a life which has remained essentially private. To know him, Virginia Woolf suggests, one must turn to his still highly-readable books.

Perhaps one could enlarge on her suggestion. Although one need not search long for a good excuse to visit a superlative hotel, suppose one arrived there with a supply of Marryat novels—novels which evoke a world of the early nineteenth century and which are still highly regarded, even if they are not regarded as masterpieces. Then an adventure in reading could effectively combine with an adventure in living.

CHEWTON GLEN HOTEL
Christchurch Road
New Milton
Hampshire BN25 6QS

Telephone: (01425) 275341   Fax: (01425) 272310

The 58 bedrooms of one of Britain's most prestigious and expensive hotels include 45 double rooms, 12 suites, and one four-poster suite, all with bathrooms, television, room service, hairdryer and trouser press, and such luxurious touches as complimentary sherry, home-made biscuits, quality toiletries, and fresh flowers in bathrooms.

The Marryat Room is the venue for superb dining.

A Romanesque swimming pool, health club, and two tennis courts are indoors.

Other pleasurable sites include the Marryat Bar, lounge, conservatory, and Billiard Room.

The unobtrusive Lake Suite is for conferences.

There is also the garden, heated outdoor swimming pool, 9-hole golf course, tennis, putting, and croquet.

ALFRED, LORD TENNYSON

at

Farringford Hotel
Freshwater Bay
Isle of Wight

...All by myself in my own dark garden ground,
Listening now to the tide in its broad-flung, shipwrecking roar,
Now to the scream of a madden'd beach dragg'd down by the
    wave.

—Maud

Perhaps because only islands offer that feeling of complete isola-
tion, perhaps because he had always had a passion for the sea,
Tennyson was strongly attracted to the Isle of Wight in answer to
his need for privacy and seclusion.

He was forty-four and famous when he came to the Isle of Wight
in the summer of 1853 with his wife. Publication in 1850 of his
enormously popular *In Memorian* (a tribute to his dear friend
Arthur Hallam, who died in 1833) had established him securely as
a poet and let to his appointment, in succession to Wordsworth, as
Poet Laureate. Also in that year, he married his long-beloved Emily
Sellwood. The times of youthful struggles were over.

The journey to his island haven was a long and arduous one,
entailing cross-country travel through Hampshire by train and
horse-bus to Lymington, then across the Solent in a rowing boat
(missing the steamer seemed inevitable) to Yarmouth and proceeding overland to his destination.

When the couple first saw Farringford, they fell in love with the
house at first sight. They had come in search of a secluded house
away from London's mad strife, and they delighted in this attractive

Georgian building with its eighteenth-century Gothic-style windows and unsurpassable view. They agreed immediately to rent it, with an option to purchase. The Tennysons, with their baby son Hallam, were ensconced by autumn. A second son, Lionel, was born the following year in the house destined to be their home for some forty years.

Located on the Freshwater Peninsula on the western end of the island, Farringford overlooks the sea from its position on a high down which is aptly named High Down. The spacious house, which then contained fifteen rooms, is now the superb three-star Farringford Hotel.

The hotel stands in Bedbury Lane about a mile from the village of Freshwater. In the Freshwater Parish Church are monuments to members of the Tennyson family, including one to Lionel, who died in 1886 on his way home from India, and another to Hallam (Lord Tennyson) who died in 1926, leaving 155 acres of cliff land to the National Trust.

Many of Tennyson's possessions at Farringford have been moved to the Tennyson Museum in Lincoln, for he was born in 1809 in the Lincolnshire village of Somersby. A few pieces of furniture, his writing desk and two chairs, are in the Isle of Wight Museum at Carisbrooke Castle.

Structural changes have been made to Farringford. The present dining room includes the large room built for parties when the house was enlarged in 1871; the library above had a winding stairway by which the poet could escape if warned of the arrival of unwelcome visitors. Also, the splendid view from the drawing room window northward to the English coast is now partially obscured by growth of trees.

The estate was a constant source of pleasure for the poet. He walked a great deal, and a favorite ramble was along the down overlooking the multicolored sands of Alum Bay to the Needles, a group of strangely-shaped rocks projecting from the sea. He worked at such physical chores as mowing the lawn and caring for the farm and garden; he made summer-houses out of rushes; and he built a wooden bridge over the lane leading to the farm.

Alfred Lord Tennyson
(1809-1892) and his
home for many years,
Farringford, Isle of Wight

He indulged in astronomy and bird watching, observed nature and the sea. And he wrote.

Maud was published in 1855, the first major poem written at Farringford. In it, he described the horrors of industrial town life where "the poor are hovell'd and hustled together, each sex like swine" and denounced the evil of the place where "the spirit of murder works in the very means of life." *Maud* also contained the spirit of Farringford, "the house half hid in the gleaming wood," and its surroundings, "the liquid azure bloom of a crescent of sea." He immortalized the beauties of his new environment:

> A Million emeralds break from the ruby-budded lime
> In the little grove where I sit—

Despite the poor critical reception, the public did buy the book and thereby enabled Tennyson to buy the spacious house.

The Charge of the Light Brigade came to him while walking on High Down. *The Idylls of the King* was also written at Farringford. Later, with the profits of *Enoch Arden*, he purchased the land between Farringford and the sea to ensure that the view would never be spoiled by building.

His popularity grew steadily. Friends and admirers flocked to this literary mecca. Invited guests included such distinguished notables as Browning, Longfellow, Fitzgerald, Lewis Carroll, and Darwin. His neighbor, Julia Cameron, photographed him. Garibaldi, the defender of Italian liberty, planted a tree in front of the house. Sir Arthur Sullivan played at Farringford, and Jenny Lind sang there.

But uninvited visitors, seeking a glimpse of the poet, made life on the island intolerable for Tennyson. They hounded him for a few words or for autographs. They accosted him walking on the downs in his familiar broad-brimmed hat and wide-flowing cloak. They continually intruded on his privacy and infuriated him. One celebrity-seeker even climbed a tree to peer through the window to see the poet at work. Because improvements in all kinds of transportation made the island less remote, it had become an easy target for all kinds of unwelcome tourists and sightseers. No, his marine retreat was no longer a secure haven from curious intruders.

He fled from them, sometimes withdrawing to his study, sometimes withdrawing into himself, but eventually to the mainland. In search of peace, Tennyson acquired, by 1869, a house on another inaccessible site, Aldworth, near Haslemere in Surrey. But he continued to reside at his beloved Farringford for several months each year. On one homeward journey to Farringford, while crossing the Solent by ferry, he composed the poem that his son Hallam considered the peak of all his poetry, *Crossing the Bar*:

> Sunset and evening star,
>   And one clear call for me!
> And may there be no moaning of the bar,
>   When I put out to sea. . .

The "bar" might have referred to a sandbank across the mouth of the harbor where the River Lymington enters the Solent. Or it might have referred to the sea barrier that separates the island from the Hampshire coast. Metaphorically of course—and this is the real meaning—it referred to Tennyson's own death. He was in his eighty-first year when he wrote it and he died a few years later, in 1892, at Aldworth.

Easy communication with the island, with ferries and hovercrafts at frequent intervals, now makes it possible for the masses to cross the bar, particularly in the overcrowded summertime, when "overners" (as mainland people are called) come to enjoy the miles of sandy beaches. But the island enjoys mild winters and is attractive throughout the year. Famous for its sheer natural beauty, other attractions include the twelfth-century Carisbrooke Castle and the royal Osborne House, built for Queen Victoria when she too evinced a need for privacy.

Tennyson's corner of the island is still a place of pilgrimage, and one can still sense his presence there. The name of High Down has been changed to Tennyson Down, and a thirty-eight-foot-high Tennyson Memorial Cross was erected on it in 1897 to honor the poet. The National Trust preserves the land which still offers exciting walks to the Needles amidst spectacular scenery with views of cliffs and colored sands across the chalk downlands and out to sea.

The secluded Farringford Hotel still has the garden gate by which Tennyson left to walk on the downs. It also has the wooden bridge built by the poet over the lane which separates the grounds from the farm. Opposite the front of the house stands the Wellingtonia tree planted by Garibaldi, now eighty feet high. And in the garden one can still hear the sound of the sea from Freshwater Bay, the same "shipwrecking roar" that the poet heard well over a century ago.

So it is not too late to accept the "Invitation to Farringford" that Tennyson himself issued in 1854 in poetic lines (actually to the Reverend F. D. Maurice, godfather to Hallam Tennyson) to come to the Isle Wight:

> Where, far from noise and smoke of town,
> I watch the twilight falling brown
>   All round a careless-ordered garden
> Close to the ridge of a noble down.

FARRINGFORD HOTEL
Bedbury Lane
Freshwater Bay
Isle of Wight PO40 9PE

Tel: (01983)752500 or 752700   Fax: (01983) 756515

Rooms: In addition to fifty-six bedrooms, all with private bathrooms, television, radio, and telephone, there are self-catering cottages and garden suites for families of up to six people.

Lounges: Tennyson Drawing Room with scenic views and the Library with Tennyson mementos and book borrowing possibilities.

Outdoor recreational facilities: Nine-hole golf course for residents only, putting green, bowling green, croquet lawn, and tennis court. Also, outdoor solar-heated swimming pool with separate children's pool and nearby sand pit and swings.

Indoor facilities: Sports pavilion for table tennis, darts, and snooker.

THE WEST COUNTRY

VIRGINIA WOOLF

at

Talland House
St. Ives
Cornwall

"Oh, how beautiful!" For the great plateful
of water was before her; the hoary Lighthouse, distant, austere, in the midst; and on
the right, as far as the eye could see, fading
and falling, in soft low pleats, the green
sand dunes with the wild flowing grasses on
them, which always seemed to be running
away into some moon country, uninhabited
of men.

—To the Lighthouse

Applying a unique and imaginative use to the fig leaf, St. Ia floated
over on it from Ireland to give St. Ives its name. She must be
credited also with finding a magnificent spot to come to, well worth
the perilous journey. The parish church, a large and attractive
fifteenth-century granite building, standing very near the sea, is
dedicated to her. The figure of St. Ia is on the roof of the church,
together with two other Irish saints, her brothers: Erc went to St.
Erth, and Uny to Lelant. In view of such a tradition of creative
power, it seems appropriate that the district should have been
discovered by artists, albeit artists of a less legendary stature.

146

Formerly known for pilchards, St. Ives is now famous for pictures. Shops brim over with the products of artists and craftsmen, who come here in droves. And throngs of tourists come to buy—from the the barefoot and hirsute to the conservative and elderly, all are equally attracted.

Life still revolves around the harbor, and the old fishing quarter known as Down-a-Long retains its charming atmosphere. Intriguing streets often have names to match—Teetotal Street, Virgin Street, Salubrious Place. Although cargoes of pilchards are no longer the characteristic catch unloaded at the quay, the fresh fish harvest includes all kinds of local fish and shellfish, from lobsters and crabs to turbots and John Dory. Sea gulls add to the bustling scene as they crowd around the quay, oblivious to the fact that the fishing industry has been superseded by the tourist industry. It makes a pretty picture with fine views out over the Atlantic, the sweep of the bay, and the Godrevy Lighthouse.

The area all around is rich in scenery. Just half an hour's walk from the center of St. Ives are wild moors—mysterious gorse-grown wastelands, secret and silent, but full of suggestions of a peopled past, with great monoliths raised by pre-Roman tribes. Prehistoric remains, cromlechs and stone circles, are abundant. Less abundant are railways, telephones and traffic, and other maladies of civilization. St. Ives, over three hundred miles from London, is endowed with sheer beauty of setting as well as with a sense of the past.

The spacious residence named Talland House stands high above the harbor within easy walking distance of beach or town. It also offers opportunities for walking and exploring the surrounding wild moors or the many coastal paths with spectacular cliff views, or for simply enjoying the local scenery, as the view of St. Ives Bay and the Godrevy Lighthouse is particularly enchanting.

To this Cornish scene, Sir Leslie Stephen came in 1881. So pleased was he with the flourishing artistic center situated on the north coast of Cornwall, that he bought Talland House one year later, in the year of his daughter Virginia's birth. Here, the Stephen family spent their summer holidays every year until 1894. Sir

Leslie had been quite a good athlete, and now the aging writer could content himself with walks across the Cornish moors.

He had married Julia Duckworth, a widow with three children, after his first wife (Thackeray's younger daughter) died. Vanessa (born in 1879), Thoby (1880), Virginia (1882), and Adrian (1883) are the children of that union.

Virginia was born into the literary environment of an upper-middle and intellectual class when Sir Leslie Stephen was fifty years old. A well-known, respected writer and biographer and the noted editor of the *Dictionary of National Biography,* it is perhaps his unhappy posthumous fate to be remembered as the father of Virginia Woolf.

Virginia was born at 22 Hyde Park Gate, Kensington, in a house that is still standing. She grew up in that house, but her happiest childhood memories of those early formative years are associated with the holiday house situated high above St. Ives Bay.

An ancient riddle asks an intriguing question:

> As I was going to St. Ives
> I met a man with seven wives;
> Seven wives had seven sacks,
> Seven sacks had seven cats,
> Seven cats had seven kits,
> Kits, cats, sacks and wives—
> How many were there going to St. Ives?

The riddle's question, applied to Talland House, is incalculable, for the house was teeming with people. It was a large, happy family with eight children, seven servants and innumerable friends and relatives. The life style was casual. The family partook of a variety of pleasurable activities such as boating, fishing, bathing, walking, playing cricket, and even night excursions to trap moths, which Virginia wrote about in her essay, *Reading*. Or they simply enjoyed the landscape. Or they wrote. The importance of the St. Ives period on her later life and work—on her writing—cannot be exaggerated; she discusses the art of writing in her *Diary* (19 December 1938) and recalls that it had been "absorbing ever since I was a little creature, scribbling a story in the manner of Hawthorne on the green plush sofa in the drawing room at St. Ives while the grown-ups dined."

At the age of ten, she was already making notes, both mental and written, of St. Ives events. She and her brother Thoby put together a hand-written weekly periodical called *The Hyde Park Gate News*. On 11 May 1892 they recorded a projected departure for St. Ives as "a heavenly prospect to the minds of the juveniles who adore St. Ives and revel in its numerous delights." On 12 September 1892 she wrote, "On Saturday morning Master Hilary Hunt and Master Basil Smith came up to Talland House and asked Master Thoby and Miss Virginia Stephen to accompany them to the lighthouse as Freeman the boatman said that there was a perfect wind and tide for going there. Master Adrian Stephen was much disappointed at not being allowed to go." That incident became a crucial element of the plot in the novel that is generally considered her masterpiece, *To the Lighthouse*.

But the happy childhood of Virginia ended with the death of her mother in May 1895. Virginia was overcome with grief and, at the age of thirteen, suffered her first breakdown. The situation was exacerbated by the demands of a distraught father who retreated into the consolation of deep mourning. Sir Leslie, finding the thought of life there without his beloved Julia unbearable, gave up Talland House.

In a sense, Virginia never really left St. Ives. Its happy memories and indelible images remained with her always, to be translated into words in her later years. In troubled times she returned to this joyful place of childhood holidays for its beneficial effects and for sustenance. When breakdowns recurred, she was nurtured by Cornish memories and helped considerably by return visits.

Her first return to St. Ives occurred in 1905 when she took a summer holiday in Carbis Bay, in what she called (in a letter to Violet Dickenson) "the divinest view in Europe." She continues:

> It is a strange dream to come back here again. The
> first night we groped our way up to Talland House
> in the dark, and just peeped at it from behind the

Escalonia hedge. It was a ghostly thing to do: it all looked quite unchanged. Old people meet us and stop and talk to us, and remember us playing on the beach.

However, it is the loveliest country, whatever age you happen to be, and really not spoilt. We went for a walk this afternoon which we used to every Sunday, and saw the Lizard and St. Michaels Mount.

And this letter to Emma Vaughan dated 17 September 1905:

Why do you go to Suffolk when you might come here? We have a little lodging house, of the most glaring description, but the divinest country all round. Moors, seas, hills, rocks, a land flowing not only with honey but with cream. Here Nessa paints all the afternoon; and I write all the morning from 10 to 1. Thoby and Adrian discuss points of law; and then take to piquet. We all walk and wander like so many disembodied ghosts. We go to tea with the people who now own Talland. They are a delightful pair of artists, with a family of the age we used to be.

Virginia had continued her practice of writing, as literary exercises, descriptions of the places she visited.

After the death of her dear brother Thoby, she made several visits to Cornwall and wrote one letter of particular interest, to Lady Ottoline Morrell, dated 11 March 1909: "I wish one could manage so that Bloomsbury was on the sea shore; and all your company sat among seahills."

In Sussex, she found a semi-detached house at Firle, near Lewes, which she rented and named Little Talland House in what some might call a fixation on her St. Ives childhood. She settled in in 1911. From Little Talland House she wrote to Clive Bell on 18 April 1911, "I've found a new walk every day. You must come here and go there with me. There are plains, rivers, downs and the sea to choose from. You will wag your head, and say 'Poor creature! Cornwall again!' "

Virginia Woolf
(1882-1941) spent her
childhood holidays on
the Cornish coast
at Talland House,
St. Ives

In 1912, at the age of thirty, she married Leonard Woolf, one of the members of the Bloomsbury group. The denigrating name was applied by outsiders to the group of notables who met in the neighborhood of Bloomsbury to share artistic purposes and friendship. Virginia and her sister Vanessa (who married Clive Bell) had been hostesses in this highbrow Bohemian world. Now Leonard and Virginia Woolf founded the Hogarth Press, and she worked actively toward the success of this publishing venture that produced much fine literature, including her own novels.

It was Cornwall again when she returned with Leonard in April 1914 for a three-week holiday to Lelant, St. Ives, and Carbis Bay. Overworked and plagued by a series of mental crises, recovery was to be fortified by a return to the West Country. Despite difficulties and frenzied moments, she found succor and a sense of calm in the nostalgic return to childhood scenes. Some years later they went househunting, but Cornwall was too far from London, and they ended up buying Monks House in Rodmell, Sussex, on the bank of the River Ouse.

Virginia's first novel, *The Voyage Out*, came out in 1915. While it may show the uncertainties of an insecure novelist, it also shows insights and meaningful commentaries on life in a plot which has the young and motherless Rachel voyage out with her aunt and uncle to a remote spot in South America. Significantly, for her sensitive examination of the voyage out into life, Virginia Woolf is comfortable in a sea setting.

"No casements are so magic, no faery lands so forlorn," Leonard Woolf philosophizes, "as those which all our lives we treasure in our memory of the summer holidays of our childhood." The influence and impact of Talland House and its environment continues unabated in the two novels which followed, *Night and Day* (1919) and *Jacob's Room* (1922).

Although *Mrs. Dalloway* (1923) is set entirely in London, the city and its characters take on sea symbols and rhythms and colors. Clarissa Dalloway expresses her state of well-being by thinking back to youth: ". . .what a morning—fresh as if issued to children on a beach. . . like the flap of a wave; the kiss of a wave. . ." Thus is Clarissa described in her silver-green dress: "But age had brushed her; even as a mermaid might behold in her glass the setting sun on some very clear evening over the waves."

In *To the Lighthouse* the seaside dominates. Preparatory to her great novel, she recorded in her *Diary* (14 May 1925) her desire to "get on to *To the Lighthouse*. This is going to be fairly short; to have father's character done complete in it; and mother's; and St. Ives; and childhood; and all the usual things I try to put in—life, death, etc."

Although the fictional aspect places the Ramsay family on a holiday in the Hebrides, the setting is unquestionably Cornwall. Some readers complained that descriptions of the fauna and flora were inaccurate—there are no elm trees in the Hebrides, for instance. Her critics were right, of course, for despite the geographical name, Virginia Woolf was describing the magic of Cornwall, the summer home of the Stephen family at St. Ives, and the Godrevy Lighthouse.

The Godrevy Lighthouse, visible from Talland House, was one of the happy childhood images indelibly etched into her imagination and being:

> Indeed they were very close to the Lighthouse now.
> There it loomed up, stark and straight, glaring, white
> and black, and one could see the waves breaking in
> white splinters like smashed glass upon the rocks.
> One could see lines and creases in the rocks. One
> could see the windows clearly; a dab of white on one
> of them, and a little tuft of green on the rock. . .the
> Lighthouse one had seen across the bay all these
> years; it was a stark tower on a bare rock.

The Waves (1931) is a poetic novel which is again haunted by sea memories and imagery. Its poetry comes from the powerful images taken from the world she loved: the ocean with its waves, the sky full of birds, driftwood on the shore, cliffs, house and garden— the world of St. Ives and Talland House.

She was always in a state of exhaustion and despair in the interval between completion of a book and its publication. The

153

possibility of a crisis was always there. After sending the corrected proofs of *The Waves* to the printer, Leonard records that she was dangerously close to a breakdown. He insisted on a holiday in the hope of finding peace and relief. He describes their visit to the West Country, to "that strange primordial somnolent Cornish peninsula between Falmouth and Helsford Passage, where the names of the villages soothe one by their strangeness—Gweek and Constantine and Mawnan Smith." They capped the two-week holiday with a visit to St. Ives and Talland House, where Virginia peered through the ground floor windows at the ghosts of her childhood. Naturally, she was also driven to write another novel.

After *The Years* (1937) was published, she asked in her *Diary*, in characteristic imagery, "Will another novel ever swim up?"

Virginia Woolf, whose concern with the flow of time in her novels and with continual change, used the flow of water to represent the flux of life. Her power transferred the vision to pages of books. Her own life ended (in 1941) with her being absorbed into the flowing waters of the River Ouse.

"Then the curtain rose" is the concluding line of her posthumous novel, *Between the Acts*. The vicissitudes of life go on. Events, like waves from the sea, keep occurring. One play, one bit of action, is ending, but another has already formed and is beginning to follow its inexorable course. For Virginia Woolf, the curtain rose in Cornwall.

TALLAND HOUSE
St. Ives
Cornwall

Telephone: (01736) 796 368

Known as Talland House Holiday Flats, the impressive white building is comprised of five self-contained, comfortably-furnished and well-equipped flats.

Minimum four-day stay.

Situated in an acre of grounds with lovely lawns and gardens, waterfalls and rock pools, it is within easy walking distance of the beach, shops, or the labyrinth of streets that form the old part of the town.

DYLAN THOMAS

at

The Lobster Pot
Mousehole
Cornwall

Polgigga is a tiny place two miles or less
from Land's End and very near Penzance
and Mousehole (really the loveliest village
in England).

--Letter to Vernon Watkins, 20 April 1936

Granted that Dylan Thomas was given to exaggeration, his
Mousehole accolade—the loveliest village in England—is
nevertheless not inaccurate. Like Laugharne, the Welsh village
with which he is generally associated, Mousehole (pronounced
Mou'zl) is a poet's place. It is a pretty fishing port which looks out
to the sea over a snug and secure harbor draped with the nets of
fishermen who crowd the village. The picturesque village is
crowded too with holiday visitors, and the narrow streets become
clogged with traffic in the busy summer season.

Once important enough to have been an embarkation port for
pilgrims sailing to the Holy Land, and in the fourteenth century the
most important fishing harbor in West Cornwall, Mousehole
appeals to sightseeing visitors. Meandering through the winding
lanes and alleys, perhaps while munching on a Cornish pasty, is
an enjoyable pastime which reveals picture-postcard cottages built
of local granite and slate—a photographer's dream. A private
home called Keigwin Manor has been restored to look like the
Elizabethan house which was destroyed when the Spaniards burnt
the village in 1595 as a reprisal after the defeat of the Armada.

Dylan Thomas
(1914-1953) and
The Lobster Pot,
Mousehole, where he
and Caitlin spent their
honeymoon

The Ship is one inviting pub, and the Lobster Pot is a genuinely old and charming hotel, a leading attraction of Mousehole.

The Lobstser Pot is believed to have been built around 1595. The rambling inn is made up of adjoining fishermen's cottages, and many of its bedrooms have sea views which are a treat. The marvellous meals, served in its justifiably famous restaurant over-hanging the harbor, feature lobsters, crayfish, crabs, and oysters from the sea just outside. With gulls perched on the steeply-pitched slate roofs, the cozy inn has the feeling of an ancient fishing village, perhaps used as the setting for a fanciful story in a book of old tales.

Although the actual story of Dylan Marlais Thomas begins and ends in Wales, Cornwall is a place of special significance for the Welsh national poet; it was in Cornwall that he and Caitlin Macnamara were married, and there they spent their honeymoon. Dylan was born in Swansea on 27 October 1914. He left at the age of twenty in order to pursue his craft or sullen art in London but returned to Wales after his marriage to live in Laugharne. After he died in New York City, on 9 November 1953, while on a lecture tour in the United States, his body was brought back for burial in St. Martin's churchyard in Laugharne.

Dylan Thomas first met Caitlin Macnamara in London in April 1936. Caitlin was a very pretty girl of twenty-three, given to eccentric dress and behavior. She had run away to London in pursuit of a career on the stage and was involved with the art of dancing, which she was learning to do in the Isadora Duncan style. Dylan had come to London to work and to see his publisher about his forthcoming second volume of poems. The couple were intro-duced in a London pub by Augustus John of the large John family with whom the Macnamara children had grown up.

Shortly after their magical meeting, Caitlin and Dylan parted. She returned to her home in Hampshire where her portrait was being painted by Augustus John. Dylan left for Cornwall, for he had accepted an invitation from Wyn Henderson to her Cornish retreat, a cottage at Polgigga, between Penzance and Land's End. Mrs. Henderson, a capable and understanding person with a special position among an artistic group, had been involved in writing and publishing and was to run Peggy Guggenheim's Bloomsbury art gallery. In Cornwall, Dylan did a lot of drinking and a little bit of writing and was well cared for by Wyn Henderson.

By June 1937, Dylan and Caitlin decided to get married in what he calls in a letter to his parents a "rash and mad scheme." He had fallen in love at the first meeting and remained in love (despite altercations and infidelities) throughout the seventeen years of his remaining life.

In the spring, he and Caitlin had gone down to Cornwall, staying in a borrowed cottage in Lamorna Cove. Wyn Henderson was by then running a guest house called the Lobster Pot, on Mousehole Harbor, in partnership with Max Chapman. The young couple moved to the Lobster Pot and were married on 11 July 1937 in the Penzance Registry Office. Dylan was destitute, as usual, and Wyn Henderson paid for the marriage licence. In a letter from the Lobster Pot to his friend Vernon Watkins, dated 15 July 1937, he wrote, "My own news is very big and simple. I was married three days ago; to Caitlin Macnamara; in Penzance registry office; with no money, no prospect of money, no attendant friends or relatives, and in complete happiness. We've been meaning to from the first day we met, and now we are free and glad."

They spent their honeymoon at the Lobster Pot, then moved to the nearby fishing village of Newlyn to a studio owned by Max Chapman. They associated with painters and writers staying in the area, which had become something of an artists' colony, and a good time was had by all. At the end of the summer they left Cornwall to visit his parents in Swansea.

From the creative point of view little happened in 1937, but Dylan Thomas did write a long poem originally entitled *Poem to Caitlin*, then *Poem (for Caitlin)*, and later known by its first line, "I make this in a warring absence." The "warring absence" refers to coldness or actual separation from one another:

> I make this in a warring absence when
> Each ancient, stone-necked minute of love's season
> Harbours my anchored tongue, slips the quaystone,
> When, praise is blessed, her pride in mast and fountain

159

Sailed and set dazzling by the handshaped ocean,
In that proud sailing tree. . .

This long, difficult, and obscure poem uses the sea and harbor images which were all around at the time of writing. The absence prevents speech, and the tongue, inactive, is like a ship tied up in the harbor. The imagery reflects Cornwall.

Despite a diminished fishing fleet and despite a throng of summer holiday makers, it is still possible to find sandy beaches and peaceful coves in an area whose very name is enchanting. It is easy to dredge up romantic images of the caves where pirates and smugglers once hid contraband goods. In this idyllic place in which pressures of time and work are dispelled, it seems so right to invoke the poetic past and recall one of the world's great poets—Dylan Thomas.

THE LOBSTER POT
Mousehole
Nr. Penzance
Cornwall TR19 6QX

Telephone: (01736) 731251   Fax: (01736) 731140

Rooms: 26, several with views of the bustling harbor.

Public Rooms: Lounge, cocktail bar, and restaurant with sea views.

KATHERINE MANSFIELD

at

Hannafore Point Hotel
West Looe
Cornwall

We drove through lanes like great flowery
loops with the sea below and huge gulls sailing over or preening themselves upon the
roof tiles, until we came to this hotel which
stands in its garden facing the open sea. It
could not be a more enchanting position.
The hotel is large, 'utterly first class,' *dread-
fully expensive.* It has a glassed-in winter
garden for bad weather with long chairs, a
verandah—the garden hung between the sun
and the sea.

—Letter to John Middleton Murry, 17 May 1918

When it was known as the Headland Hotel, Katherine Mansfield
came to it to recover from her illness. Set on the glorious Cornish
coastline in an area of great natural beauty, the hotel is a perfect
haven for health and for happiness. Alas, Katherine Mansfield
found neither.

She first came to England in 1903 to complete her education at
Queen's College in London. Upon returning home to New Zealand,
where she was born on 14 October 1888, she found the atmosphere
narrow and stifling and begged to be allowed to return to London.
At last her parents yielded, and the twenty-year-old girl left the
place of her birth never to return.

In London she entered a Bohemian world and she entered a
marriage which she left the very next day. She had succumbed to

161

the persuasive charms of the man whom she married when she found herself pregnant and rejected by another. But her marital motive, an impulsive bid for security, had a predictably unhappy ending. She left her husband and the world of promising bourgeois possibilities. In Bavaria shortly thereafter, where she was so intolerably miserable that she relied on drugs for relief, she suffered a miscarriage. Her first book contained the cynical stories emanating from that dreadful time in her life; *In a German Pension,* published in 1911, expresses the feelings of an outsider in a hostile world.

A complex person who donned many masks and roles, Katherine Mansfield continued to have love affairs. On her return to London, there was a second pregnancy and an abortion. She seemed always to be seeking intensive experiences from which she might shape the stories which would bring her closer to becoming the well-known and creative writer she had long before determined to be.

She first met John Middleton Murry in 1911 after he wrote to her asking her to send a story to the Oxford undergraduate magazine of which he was editor. Her story appeared in *Rhythm* in the spring issue of 1912. She and Murry became good friends. By Easter he moved into her flat, and they both worked on the quarterly magazine which included stories, essays, and reviews by Murry, Mansfield, and their friends.

Finally, she no longer felt isolated and lonely—no longer an alien. She could share life with someone she loved, someone who was also her critic and confidant. They married on 3 May 1918, a few days after she obtained a divorce ending that first disastrous marriage.

But the chance for marital happiness was marred by the onset of tuberculosis. Although happy in London with her husband, her health steadily declined. Illness made it essential for her to leave England every winter. She had spent one winter in the milder climate of the south of France but returned to England in even poorer health than before she left. Frequent separations from Murry and worries over financial problems no doubt contributed a deleterious effect to her physical condition.

Katherine Mansfield
(1888-1923) went to the
Headlands Hotel, now
Hannafore Point Hotel,
West Looe, in hopes of
a cure for her illness

Murry was unable to convince her to enter a sanatorium, but he was able to convince her to go to Cornwall. After only a few weeks of marriage, in the middle of May, she went to the luxurious Headland Hotel in Looe, recommended by a friend. A letter to Murry dated 19 May 1918 underscores the ironies and contingencies of life: ". . . the divine sea is here, the haze and brightness mingled. I stare at that and wonder about the gulls, and wonder why I must be ill."

She also expresses anxiety, in letters to Murry, about the acceptance of *Bliss*, one of her best-known short stories. Written at a time of illness and wretchedness, the story deals with the familiar theme of the heroine's happiness so suddenly and unjustly demolished. The young woman of the story feels the beauty of a spring day with the pear tree in full bloom in the garden. In a state of bliss, she senses something wonderful about to happen. But her hopes are cruelly destroyed, while nature remains untouched by her tragedy: "But the pear tree was as lovely as ever and as full of flower and as still."

It should have been a happy stay in Cornwall. Indeed her letters from Looe were cheerful enough at first, as in this of 1 June 1918, to Murry: "I've not moved from my balcony all day. If you could see the water, half green half a tender violet, and just moving. It is unbelievably exquisite."

But when overwhelming depression took over, the world became ugly. In a letter to Lady Ottoline Morrell she writes, "the sea stank—great gray crabs scuttled over the rocks—all the private paths and nooks had been fouled by human cattle—there were rags of newspaper in the hedges. . . ."

She was especially taken with an angel of a chambermaid, Mrs. Honey, who was completely devoted to her. A letter of 18 May 1918 to Murry playfully describes the maid: "The old woman who looks after me is about 106, nimble and small, with the loveliest *skin*—pink rubbed over cream—and she has blue eyes and white hair and *one tooth*, a sort of family monument to all the 31 departed ones. Her soft Cornish cream voice is a delight. . . ." Mrs. Honey was actually sixty-eight and full of tender care and concern for Katherine. Despite good care, Katherine entered this wry description of a sleepless night in her journal: "The man in the room next to mine has the same complaint as I. When I wake in the night I hear him turning. And then he coughs. And I cough. And after a silence I cough. And he coughs again. This goes on for a long time. Until I feel we are like two roosters calling each other at false dawn. From far-away hidden farms."

Despite the sea and sun, she became disillusioned. Her initial contentment turned to bitterness and despair. She missed Murry and was in constant pain, clinging desperately to love and life. A projected stay of three months was reduced to five weeks. Murry came down to bring her home in the third week of June. They had found in Hampstead the house which they called "The Elephant" (now marked by a blue plaque) and were able to move into it at the end of August of 1918. *Bliss* was published in the prestigious *English Review*.

Very little writing survives of Katherine Mansfield's stay in Cornwall. Part she destroyed herself, part was lost—a journal of her observations. There is the complete story *Carnation* plus a few fragmentary pieces.

But after her stay in Cornwall, Katherine Mansfield began a period of intensive writing, and many of her mature stories present a world of beauty suddenly shattered by the inexplicable and capricious entry of evil into a world indifferent to human suffering. When she was not feeling debilitated by disease, her feverish application to work during the final years resulted in artistic triumph over physical disability.

In 1920 the volume *Bliss and Other Stories* was published and in 1922 *The Garden Party and Other Stories*. She was now financially secure and famous. Her reputation remains untarnished as critics continue to appreciate and respect her enormous influence on the art of the short story.

She and Murry returned to London to live, but she kept going abroad for health reasons—the Italian Riviera, the French Riviera, Switzerland, Paris. She resumed the journey of the consumptive seeking health, the journey made by Keats, Chekhov and Lawrence. She moved about from place to place in search of a cure and underwent quack treatments, radiation therapy, and, finally, even a kind of mystical or faith healing. After five years of illness and suffering, her premature death at the age of thirty-four came in France on 9 January 1923.

But the world of beauty in which the hotel exists remains unchanged. The name of the hotel is changed, but not the qualities which make it special. The Headland Hotel became the Hannafore Point Hotel in the 1950s, but its venue remains altogether joyous in its "enchanting position."

Most important is "all that sea and air outside" which Katherine Mansfield speaks of in her letters and in her journal. In a letter to Lady Ottoline Morrell of 24 May 1918, she tries to banish despair and fits of weeping: "My tiny world tinkles: 'Of course, with all that sea and air outside and all that butter, milk and cream *in* you'll be as fit as a fiddle in no time '."

When she was feeling well enough to go out, she did get about and responded with pleasure and vigor to her surroundings. She describes to Virginia Woolf the little town of Looe "built on both banks of a deep river and joined by an extremely 'paintable' bridge. And seagulls, and flowers—and *so on*."

East Looe and West Looe are joined by an attractive Victorian bridge, erected to replace the earlier fifteenth-century bridge of thirteen arches. The hotel is in West Looe, but the main part of the village clusters around the quay. In one of the appealing old streets of East Looe is a sixteenth-century guildhall, now a museum.

Katherine Mansfield describes the nearby picturesque fishing village of Polperro with its "lovely little black and white and grey houses—houses that might have been built by sea-gulls *for* sea-gulls. But you must see this yourself. You'll *not* believe it. I didn't, and can't even now. It was a divine afternoon, foxgloves everywhere, AND we found the most SUPERB fresh strawberries." It is still a charming village with fascinating streets. Around the harbor, simple color-washed Georgian houses are reflected in the water. A long history of smuggling activity makes it even more colorful, and a smuggler's museum is located in the cellar of a house near the center of the village.

Nowadays, the area around Looe boasts of such unusual attractions as an organ museum and a monkey sanctuary as well as the usual attractions of golf, boating, and sea bathing. But the unchanging aspect of the area includes ancient stone circles and simply gorgeous scenery.

Katherine Mansfield's description of an "ideal beach, really ideal. . ." might make anyone dash off to explore the Cornish area: "This is the most astounding place. Where we were was absolutely deserted—it might have been an island—and just behind us there were great woods and fields. . . ."

But perhaps the last word for visiting Looe with its timeless sense of the past, including Katherine Mansfield's presence, can best be left to her lyrical and evocative description from this journal entry of 22 May 1918: "The sea here is real sea. It rises and falls with a loud noise, has a long, silky roll on it as though it purred, seems sometimes to climb half up into the sky and you see the sail boats perched upon clouds—like flying cherubs."

HANNAFORE POINT HOTEL
Marine Drive
West Looe
Cornwall PL13 2DG

Telephone: (01503) 263273   Fax: (01503) 263272

Best Western Hotels.
All 38 bedrooms have private bathrooms, tea/coffee making facilities, and television. The majority also have panoramic views along the Cornish coastline and many have balconies overlooking Looe Bay.

A Leisure Centre Complex comprises heated indoor swimming pool, squash court, gymnasium, steam room, saunas, solarium, and club lounge.

The hotel is located in southeast Cornwall just a few miles from the bustling city of Plymouth.

KENNETH GRAHAME

at

The Greenbank Hotel
Falmouth
Cornwall

He marched into the inn, ordered the best
luncheon that could be provided at so short
a notice, and sat down to eat it in the coffee-
room.

—The Wind in the Willows

When Kenneth Grahame wrote the famous children's classic which
has gone into over a hundred editions since its publication in 1908,
he had already achieved fame as a writer. He had created an
idealized picture of childhood in two extremely popular works, *The
Golden Age* and *Dream Days*. A more unlikely candidate for the
author of *The Wind in the Willows* would be hard to imagine.

He was born in Edinburgh on 8 March 1859. His mother died
when he was five, and the four Grahame children were sent by their
father to live with their maternal grandmother at Cookham Dene
in Berkshire. He developed a love of nature and a love for the
Berkshire portion of the River Thames, which he used as the home
of his animal characters. Years later, after a career in London,
Grahame was to return to Cookham Dene with his wife and son.
Like the character he created, Mole, a mysterious call reached him:
"Home! That was what they meant, those caressing appeals, those
soft touches wafted through the air, those invisible little hands
pulling and tugging, all one way!"

Not permitted to go to Oxford, the young Grahame entered into
a clerkship in the Bank of England on the first day of 1879. The
condemned man resented all his life the denial of a university

education and the career decision which was made for him. But he stayed with the Old Lady of Threadneedle Street for nearly thirty years and found solace in holidays, both in England and abroad; in particular, he discovered and fell in love with Cornwall, returning to it often.

He was making a success of life. He advanced in his career, and he wrote essays, a selection of which were published as *Pagan Papers* in 1893. He may even be credited as an early feminist writer for his single adult short story, *The Headswoman* (which appeared in *The Yellow Book* in 1894). Written at a time of controversy over the employment of women at the Bank, this satirical story was about a woman claiming her rights to a hereditary position as executioner in a sixteenth-century French village. But *The Golden Age* (1895), a collection of eighteen articles about children, made him famous overnight.

The year 1898 was a highly successful one in both his professional and literary life. At the age of thirty-nine, he became Secretary of the Bank of England. And *Dream Days* was published in December to enthusiastic reviews. Now he was a financially secure and highly eligible bachelor of nearly forty. His house-keeper, in his quarters in Kensington Crescent, conceived of him as a Mr. Jekyll who went to the Bank of England and Mr. Hyde "who wrote bits in the papers."

Indeed, the idea of a person serving in the Bank conjures up a picture of solid respectability—a stodgy man in formal attire, with black umbrella and silk top hat, stiff and uncomfortable with children. A colleague at the Bank purchased *The Golden Age* believing it to be about bullion or currency. Both the colleague and the image were wrong.

Elspeth Thomson entered his life in 1897, and the friendship culminated in marriage. She came down to Fowey in Cornwall when he was convalescing from an illness, and they were married there on 22 July 1899. Unfortunately, it was to be a disappointing and unhappy marriage for both partners.

Their only child was born on 12 May 1900. He was blind in one eye with a squint in the other, and he was destined to be spoiled, unhappy, and unable to live up to the level of expectations set for him. His father's repressed imagination and creative impulses found release by focusing on Alistair—"Mouse" as their young son was affectionately called.

The Wind in the Willows evolved from the bedtime stories Kenneth Grahame told his son over a three-year period, beginning in early 1904. He writes in a letter of 15 May 1904 that Alistair had a fit of crying, "...and I had to tell him stories about moles, giraffes & water-rats till after 12." In that same month, the maid, asked by Elspeth why the master was late when they were going out to dinner, replied, "Oh, he's up in the night-nursery, telling Master Mouse some ditty or another about a toad."

While the giraffe was dropped from the cast of characters, a guest shamelessly eavesdropping in rapt fascination to the story Grahame was telling Alistair, reported in August 1905 that a badger had been added.

In May 1907, Alistair was sent to Littlehampton with his governess on a seven-week seaside holiday. To placate the child, his father promised to send letters containing the continuing saga of the adventures of the toad so that Mouse would not miss the bedtime stories. While the child was enjoying the sea and sand, his parents left for Cornwall. They spent some ten days at the Greenbank Hotel in Falmouth before going on to Fowey. Then Elspeth returned in mid-June to be with Alistair, who was now back at home in Cookham Dene, but Grahame (for some inexplicable reason) stayed at their London pied-à-terre until September, returning to Cookham Dene for weekends.

It is during the period of time from the spring to the autumn of 1907 that Kenneth Grahame wrote the letters which the governess read to Alistair at bedtime. Fortunately, she also preserved them, for they contained the basic narrative of Toad's adventures. A letter of 10 May from the Greenbank Hotel begins, "Have you heard about the Toad?" and ends, "I fear he is a bad, low animal."

When *The Wind in the Willows* was published, not many people realized what a strong and lasting wind blew. The book had a slow and indifferent reception and was initially appreciated by few. Arnold Bennett reviewed it and pointed out its value, speaking of its characters—the Rat, the Mole, the Toad—as human beings.

Kenneth Grahame (1859-1932)
wrote letters to his son
containing the adventures
of Toad from
The Greenbank Hotel,
Falmouth

Toad does have the appeal of the ever-popular bad boy, wild and boastful, but full of spirit and fully confident of finding a way out of his predicament.

The story is set mainly in the geographical area of the Thames from Marlow to Pangbourne, especially around Cookham Dene. Grahame knew the area as a child and returned to it in middle age for his escape into an ideal social world. By drawing on actual memories for some of his descriptions, he gave a powerful feeling of reality. "As you went along in the stillness, every now and then masses of snow slid off the branches suddenly with a *flop* ! making you jump and run for cover."

In a letter dated 10 October 1908 to one of his many enthusiastic fans, President Theodore Roosevelt, he wrote of *The Wind in the Willows*: "Its qualities, if any, are mostly negative—i.e., no problems, no sex, no second meaning—it is only an expression of the very simplest joys of life as lived by the simplest beings of a class that you are specially familiar with and will not understand." This effacing statement is denied by critics who find significant, latent meanings as they delve into the characters of Grahame's private world. Although he displayed outward conformity to society, inwardly he found revenge in satire and fantasy. He found relief in a world of childhood.

Kenneth Grahame retired prematurely from the Bank in June 1908. He did a great deal of traveling but never went to the United States. He never accepted the invitation extended by Theodore Roosevelt to visit him at the White House, but the two met when Roosevelt came to Oxford to lecture several years later. In his travels, Cornwall always remained a special haven. "I want Mouse to make the acquaintance of my Cornish haunts, and friends," he wrote, "before he goes to school."

Alistair's days at school were sheer misery. He was semi-blind, awkward, and friendless and went from one emotional crisis to another. He continued to be unhappy at Oxford when he went up to Christ Church in the spring term of 1918. Then on 7 May 1920 tragedy struck. Out on an evening walk by himself, while crossing railway tracks, he was killed by an oncoming train. Although a coroner's jury returned a verdict of accidental death, doubts remain. (Why did he indulge in an unaccustomed glass of port before going out? Aware that his vision was poor, why did he not choose the proper crossing instead of a spot some distance from it? Even if he could not see well, could he not *hear* the train approaching?) In any case, the recipient of those comforting bedtime tales was dead at twenty.

The Grahames made their last home at Church Cottage, Pangbourne, in the Berkshire countryside which Kenneth loved. He wrote a little, traveled, and lived out his final years quietly. He died on 6 July 1932.

The world he created continues to enchant, as does the actual world in which he lived, a world which goes through the Berkshire landscape on to Cornwall. As Rat expresses it, "Beyond the Wild Wood comes the Wide World."

And in the wide world is Falmouth, a lovely seaport with a climate so mild that oranges and bananas have been grown, and tropical plants thrive in public gardens. And at the mouth of the Penryn River is the Greenbank Hotel, looking across the harbor towards St. Mawes. Henry VIII built castles at Falmouth and at St. Mawes to guard the entrance of the estuary from possible attack; they are among the best preserved Tudor castles in the land.

History and romance conspire at the Greenbank Hotel as it overlooks the harbor from which packet ships and sea clippers once sailed across vast oceans to achieve fame and fortune. The names of those ships and their captains are on the doors of each of the guest rooms, many with spectacular waterfront views.

The hotel itself has a long history, for the original building dates from at least 1640. It was a private residence before becoming the Ship Inn and later the King's Arms Inn. Thomas Selley became its proprietor in June 1813 and renamed his establishment the Green Bank, making it a gentlemen's residence where packet captains stayed. In 1869 it came into the hands of the Mitchell family, after whom the present dining room is named.

In the nineteenth century, the Greenbank Hotel was an important stop for coaches leaving for Plymouth, Exeter, London, Bath, and Bristol. Still in the nineteenth century, another well-known visitor stayed here—Florence Nightingale.

The public rooms, two lovely lounges and two bars, display collections of seafaring memorabilia: models of ships, prints, and early photographs. It is only appropriate that nautical associations dominate, but the literary association is not neglected. In the reception area are the framed letters written by Kenneth Grahame which form the basis for *The Wind in the Willows*.

From the Greenbank Hotel, the guest can look out at the vista and wonder, as did Rat, "What seas lay beyond, green, leaping, and crested! What sun-bathed coasts, along which the white villas glittered against the olive woods! What quiet harbours, thronged with gallant shipping bound for purple islands of wine and spice, islands set low in languorous waters!"

THE GREENBANK HOTEL
Harbourside
Falmouth
Cornwall TR11 2SR

Telephone: (01326) 312440   Fax: (01326) 211362

61 rooms, the best overlooking the harbor. All offer en-suite bathrooms, satellite television, radio, and tea and coffee making facilities. A 17-bedroom wing opened in 1991, and the bar has been modernized with picture windows since Kenneth Grahame's days.

Nightingale's Restaurant is an elegant setting for dinner with spectacular views across the world's largest natural harbor toward Flushing on the far bank.

Amenities include garden, private quay mooring, sauna, solarium, and gym.

ELIZABETH BARRETT BROWNING

at

Regina Hotel

Torquay

Devon

My lonely chamber next the sea,
Is full of many flowers set free
By summer's earliest duty;
Dear friends upon the garden-walk
Might stop amid their fondest talk,
To pull the least in beauty.

—A Flower in a Letter (1839)

Torquay, the large and flourishing seaside resort on the southern
Devonshire coast, is a place of palm trees and sub-tropical vegeta-
tion. With a very mild climate, a superb panoramic setting, and a
variety of holiday attractions, it has won the accolade as the French
Riviera of England. Yet Torquay is also the scene of what were
undoubtedly the unhappiest years in the life of Elizabeth Barrett
Browning.

Elizabeth was born on 6 March 1806 at Coxhoe Hall in the
county of Durham. Three years later, after a son and another
daughter were born to Edward and Mary Moulton Barrett, the
family moved to Hope End. That house (now the site of the Hope
End Country House Hotel), near the delightful market town of
Ledbury in Herefordshire, is the home of Elizabeth's childhood and
youth and the place where literary foundations and aspirations were
laid. It is also the place where the family greatly increased in size,
with the birth of two more daughters and seven more sons, and the

place where the first attack occurred of the long and serious illness which plagued Elizabeth throughout her life.

Despite her illness and despite the unexpected death of her mother when Elizabeth was twenty-two, the Hope End period was essentially a happy one. But severe financial setbacks forced the family to relinquish a comfortable life style and to give up the paradisiacal setting in the Malvern Hills. Hope End was sold in 1832.

The Barretts lived in Sidmouth in Devon for nearly three years before taking up residence in London, where they rented a house in Gloucester Place. Then Mr. Edward Barrett found the house he wanted—50 Wimpole Street—*the* house associated with Elizabeth. The Barrett family moved into it in the spring of 1838. In London, Elizabeth's frail health broke down and her invalidism dates from that time. Confined largely to her room, she wrote incessantly, and the result was the publication of *The Seraphim, and Other Poems*, a volume which firmly established her literary reputation.

When doctors advised a warmer climate for the winter, Torquay was chosen in the hope that the sea air would restore her strength. She left unhappily and unwillingly, sentenced by an illness so serious that she might never return. Her favorite brother Edward, affectionately nicknamed Bro, accompanied her in the autumn of 1838, and various members of the family joined her from time to time.

At first they lived in the northern part of Torquay with an aunt and uncle. Then she moved to 3 Beacon Terrace, the warmest situation in the town, with an ideal location which she describes in a letter of October 1838 to Mary Mitford:

> Here, we are immediately *upon* the lovely bay—a few paces dividing our door from its waves—and nothing but the "sweet south" and congenial west wind can reach us—and *they* must first soften their footsteps upon the waters. Behind us—so close as to darken the back windows—rises an abrupt rock crowned with the slant woods of Beacon Hill—and

thus though the North and East wind blow their fiercest, we are in an awful silence and only guess at their doings.

But Number 1 Beacon Terrace offered an even warmer residence, as she reveals in a letter of 30 October 1839, and she again moved. "The new house is warm and in all ways or *most*, superior to the last." That house, now the Hotel Regina, is where she lived for two years.

The name of the hotel has undergone several changes since the first baths in Torquay were installed in 1817. The building was then given its original and appropriate name of Bath House. Indeed, excavations made in 1929 to install a lift uncovered some of the old baths underneath the drawing room. After 1857, it was known as Victoria House, later as Sea Lawn, and finally as the Regina Hotel. It had everything going for it then, as now.

The Regina Hotel sounds queenly enough and does command a royal position on the road which runs alongside the seafront on the English Channel. But the unpretentious little place has been renovated recently, modernized and enlarged to contain over seventy bedrooms to suit the needs of the growing clientele which fills the house, especially in the overcrowded summer months. It emphasizes the presence of the poetess by a Browning Bar embellished with pictures of Elizabeth Barrett Browning.

Pleasure craft fill the busy harbor, and an attractive scene offers many summer activities as well as a warm winter haven. But for Elizabeth Barrett, "the lovely bay" became "this dreadful place." Illness and tragedy marred the offerings of an ever-popular seaside resort.

In Torquay, she remained in a state of poor health, nearly always bedridden in a room facing the bay. Although her health seemed at first to improve, she suffered a relapse in January 1839, followed by partial recovery in the spring. Her up-and-down curve ended in a relapse and serious illness for the rest of her stay in Torquay. Confined to bed in a state of feeble health, her letters often express the hope of leaving. The poems written during this period of

ignominious exile indicate her unhappy outlook rather than enjoyment or inspiration derived from an attractive seaside location.

In *The Cry of the Human*, one of the short poems written
at Torquay, she speaks of the tempest. . . the plague. . .the curse
. . .the corpse. . .terrors":

> The city's golden spire it was,
> When hope and health were strongest,
> But now it is the churchyard grass,
> We look upon the longest.

News of the death of her brother Sam in Jamaica in February
1840 caused a near-total collapse. Then came the tragedy from
which she never recovered, the death of her beloved brother
Edward, drowned in a boating accident on 11 July 1840. He
was on a sailing expedition with friends when a sudden squall
caused the boat to capsize in Babbacombe Bay. The bodies were
discovered washed ashore days later and buried in Tor
Churchyard in Torquay. The effect on Elizabeth was disastrous.
Grief was exacerbated by guilt. She loved him deeply, and he was
in Torquay because of her.

She was left prostrate by the tragedy. When she finally rallied
and regained a will to live, she lived only to be released from
incarceration in Torquay with its dark associations. But she was
simply too unwell to undertake the journey.

In a letter of 12 June 1841 to Richard Horne, she expresses her
intense need to go home and speaks of the patent carriage "with a
thousand springs" that will carry her to London, to Wimpole Street.

The last letter she wrote from Torquay makes a slip-of-the-pen
error in its date: 31 August 1831. How she must have wished to
turn the clock back some ten years! That letter also contains a
passage revealing that "the associations of this place lie upon me,
struggle as I may, like the oppression of a perpetual nightmare. It
is an instinct of self-preservation which impels me to escape—or
try to escape."

Finally, she was allowed to make the journey home to London
in an invalid carriage on 1 September 1841. A bed was fitted into

Elizabeth Barrett Browning (1806-1861) and Hotel Regina, formerly 1 Beacon Terrace, Torquay, where she lived for two years before her elopement

the conveyance which took her by slow stages to Wimpole Street, arriving there on 11 September. In a letter to Miss Mitford, written from Wimpole Street, she refers to the recent past: "The scars of that anguish I shall take down with me to the grave."

In London she resided in a bedroom of the house, dominated by an authoritarian, possessive, and unreasonable father. She received few visitors and remained ill but not idle. She wrote critiques and reviews, and she wrote poetry and letters. She had the attentions of a large and caring family but lived a quiet life and seemed destined to continue to do so—until a letter arrived from Robert Browning.

In Wimpole Street, she had composed the two-volume *Poems*, published in 1844. One of the poems of the collection, *Lady Geraldine's Courtship,* contained a compliment to Robert Browning, whose position and popularity as a major poet was not then so well established as her own. Her hero reads to his lady from a variety of poets and refers favorably to the work of the unknown Browning.

Browning returned the compliment in a letter of 10 January 1845, which lacks the conventional salutation but rushes headlong into this effusive opening: "I love your verses with all my heart, dear Miss Barrett. . . ." As if foretelling the future, he continued, "I do, as I say, love these books with all my heart— and I love you too."

He was thirty-two and she was thirty-eight when Browning wrote the first of nearly six hundred letters which passed between them. The mutual respect and friendship deepened into love after they met, for the first time, on 20 May 1845.

Under Browning's guidance and encouragement, her health improved rapidly. But the match could never receive the approval of an imperious father who was simply opposed to the marriage of any of his children. The couple were secretly married on 12 September 1845, and they eloped to Italy on the 19th, living happily in Florence, and writing poetry, until she died peacefully in his arms on 29 June 1861.

Elizabeth Barrett Browning was a fortunate woman, able to overcome grief and ill health by an inner strength and integrity. She enjoyed a happy childhood and had an affectionate, admiring family. She derived great satisfaction from being immersed in the study of language and literature and was able to indulge freely. In middle life, the best was yet to be. An apparently incurable invalid, she met and married the devoted poet, regained her health, had a child, lived in a delightful city, and relished the company of many good friends. Perhaps what is more important, she was a successful and loved human being and poet.

HOTEL REGINA
Victoria Parade
Torquay
Devon TQ1 2BE

Telephone: (01803) 292904   Fax: (01803) 214014

76 rooms, most with private bathrooms, and most accessible by the lift. All with television, radio, and tea/coffee making facilities.

Reception lounge and two bars including the Browning Bar. Entertainment several evenings of the week.

An ideal location overlooking the harbor, just one hundred yards from the Beacon Leisure Complex and close to shopping center.

EVELYN WAUGH

at

Easton Court Hotel
Chagford
Devon

I came to Chagford with the intention of
starting on an ambitious novel tomorrow
morning. I still have a cold and am low in
spirits but I feel full of literary power which
only this evening gives place to qualms of
impotence.

—*Diary*, 31 January 1944

Imagine a small thatched Tudor house of the fifteenth century set
in a lovely garden presided over by a flowering chestnut tree.
Imagine it surrounded by the serene and unspoiled countryside of
Devon. Imagine an interior of enormous charm and character with
log fires, comfortable chairs, and original oak beams. Now imagine
that a well-known writer wanted to escape to the peace and quiet
and comfort of a place conducive to his getting on with his work.
Unreal? Perhaps. But the elements pieced together make up the real
story of Evelyn Waugh at the Easton Court Hotel.

Recommendations are the best way of discovering a good hotel
suitable to one's needs, and the Easton Court Hotel was recommended to Evelyn by his brother Alec who had discovered it while
touring the west country with friends. A maid became infatuated
with their chauffeur, and the chauffeur persuaded the group to make
the hotel their base. Poetic justice was done when the group became
infatuated with the hotel.

Evelyn Waugh
(1903-1966) retired
frequently to the
tranquility of the
Easton Court Hotel,
Chagford, to write

Both brothers, the only children of publisher and literary critic Arthur Waugh, achieved literary fame. Alec, five years older, began to use the hotel as a retreat for his own writing. It was a cozy place with a country house atmosphere run by Mrs. Carolyn Cobb, an American, who had a fine appreciation of writers and their needs. And the many writers who came to the hotel had a great respect for her in turn.

The hotel has changed hands since the days of Mrs. Cobb but remains essentially unchanged. A sitting room with a great stone fireplace, a bar, and a well-stocked library have antique oak furniture and log fires. Eight bedrooms are individually and tastefully furnished. The meals, served by candle light in a handsome dining room, feature local game and fish and fresh produce. Cheese and Devonshire cream come from a local farm.

On entering the village, a signpost declares: "Chagford, Ancient Stannery Town, 1305"—and the treat begins. In the center of Chagford is an attractive octagonal Victorian market building which blends in with Tudor and Georgian houses. Older thatched cottages and a sixteenth-century bridge over the River Teign make this appealing village on the edge of Dartmoor a delightful center for exploration. The hotel is situated a mile from the village.

The scenery is glorious, and the possibilities of delightful walks, endless. Stone circles, cromlechs, and Bronze Age settlements are there. The River Teign, known for its salmon and trout fishing, winds through the area and is just a few hundred yards from the hotel. By contrast, the great cathedral city of Exeter is just eighteen miles away. Facilities for horse riding, golf, hunting, and fishing are plentiful. One might append writing to the list of activities, for the setting has been an inspiration to the creative process of many.

Evelyn Waugh's reputation as a leading novelist was already secure when he first came to Chagford. His writing career was launched in 1928 with his first novel, *Decline and Fall*, which was a success. Also in that year came his first marriage, which was a failure. He busied himself in the following years by traveling a great deal and writing a great deal. In addition to his travel books and biographies, the novels of this period include *Vile Bodies*

(1930), *Black Mischief* (1932), *A Handful of Dust* (1934), and *Scoop* (1938).

In 1937 he married Laura Herbert and settled into Piers Court in the Gloucestershire Cotswolds for nearly twenty years. Laura pottered about the farm which produced milk, cream, butter, and eggs. They traveled, and a trip to Hollywood (where he refused a film offer for *Brideshead Revisited*) resulted in *The Loved One* (1948).

They moved to the west country, to Combe Florey near Taunton, with a large family which by then included six children. Over the final ten-year period at his country home, he declined and fell, and death came on 10 April 1966 at the age of sixty-three.

Although his rate of writing and his energy diminished in his last ten years, he produced four more books. He never stopped writing. Although he put out remarkable quantities of material in his peak period and claims to have written *Put Out More Flags* while on a troopship returning to England in 1941, Evelyn Waugh seems to have needed a comfortable writing place free from distractions. As early as 1931, he expresses in a letter his intention to go to the Easton Court Hotel: "Well at Chagford I pretend to my London chums that I am going to hunt stags but to you who are intimates & confidantes I dont mind saying that I shall sit all day in my bedroom writing books, articles, short stories, reviews, plays, cinema scenarios, etc. etc. until I have got a lot more money."

Apparently he succeeded, for he kept returning to the hotel. He was back in Chagford in April 1932 finishing *Black Mischief,* and he came again and again whenever he needed to get writing done. A letter from the hotel written in 1934 divulges an interesting bit of news: "I am back & this is my address until the novel is finished. . . .The name of the novel is A HANDFUL OF ASHES." He later changed the title, but not the venue.

These entries written in the *Diaries* in October 1939 indicate his work habits at the hotel in Chagford:

Tuesday 24 October: Wrote all morning. The second chapter taking shape and more important ideas springing. A long and lonely walk in the afternoon. A little more work.

185

Wednesday 25 October: Wrote all the morning and some of the afternoon. Eight-mile walk...

Thursday 26 October: Working well. Over 4,000 words done since I arrived...

Friday 27 October: Working well...

But it was not all work and no play. He did take exhilarating walks, and Laura often came down to meet him and sometimes to spend the day with him in Exeter. On Sundays he generally attended church services in the tiny village of Gidleigh. And there was the occasional happy telephone interruption, once with a message to announce that Laura had given birth.

However, it was not always perfection at the hotel, as this *Diary* excerpt of February 1944 suggests: "The hotel is full of elderly women who do not distract me from my work. Carolyn has given me the room they call 'the middle lounge' for a private sitting room but the fire smokes so badly that I must choose between freezing and going blind."

When he was ready to begin his "ambitious novel," *Brideshead Revisited,* Evelyn Waugh revisited this simple country place which is a far cry from the half-legendary stately home of England that he calls Brideshead. Again, a few extracts from the *Diaries* of 1944 record the successful piling up of words at Easton Court:

Wednesday 2 February: Score at close of play 3,000 words odd.

Tuesday 8 February: Working steadily...

Sunday 13 February: ...rewriting...

Monday 14 February: 3,000 words in three hours. I shall have the third chapter done before I go to bed.

Friday 18 February-Wednesday 23 February: Laura came to stay with me. . .

Saturday 26 February: This morning I finished my third chapter, 33,000 words in all, and took it in high good humour to the post office. . .

A footnote to the completed manuscript of *Brideshead Revisited* reads, "Chagford (Devon), Feb-June 1944."

To say that the Easton Court Hotel played a great role in the life of Evelyn Waugh would be to understate the truth. More accurately, it was part author of the novels. It presents a record of work well done in a congenial atmosphere. Other artists would agree, for the guest book is signed by such illustrious names as John Betjeman, John Gielgud, Dr. Margaret Meade, Ralph Richardson, C.P. Snow, and John Steinbeck.

The temptation is to think that one need only repair to the Easton Court Hotel for the words to pile up. While the proprietors do not guarantee that their guests will produce novels of distinction, they do promise a charming Tudor house in a gorgeous country spot which serves as an excellent center from which to explore Dartmoor in Devon. And at the very least, the guest may write a postcard or two telling of a memorable holiday experience.

187

THE EASTON COURT HOTEL
Chagford
Devon TQ13 8JL

Telephone/Fax: (01647) 433469

Rooms: Eight, each with en suite bath or shower and tea/coffee making unit.

Public Rooms: Sitting room with open fireplace complete with bread oven, and library complete with good collection of old books. The restaurant offers traditional English cuisine using fresh local produce.

Nearby facilities: Eighteen-hole golf course, tennis, and swimming (in open-air pool or sea). Salmon or trout fishing in the River Teign (which runs only a few hundred yards from the hotel) or trout fishing in Fernworthy and Hennock reservoirs. Several riding schools in the area provide lessons and horses.

How to get there: Railway and coach lines serve Exeter (170 miles southwest of London), where taxis or rental cars are available. Arrangements can be made for the hotel to meet guests by car. Flights from Exeter Airport connect with Heathrow and Gatwick.

GEORGE BERNARD SHAW

at

The Victoria Hotel

Sidmouth

Devon

Well, what more could anyone ask but a
nice hotel? All the housekeeping done for
us: no trouble with the servants: no rates nor
taxes. I have never had any peace except in
a hotel. . . .

--The Millionairess

George Bernard Shaw was eighty-two when he first came to the
Victoria Hotel in Sidmouth in 1938. His wife and friends cajoled
and conspired to get him to go at a time when he was feeling worn
out and unwell. And no wonder! So prolific, so active and creative
was he throughout his life, that it is meaningless to say that he is
famous or popular or talented. He wrote five novels, about fifty
plays, innumerable pieces of journalism and vast amounts of drama
and music criticism. He was a lecturer and a member of the Fabian
Society.

Born in Dublin on 26 July 1856, he left for London in 1876
determined to become a successful writer. He had a long apprenticeship, and fame eluded him until he was fifty. When it came,
his success was stupendous, culminating in the Nobel Prize for
Literature awarded in 1926 when he was seventy.

His first play, *Widowers' Houses*, was performed in 1892. Then
came *The Philanderer*, *Mrs. Warren's Profession*, and *Arms and
the Man*. His fifth play, *Candida*, ushered in a long line of plays
with hardly a pause—*The Man of Destiny*, *You Never Can Tell*, *The
Devil's Disciple*, *Caesar and Cleopatra*. . . .

189

The important man of the theatre became involved with several attractive and important ladies of the theatre. Always in search of leading ladies for his plays, his attempts to win them over knew no bounds. He often fell in love with them. Fascinated by the acting of Ellen Terry, he wrote letters to her as early as 1892, and he later wrote *Captain Brassbound's Conversion* for her. During his years as a drama critic for the *Saturday Review*, he came to admire Mrs. Patrick Campbell for her beauty and for her talent as an actress. In August 1912, he began a correspondence of love letters with her—Stella—and of course he wrote plays for her.

Shaw was busy with his correspondence with Ellen Terry when he met Charlotte Frances Payne-Townshend. She became his secretary by the beginning of 1898 and his wife in June of that year. She was seen by many as a nurse and mother to him, but they got along splendidly together, sharing interests and a long life. The couple lived in such places as Haslemere and Hindhead before settling in 1906 into "Shaw's Corner" in Ayot St. Lawrence, a pretty, little, isolated village in Hertfordshire of the kind one is in danger of missing by blinking an eye. Shaw disliked the house but stayed on rather than undertake the bothersome alternative of leaving it.

Shaw's Corner is an unpretentious but delightful house now run by the National Trust and open to visitors who make their way to it via difficult single-track country lanes. The four downstairs rooms and their contents remain as they were in Shaw's lifetime with such personal treasures and effects on display as his pens, typewriter, and desk. Upstairs, Shaw's bedroom and bathroom are open on weekdays. His hats hang on a rack in the entrance hall as if in readiness to be picked up by him on his way out for a long walk or a long bicycle ride. In the garden is the summerhouse retreat in which he did his writing. At Shaw's Corner, Shaw could relax as well as work.

Charlotte was not musical, nor was she greatly interested in theatre. And she abhorred the hero-worshippers who fawned, no matter where they went, on the author of *Man and Superman, Major Barbara, Misalliance, Pygmalion, Heartbreak House, Saint Joan, The Millionairess.* But it was a long and successful marriage and one based on her condition that the marriage should not be consummated.

Other eccentricities might include the fact that Shaw was a vegetarian and a teetotaller with a strong aversion to tobacco. His idea of a holiday was a change in work, and he did not indulge in travel. Charlotte, on the other hand, had a passion for travel. Perhaps it was her total distaste for housekeeping that made her prefer hotel life. Nevertheless, Shaw agreed to go to Sidmouth.

The nature of his illness was unknown. He had been overworking in 1937, as usual, and was feeling tired and irritable; Charlotte became concerned and enlisted the aid of friends. Nora and St. John Ervine investigated several hotels before selecting the Victoria Hotel in Sidmouth as the one that would meet their requirements. Their comfortable suite at the hotel consisted of two bedrooms and a sitting room. The manager was so helpful and solicitous that they returned to his care at a later date.

At the Victoria, Shaw resented being gaped at by guests who recognized his gaunt figure, and he developed the habit of using the fire-escape to enter or leave his sitting room, thereby upsetting several elderly ladies.

In order to distract Shaw from his illness, various jaunts were made. One excursion took them to Ashe House in nearby Musbury, the house in which the Duke of Marlborough was born. But Shaw displayed more interest in the archery range than in the house. He also exhibited a complete indifference to nature. They drove through a beautiful valley, thick and blue with flowers. "Did you see the bluebells, GBS?" asked Charlotte. He replied, "What bluebells?" Indeed, his works contain few references to the beauties of nature.

He had arrived in Sidmouth at the end of April 1938, and during the several weeks spent at the Victoria his health seemed to improve. But by May his condition deteriorated, and Charlotte insisted on a doctor. The diagnosis was pernicious anemia, and he had to undergo a course of liver injections in opposition to his vegetarian principles. He was in his eighties, but he rallied and was quite well by October.

Charlotte died in 1943, aged eighty-six. Shaw continued to write, largely political works. His last completed play, *Buoyant Billions*, was written in 1946 at the age of ninety. In 1949 he wrote *Farfetched Fables* and *Sixteen Self Sketches*.

One day, at the age of ninety-four, he went into his garden to prune trees and had the accident which ended his life. He stepped back from a tree, slipped, fell and broke his leg. At home after being treated in hospital, he did not recover. Death came on 2 November 1950.

The wit and humor of his works make it a pleasure to recall George Bernard Shaw. It is a particular pleasure to remember him at Sidmouth, an attractive seaside resort with Regency and early Victorian architecture. Sidmouth was once a popular watering place and retreat for the aristocracy. Queen Victoria made her first visit to it as an infant, in 1819.

From the hotel, the town center is within easy walking distance, and surrounding the town is a wealth and a variety of natural beauty. Walking is a good pastime, especially along the cliff-top paths which overlook the beaches and coastline.

The fine Edwardian hotel has been offering high standards of comfort and service since it opened its doors to guests in 1904. Bedrooms are individually designed. Many have balconies and most have views of the sea.

Set in five acres of gardens overlooking the picturesque bay of Sidmouth, the appealing haven is well maintained and refurbished, with every amenity available.

Let us allow a character in Shaw's *The Millionairess* (written only two years before Shaw came to the Victoria Hotel) have the final words: "This is what home ought to be, though it's only a hotel."

George Bernard
Shaw (1856-1950)
used the fire-escape
to avoid appearing
publicly at
The Victoria Hotel,
Sidmouth

193

VICTORIA HOTEL
The Esplanade
Sidmouth
Devon EX10 8RY

Telephone: (01395) 512651   Fax: (01395) 579154

Member of Brend Hotel Group

Rooms: All 62 guest rooms have private bathrooms, color television, and direct dial telephone. Most are south facing with sea and coastal views, and a few have private balconies. Twenty-four hour room service is available.

Restaurant: Dinner, accompanied by the resident orchestra, may be ordered from table d'hote or a la carte menus.

Public Rooms: Bright and airy sun lounge with views across the gardens to Sidmouth Bay; lounge bar for light lunches; writing room.

Amenities: Outdoor swimming pool with changing rooms and access to Hunting Lodge Bar and buttery. Tennis court and two eighteen-hole putting greens. Beach terrace. Indoor leisure complex with heated swimming pool, sauna, table tennis, fitness area. Hairdressing salon.

Location: A short walk from the town center and within easy reach of the cathedral city of Exeter.

CHARLES KINGSLEY

at

The Royal Hotel
Bideford
North Devon

All who have travelled through the delicious
scenery of North Devon must needs know
the little white town of Bideford, which
slopes upwards from its broad tide-river
paved with yellow sands, and many-arched
old bridge where salmon wait for Autumn
floods, toward the pleasant upland on the
west.

--Westward Ho!

There is no seaside town in Dorset called French Lieutenant's
Woman—or even Persuasion. But there is a seaside town in Devon
called Westward Ho!

An obscure place until it was given the name of Charles
Kingsley's popular novel, Westward Ho! is a resort town consisting
mostly of holiday homes, amusement or leisure centers, good
bathing beaches, and a golf course. Located on the northern
Devonshire coast, it is in effect an extension of Bideford, the town
in which Charles Kingsley lived in 1854 when he wrote *Westward
Ho!*.

Born on 12 June 1819 at the parsonage in Holne, one of the most
attractive villages of Devonshire, Charles Kingsley learned to love
the sea, the country, and the outdoor life. As a child, he was moved
about from place to place whenever his father, a vicar, received a
new appointment. Barnack in the fens of Lincolnshire and the
lovely picture-book Devon village of Clovelly were later to appear

in his writing. The mystery and charm of the fenlands is described in his final novel of 1866, *Hereward the Wake*, and Clovelly appeared disguised as Aberalva in *Two Years Ago*.

When he was seventeen, the family emigrated to London. Charles deeply regretted the loss of open country and returned to his native Devon whenever he could. He entered King's College, London, and afterwards, Magdalene College, Cambridge. Ordained as an Anglican clergyman at the age of twenty-three, he was appointed rector at Eversley in Hampshire. Together with his loving wife Fanny, whom he married early in 1844, he was to make Eversley his permanent home for the next thirty-three years, until his death on 23 January 1876.

From his childhood, Charles Kingsley had written poetry. His principal poetic works are *The Saint's Tragedy* (1848), a drama of Elizabeth of Hungary as she is torn between her natural desires and her religious duties, and *Andromeda* (1858), which deals with classical myth. But it was as a novelist that he made his literary mark.

A man of action with a deep concern about social conditions of England, Charles Kingsley put his ideas into fictional form. *Yeast* was originally written in installments for *Fraser's Magazine* and published in book form in 1851. In *Alton Locke* (1850), he continued his fight to improve conditions for the poor working classes. His novels had the purpose of instructing, arousing public opinion, and changing conditions; but his main fault is that he preaches. He gave sermons from his pulpit and he gave sermons in his novels, and although *Hypatia* (1853) was an historical novel set in fifth-century Alexandria, it too included topics of current concern and aroused wide public interest.

Winters were hard in Eversley, and the damp and cold Eversley rectory aggravated Fanny's precarious state of health. In July 1854, the Kingsley family moved temporarily to a house in Bideford in the hope that the change of climate would be beneficial to her. Furthermore, Charles Kingsley wanted to be near the scene of the novel he was writing. Bideford was a total success. Mrs. Kingsley's health improved, and *Westward Ho!* was published early in 1855.

Charles Kingsley
(1819-1875) wrote his
novel *Westward Ho!*
in an upstairs study
of a rented house in
Bideford, now part of
The Royal Hotel

Bideford was the principal port of North Devon from the time Sir Richard Grenville secured a charter from Queen Elizabeth. Kingsley extracted the local color of Bideford for his adventure story set in an earlier age: "Pleasantly the old town stands there . . . fanned day and night by the fresh ocean breeze, which forbids alike the keen winter frosts, and the fierce thunder heats of the midland; and pleasantly it has stood there for now, perhaps, eight hundred years. . . ."

He used scenes of the surrounding countryside and coast which he knew and loved to present vivid pictures of Elizabethan heroes who appear in the pages of his novel—Drake, Raleigh, Frobisher. His accurate historical account and excellent descriptive power made the book immensely successful. Although he needed to confine the setting of his stories to places familiar to him, it is curious that he also did a superb job of painting the scenery of the West Indies, which he was not to know until he visited some fourteen years later.

Curiously too, *Westward Ho!*, full of sword fights and galloping horses, has survived primarily as an adventure story for boys rather than as a polemical Protestant tract and perhaps his most violently propagandist novel. His prejudiced viewpoint did not allow him to be fair to Catholicism. It dwells on Spanish atrocities and glosses over English ones. The bloodthirsty massacres are extreme, and he himself called it a "sanguinary" book.

Kingsley wanted to inspire young Englishmen to be as heroic as the models of the past. Many regarded it not only as a stirring adventure story but as recruiting propaganda at a time when England was engaged in the Crimean War. The public approved of his views and the book met with popular and critical success, making him a leading novelist of the day.

Kingsley worked on *Westward Ho!* in an upstairs study of his rented Bideford house. Built by a wealthy merchant in 1688, the house has since been incorporated into what is now the Royal Hotel.

The Royal Hotel stands on a busy corner of the town, overlooking the River Torridge and the "many-arched old bridge." With its twenty-four arches, the Bideford Bridge is the town's most prominent sight. Here are two reminders that nothing is wasted in England: the bridge, which was widened in 1925, incorporates part of the ancient bridge of 1460; and the Royal Hotel, which opened in 1888, encompasses the original house of 1688 in which Kingsley wrote.

The hotel retains the large oak-paneled room with a magnificent molded plaster ceiling, appropriately named the Kingsley Room, for in it the author worked hard on his famous novel. Across the corridor is the Kingsley Bedroom with marble fireplace surround and plasterwork ceiling, nicely furnished to evoke a feeling of the author's presence. The grand oak staircase leading to these rooms is another original part of the merchant's mansion.

Many other features give the hotel the interest and charm of age. The covered courtyard of the hotel was formerly the stable yard of the old mansion and is now the ballroom, while the present dining room occupies the site of the stables. Part of the old building was once used as a workhouse and later as a prison. Three cells remain with heavy double-planked doors and sliding peep holes.

An old-fashioned hotel in an old-fashioned town, the Royal has recently been refurbished. Though a bit tired, the town has character. Several seventeenth-century buildings of architectural interest can be seen in Bridgeland Road, and a Pannier Market is held on Tuesdays and Saturdays.

No escape is possible from reminders of the author's presence. Alongside the river and near the end of the quay the inevitable statue stands, predictably in Kingsley Road. All about are tributes to his name—Kingsley Plumbing, Kingsley Car Sales, Kingsley Pet Stores, Kingsley Dry Cleaners, Kingsley Insurance. . . .

After *Westward Ho!* Kingsley wrote *Two Years Ago*, a novel which takes place in 1854 and deals with a cholera epidemic and the young doctor who attempts to halt it by improving sanitation. The author had actually campaigned for better sanitary conditions to prevent cholera outbreaks.

Kingsley is also remembered for *The Water Babies*, a children's story of a chimney sweep who escapes a tyrannical master to live in a watery world. Like many other complex and lasting children's stories, this minor masterpiece can take on added levels of meaning to give satisfaction to adult readers.

Many of his other works cover history and sermons which are remarkable for style and diversity of subject. *At Last* (1871) records the realization of a travel dream which was at last fulfilled when he visited the West Indies, his mother's home, in 1869.

Although Kingsley was also known as a social reformer, sanitary reformer, editor, critic and reviewer, naturalist and popularizer of geology and zoology, although he became Canon of Chester and of Westminster, Chaplain to the Queen, and professor of history at Cambridge, he achieved prominence primarily as an author of novels and particularly as the author of *Westward Ho!* To him we owe the existence of perhaps the only town in the world with an exclamation mark in its name!

THE ROYAL HOTEL
Barnstaple Street
Bideford
North Devon EX39 4AE

Telephone: (01237) 472005   Fax: (01237) 478957

Member of the Brend Hotel Group

Rooms: All rooms have private bathroom, color television and radio, direct dial telephone, tea and coffee making facilities.

Public rooms: Bar and spacious lounge where Devon cream tea may be enjoyed.

Restaurant: Serves full English breakfast, lunch, and dinner with table d'hote or a la carte menus.

Location: Near the quay of the historic port of Bideford, a few minutes driving time from the M5 Motorway, and 205 miles from London.

COLERIDGE AND THE WORDSWORTHS

at

Alfoxton Park Hotel

Holford

Somerset

But never elsewhere in one place I knew
So many nightingales.
>   —*The Nightingale*
> Samuel Taylor Coleridge

It is the first mild day of March.
Each minute, sweeter than before,
The redbreast sings from the tall larch
That stands beside our door.
>   —*To My Sister*
> William Wordsworth

A very bright moonlight night. Venus
like another moon. Lost to us at
Alfoxden long before she goes down the
large white sea.
>   —*The Alfoxden Journal*
> Dorothy Wordsworth

Although associated primarily with the Lake District, Wordsworth—together with his close friend Coleridge—can be said to have started poetic life in Somerset, in the west country rather than in the lakes.

In 1795 Wordsworth and Coleridge met at Bristol, and the meeting was to bring about a literary revolution. Samuel Taylor Coleridge moved, in 1796, with his wife and infant son to Nether Stowey in Somerset, to a small cottage in Lime Street now maintained by the National Trust. Before long, William Wordsworth moved with his sister Dorothy from Racedown in Dorset to Holford in Somerset to be near Coleridge. Wordsworth was in a state of severe depression and despair brought on by lost ideals pertaining to the French Revolution and by guilt incurred by the need to leave Annette Vallon and their child behind in France.

William and Dorothy rented Alfoxden House, half a mile west of the village of Holford, just a few miles from Nether Stowey. They installed themselves in the early eighteenth-century manor house of the St. Albyn family in July 1797, and Coleridge stayed with them during their first week at Alfoxden. Thus began an idyllic year in which the three were virtually inseparable.

Dorothy loved the spacious and elegant house and called it "that dear and beautiful place." William wrote of its "enchanting beauty." Their Alfoxden home (as spelled by Dorothy in her Journal but pronounced Allfoxen by the locals) became the Alfoxton Park Hotel in the early 1960s.

The present gracious white house, with roof of bluish slate, is set in grounds which consist of fifty acres of gardens and woods; the grounds also include an outdoor heated swimming pool and tennis court. The front door opened onto a grass court and gravel path on which Wordsworth paced when he was creating poetry. Gone is the larch, with its resident redbreast, that stood near the door.

The comfortable, family-run hotel faces the Quantock hills and commands a wonderful view of the Bristol Channel with Wales on the far side. From their dining room, the Wordsworths could feast on a pastoral landscape which took in the view of the sea. Walkers still encounter sheep grazing on the slopes; their owners are still given rights of free pasture.

The walled kitchen garden which Dorothy once tended, and which produced lettuces and other basic provisions for the meals she prepared, now supplies some of the ingredients which go into the chef's good meals, served in the Georgian Dining Room.

The mansion, as Dorothy called it, had nine bedrooms; but after the Wordsworths left, an extension was added on the north side. Today the hotel has twenty bedrooms.

The Oak Room Bar was Wordsworth's library. In the long paneled parlor to the right of the entrance, Coleridge gave his first reading of *The Ancient Mariner* by the warmth of a fireplace decorated with blue and white Dutch tiles picturing windmills and ships. The Wordsworths paid £23 rent for the idyllic year, a sum that would today only partially cover a single idyllic day. Dorothy wrote of the area in a letter: "There is everything here; sea, woods wild as fancy ever painted, brooks clear and pebbly as in Cumberland, villages so romantic; and William and I, in a wander by ourselves, found out a sequestered waterfall in a dell formed by steep hills covered with full-grown timber trees." There was everything there. Primarily, there was Coleridge. "We are three people, but only one soul," said Coleridge. They were together almost daily; they walked, read, discussed poetry, enjoyed sunshine, gazed at views, exchanged ideas and thoughts.

The friends were continually wandering over the Quantocks, and the contemporary wanderer can seek inspiration by following their footsteps, perhaps with Dorothy's *Alfoxden Journal* as guide: "On the hill-tops. . .through the wood to Holford. . . followed the sheep tracks. . .to Stowey. . .to Woodlands, and to the waterfall . . .into the Coombe. . .walked. . .walked by moonlight . . .walked to the sea-side. . .walked to Cheddar. . . ."

Coleridge and Wordsworth collaborated on the *Lyrical Ballads*, which inaugurates the Romantic movement in English literature. Almost all of the poems of that volume were written in the spring and summer of 1798.

At Alfoxden, Coleridge had listened to "delicious notes" and wrote *The Nightingale* for the *Lyrical Ballads*. Confined to his cottage when his wife accidentally spilled a pan of scalding milk over his foot, Coleridge imagined in "This Lime-Tree Bower, My Prison" the wanderings of Dorothy and William over hilltops with their visitor, Charles Lamb. Coleridge's *Rime of the Ancient Mariner* is a reminder that the sea was only about two miles away; one of their walks took in the ancient little port of Watchet, the supposed prototype of the ancient mariner's harbor. *Christabel* and

Before William Wordsworth (1770-1850) became associated with the Lake District, he lived in Somerset with his sister Dorothy, at Alfoxton House; Samuel Taylor Coleridge (1772-1834) stayed with them in what is now the Alfoxton Park Hotel

Kubla Khan are among the greatest of his poems, all of which were written during this happy period.

Wordsworth expressed his joy in nature, which outweighs the evils in man, in *Lines Written in Early Spring*. And in the spring he composed the companion pieces, *Expostulation and Reply* and *The Tables Turned*, in front of the house at Alfoxden.

Nor can Dorothy's influence on both poets be overestimated. For Coleridge, Dorothy was "exquisite in mind and heart." For Wordsworth, she was a source of ideas. Consider, for example, this extract from her *Journal*: "25 January 1798—Went to Poole's after tea. The sky spread over with one continuous cloud, whitened by the light of the moon, which, though her dim shape was seen, did not throw forth so strong a light as to chequer the earth with shadows. At once the clouds seemed to cleave asunder, and left her in the centre of a black-blue vault."

Wordsworth adopted the imagery for his poem, *A Night-piece*:

> The sky is overcast
> With a continuous cloud of texture close,
> Heavy and wan, all whitened by the Moon,
> Which through that veil is indistinctly seen,
> A dull, contracted circle, yielding light
> So feebly spread that not a shadow falls,
> Chequering the ground—from rock, plant, tree, or tower.
> At length a pleasant instantaneous gleam
> Startles the pensive traveller while he treads
> His lonesome path, with unobserving eye
> Bent earthwards; he looks up—the clouds are split
> Asunder,—and above his head he sees
> The clear Moon, and the glory of the heavens.
> There in a black-blue vault she sails along,
> Followed by multitudes of stars. . .

When their one-year lease expired in July 1798, the Wordsworths were refused a renewal and forced to leave because of their questionable activities. They had done so much walking, including nocturnal rambles, that they were suspected of being spies at a time when everyone feared invasion by the French. Even Coleridge had expressed his forebodings and anxieties in *Fears in Solitude* in April of that year.

But the year had worked its wonders. Coleridge reached the peak of his creative power during this, the happiest year of his life. Dorothy too had enjoyed her least troubled time, a year full of the contentment and health that later years would lack. And Wordsworth left cured of depression, with self-confidence and happiness restored, and with his destiny as a poet ensured.

What became of the threesome? In a state of poor health, Coleridge had been taking opium for relief of pain and suffered the effects of addiction. At the age of forty-three, he put himself into the hands and home of a London physician for the remaining years of his life, continuing to produce important work. When he died in 1834, Wordsworth mourned him as the "most *wonderful* man" he had ever known.

Born in 1770 in the Lake District town of Cockermouth, Wordsworth returned with Dorothy to the Lakes in 1799 to settle there finally.

Curiously enough, both Coleridge and Wordsworth returned to Alfoxden. Coleridge visited his friend Tom Poole in Nether Stowey around 1807 for the last time. The visit that was to last two weeks took two months. He and Poole rode together over the Quantocks and around Alfoxden, recalling those old walks and blissful months with Dorothy and William.

Wordsworth returned forty-three years later to visit his youthful haunts. In 1841, he had gone with his wife, Mary Hutchinson, to Bath where he stayed with their good friend Miss Isabella Fenwick in a house in North Parade. A tablet on the front of the building bears the inscription: "Here dwelt William Wordsworth." The Wordsworths drove from Bath to Ashcott to have breakfast at Piper's Inn with their newly-married daughter Dora and her husband. Afterwards they all went to Alfoxden where he sought nostalgic reminiscences of the past.

Who knows what poetry or great thoughts may inspire today's visitor to the lovely Alfoxton Park Hotel? The influence on Wordsworth was ever present. In the last book of the *Prelude* written in 1850, the year of his death, he refers to that crucial and idyllic summer with Coleridge:

> . . .but, beloved Friend!
> When, looking back, thou seest, in clearer view
> Than any liveliest sight of yesterday,
> That summer, under whose indulgent skies,
> Upon smooth Quantock's airy ridge we roved
> Unchecked, or loitered 'mid her sylvan combs,
> Thou in bewitching words, with happy heart,
> Didst chaunt the vision of that Ancient Man,
> The bright-eyed Mariner, and rueful woes
> Didst utter of the Lady Christabel.

ALFOXTON PARK HOTEL
Holford
Somerset TA5 1SG

Telephone: (01278) 741 211

All twenty rooms, including one with a fourposter bed, have private bathrooms as well as television, radio, and tea/coffee facilities.

Public rooms include bar, lounge, and dining room.

Extensive grounds provide views to the Bristol Channel.

Closed from end of November to late March.

BENJAMIN DISRAELI

at

The Royal Bath Hotel

Bournemouth

Dorset

I am going to Bournemouth—the Bath
Hotel—some rooms on the first floor, I hope
pretty good as Rothschilds have them now.

--Letter to Lady Bradford, 23 November 1874

Benjamin Disraeli was an author long before he was a politician.
He produced his first novel when he was in his early twenties, and
he went on writing throughout his life. From *Vivian Grey* in 1826,
when he was twenty-two, to *Endymion* in 1880, the year before he
died, he had a long, prolific, and diverse literary career. In addition
to his eleven novels, he wrote short stories, poems, a biography, a
play, and essays.

As a Prime Minister who wrote novels, Disraeli is generally
accepted today as a skillful and accomplished writer whose
neglected works deserve a better fate. Perhaps his powerful
political career obscured the merits of his literary output. The noted
critic F. R. Leavis has said that he deserves to be revived as a
novelist and that his so-called "Young England" trilogy expresses
"the interests of a supremely intelligent politician who has a
sociologist's understanding of civilisation and its movement in his
time."

His oeuvre is generally divided into three groups—those books
written in his pre-parliamentary days, the trilogy written in the
midst of his political career, and the last two novels produced after
he became Prime Minister.

The first phase begins with *Vivian Grey* which features a clever and ambitious hero whose schemes are defeated. It was followed in 1831 by Disraeli's rendition of fashionable life, *The Young Duke*, which he himself described as half fashion and half passion. A sixteen-month tour of the Near East gave him the atmosphere for *Contarini Fleming* in 1832 and *Alroy* in 1833. He wrote both *Henrietta Temple* (a novel of love and manners) and *Venetia* (a fictional account of the lives of Byron and Shelley) in 1837 to relieve financial pressure. That was also the year in which he won a seat in Parliament and shortly thereafter, in 1839, married Mary Anne Lewis, a widow.

The trio of novels of the 1840s belonging to the second group are considered by most critics to be the most significant: *Coningsby* (1844), *Sybil* (1845), and *Tancred* (1847).

Coningsby encompasses the period from the passing of the Reform Bill in 1832 to the Tory victory in 1841 and ends with Harry Coningsby's election to Parliament. In *Sybil, or The Two Nations*, the two nations of the alternate title are identified as the rich and the poor, and Disraeli exposes the oppressive tyranny of an industrial system which causes human misery. The eponymous hero of *Tancred* is a young, religious enthusiast who goes to the Holy Land in search of revelation and truth, and the central theme is the discovery of religious faith.

Taken together, the trilogy expressed the ideals of a group of bright, young, and dynamic Parliamentarians who made up the "Young England" movement. Greatly concerned with the well-being of man, they called for past ideals to be applied to present Tory party principles and chose Disraeli to describe their aims. This he did in the trilogy, thereby extending his political ideology into the realm of imaginative writing. The novels deal with the social problems of the time. They give the daily workings of politics and embody Disraeli's own experiences of political intrigue.

After a long interval of twenty-three years, Disraeli returned to the novel in 1870 with *Lothair*, followed in 1880 by *Endymion*. He wrote the final novel when he was seventy-seven and out of office, and he was hard at work on another at the time of his death.

Benjamin Disraeli
(1804-1881)
nursed his gout at
The Royal Bath
Hotel, Bournemouth

With his vivid accounts of English political life, his acute observations, and his talent for narrative and witty dialogue, his works are good enough to be remembered in literary annals even if he had never been a statesman. But he did become a powerful statesman—leader of the Tory party and Prime Minister of England.

Disraeli was first elected to Parliament in 1837 after five unsuccessful attempts. The long hiatus that occurred in his writing career would seem to be due to total absorption in his life as a statesman. In 1852 he became Chancellor of the Exchequer for just a few months and again in 1858 and in 1866. Two years later he became Prime Minister, for a short term of eleven months, and then leader of the opposition for six years. It was during his second term of office as Prime Minister, from 1874 to 1880, that he stayed at the Royal Bath Hotel in Bournemouth.

Disraeli suffered from a case of acute gout throughout 1874, which was first diagnosed in that February. He had several attacks and was often too ill to be present at Parliamentary sessions. Because of his poor physical condition, Queen Victoria recommended "the very salubrious air of Bournemouth." She had not herself been there, but Sir James Clark, her physician and a resident of Bournemouth, believed in the efficacy of the sea air to produce a cure. Disraeli stayed at the hotel from November 1874 to January 1875 and, although he was extremely unwell when he arrived, was able to report to the Queen on his return for the January cabinet meetings that his health was greatly improved.

But Disraeli had to be cajoled and persuaded to go to Bournemouth. A letter to Lady Bradford written on 18 November 1874 expresses his dislike of hotels in general: "There is a great discomfort for a person like me in an hotel life—forced to order and eat dinners and drink wines and live in rooms like barracks, and no comforts and accommodations. It is horrid. . ." He was predisposed to complain, and complain he did—about the food (frightful), the weather (savage climate), and the resort itself (a large overgrown watering place). He missed the comforts of his Hughenden home, with his books and beeches, and later expressed regret at not having gone instead to Hughenden, the country estate in Buckinghamshire to which he had moved in 1848. Nevertheless he expressed to Queen Victoria, from Bournemouth on 10 December 1874, the certainty that "...the visit to this place, which your Majesty yourself deigned to recommend, will turn out a great success."

Bournemouth was promoted by physicians for its healthy sea air and good climate, but weather conditions were harsh that season. Disraeli writes in a Christmas Eve letter to Lady Bradford: "The severe weather has been very trying to me; but I hope it has not materially thrown me back and now the front has vanished."

There are further complaints, in a letter of December 1874 to Lady Chesterfield, about having to remain indoors due to adverse weather conditions: "Everything is white, the crust on the earth thick and hard and an Easterly wind always."

He improved in the new year with the change to milder weather and wrote to Lady Chesterfield on 3 January 1875 that "the thaw has quite revived me and removed all my *malaise*." He added, no doubt with relief, that he expected to be in London around the 9th.

It was while he was in Bournemouth that Disraeli wrote advising the Queen to confer the highest distinction for literary eminence: a GCB—the Grand Cross of the Order of the Bath—and a pension on Carlyle, and a baronetcy on Tennyson.

He seems to have written no fiction at the Royal Bath Hotel, but he wrote many letters which he posted from a box, now displayed at the Russell-Cotes Museum, very near the hotel. When Bournemouth's first letter box, red with the initials *VR*, stood at the corner of Bath Road, it was, we are informed, used by the eminent political opponents Disraeli and Gladstone. Gladstone, too, came to this Victorian resort for the well-to-do, and he also stayed at the Royal Bath.

From the time the Bath Hotel opened on Queen Victoria's Coronation Day, 28 June 1838, it has sheltered a long list of distinguished guests—Prince Oscar of Sweden, Paderewski, Sir Henry Irving and his leading lady Miss Ellen Terry, Empress Eugenie, and Oscar Wilde. But it only became "Royal" when royalty visited on 23 September 1856 in the form of the Prince of Wales, later King Edward VII.

The building was acquired in 1876 by Mr. Merton Russell-Cotes, who had it redecorated, reconstructed, and enlarged. He became Mayor of Bournemouth in 1894, opened the first public library in the town, and founded the Russell-Cotes Art Gallery and Museum before being knighted in 1911. After he died in 1921, the hotel remained in family control until it was taken over by DeVere Enterprises in 1963.

For a royal treat, the de luxe five-star Royal Bath Hotel is still the place to go. Set in its own gardens overlooking the bay, the hotel is ideally situated. It makes a good center for seeing such places of interest as Stonehenge, Beaulieu, Salisbury, Longleat, and Corfe Castle, or for visiting the town itself, the Sandbourne of Thomas Hardy's Wessex.

In addition to its luxury bedrooms, the hotel offers a variety of facilities, including a fine restaurant, which, Disraeli's negative comments notwithstanding, offers superb dishes in a sumptuous setting.

On the way out to the Royal Bath Hotel from London, the visitor could perhaps arrange to stop at Hughenden Manor near High Wycombe in Buckinghamshire. The late eighteenth-century white building in which Disraeli lived the life of a country gentleman is now maintained for the public by the National Trust.

For a memorable holiday and a continuation of that style of graceful living which Disraeli loved—not necessarily by royal command and preferably without gout—stay awhile at Bournemouth's Royal Bath Hotel.

THE ROYAL BATH HOTEL
Bath Road
Bournemouth
Dorset BH1 2EW

Telephone:(01202) 555555   Fax: (01202) 554158

5 stars. Member of DeVere Hotels.

131 bedrooms, no two identical in decor and furnishing, have private bathrooms and television, and most have sea views.

The main lounge, with classic columns and fine plaster ceiling, is commodious and comfortable.

The handsome Disraeli's Bar, warmly decorated in deep red tones and enhanced with pictures and a name to honor the distinguished guest, offers a plunge into the Victorian past. The Buccaneer Bar is more contemporary.

Two restaurants are Oscar's and the Garden Restaurant.

The Oak Room is for small conferences, and the DeVere Suite is for larger ones.

Among the amenities is the Leisure Pavilion with swimming pool and spa bath, sauna, solarium, and gymnasium. There is also a heated outdoor swimming pool, hairdressing for ladies and gentlemen, and cliff top gardens overlooking the sea.

SIEGFRIED SASSOON

at

The King's Arms
Dorchestser
Dorset

This has been my most satisfactory visit to Dorchester.

—Siegfried Sassoon *Diaries* 1920-1922

The story of Siegfried Sassoon in Dorchester is the story of one poet visiting another. Born in 1886 and named for the hero of Wagner's great *Ring Cycle* which his mother greatly admired, Sassoon became himself a hero and a poet. He enlisted at the outbreak of war in 1914 and fought in France, performing courageous exploits. Decorated for gallantry, he threw the coveted Military Cross into the Mersey. He had acquired a hatred for the war and expressed loathing and outrage at the enormous waste of lives in volumes of antiwar poems. Sassoon had his own hero— Thomas Hardy.

Sassoon sojourned to Dorchester on several occasions because Dorchester was the home of Thomas Hardy. Pilgrims still arrive in large numbers to view the statue of Thomas Hardy in the main street, to visit the museum with its collection of manuscripts and reconstruction of the novelist's study, to inspect the cottage in Bockhampton where Hardy was born and Max Gate where he lived, and to explore the surrounding Wessex countryside of the literature in which Dorchester was called Casterbridge.

But Siegfried Sassoon was more than a pilgrim to Thomas Hardy country. He was an avid admirer who became a very good friend. In his *Diaries* and volumes of autobiography, Sassoon describes the growing and genuine friendship which developed

When Siegfried
Sassoon (1886-1967)
came to Dorchester
to visit Thomas
Hardy, he stayed at
The King's Arms
in the High Street

between the two men from the time Sassoon first traveled to Dorchester to visit the venerated writer.

The association began early in 1917 when Sassoon wrote to Hardy asking him to accept the dedication of his first published book, a volume of thirty-five poems called *The Old Huntsman*. The two men communicated, but the war put off the possibility of their initial meeting until the following year. Sassoon first met Hardy at his Max Gate home in November 1918. He records in his autobiography, *Siegfried's Journey*, his impression of the eminent writer of seventy-eight, a modest and gentle genius "who had transmuted the Wessex country into a cosmogony of his imagination."

The Old Huntsman contained the best pictures of trench life ever written, according to another war poet, Wilfred Owen. (The two men met when they were fellow patients in a military hospital near Edinburgh.) The volume of poems is the first of three volumes of war verse which permanently established his reputation as a powerful war poet. In *Counter-Attack* (1918) and *War Poems* (1919), Sassoon continued to write savage denunciations of the war he so deplored, exposing its stupidities and senseless slaughter. Altogether, he published eight volumes of verse in his lifetime.

Sassoon had been writing poetry for twenty years before he turned to prose, the great achievement of his middle years. The semi-autobiographical novel, *Memoirs of a Fox-Hunting Man*, appeared in 1928 and created the figure of George Sherston to represent the lost generation, while sporting life reflected the development of character. Sassoon needed to examine his inner self after the war, and he expressed the growing disillusionment of the young hero in his first prose work, an integral part of a trilogy. It achieved great popularity, perhaps because it took readers back to the happy and rustic past of the Edwardian age in which everyone remembered having a comfortable place.

Sassoon continued the fictional sequence in *Memoirs of an Infantry Officer* (1930) and *Sherston's Progress* (1936). The horrors of war have a disrupting effect on Sherston, who grows into a compassionate and anguished figure.

Volumes of straight biography—*The Old Century, The Weald of Youth*, and *Siegfried's Journey*—continue to confirm his reputation as an excellent recorder of character and feelings. Indeed, many consider the prose output to be his highest achievement. His *Diaries* were published posthumously. Siegfried Sassoon, alias George Sherston, died on September 1, 1967.

After his first meeting with Hardy, Sassoon made a number of return visits to Max Gate, receiving advice and inspiration from the master. They talked mainly of poets and poetry, and Hardy's humility and humanity always came through.

Sassoon was among many young writers who came to Max Gate in the last decade or so of Hardy's life, which ended in 1928. But only the sensitive Sassoon saw the poet's distraction when he came down for tea and commented on it in his poem, "At Max Gate":

"Hardy, the Wessex wizard, wasn't there."

The poem presents Sassoon's impression during one of his sessions with "old Mr. Hardy":

Head propped on hand, he sat with me alone,
Silent, the log fire flickering on his face.
Here was the seer whose words the world had known.
Someone had taken Mr. Hardy's place.

Sassoon was instrumental in preparing a surprise birthday tribute from a group of younger poets who wanted to pay homage to Hardy. Too eager and impatient to wait for Hardy's eightieth birthday for the special dedication, Sassoon journeyed again to Max Gate in 1919 to present personally the Poets' Tribute on Hardy's seventy-ninth birthday. Sensitive and caring, he worried about the physical condition of the septuagenarian writer, noting small changes whenever he came and being careful not to cause weariness with too much talk. He writes in *Siegfried's Journey*: "In his latest years I stayed at an hotel in Dorchester, so as to avoid tiring him in the evening."

The hotel at which Sassoon stayed is the King's Arms in the High Street of Dorchester. It is also the hotel in which readers of Hardy's novel first meet the Mayor of Casterbridge. From the hotel,

Sassoon was able to walk to Max Gate for his talks with Hardy. His Diary refers to a wet morning in June 1922 when he stayed in his room reading *Coriolanus* before leaving for lunch at Max Gate. Another *Diary* entry of June 28 reports the advantage of being at the hotel:

> This has been my most satisfactory visit to Dorchester. . . . I am carrying away a much clearer impression of him than ever before, having been half-detached from the Max Gate atmosphere. It is no doubt one of the very precious experiences of my life.

Sassoon was again in Dorchester when Hardy was eighty-four, staying this time at the Antelope, which figures in *The Mayor of Casterbridge* as the hotel where Henchard is asked to meet Lucetta with a packet of her letters when the coach stops to change horses. The Antelope has only recently ceased to function as a hotel; but the building, located just off the High Street in the newly-pedestrianized South Street, still sports a sign announcing, "Stagecoaches to All Parts."

It is the King's Arms which must be singled out due to its connection with poets. A.E. Housman stayed in the summer of 1898. It seems that Hardy himself also stayed here. When Brander Matthews, the American author and professor, requested information preparatory to a visit to Dorchester in July 1883, Hardy responded: "I do not know much about the Dorchester Hotels. I have stayed at the Kings Arms—& was fairly comfortable."

The King's Arms is indeed a comfortable hotel. Completely refurbished in the 1980s, it has a history dating back over three hundred years. An old town map shows the existence of the building in 1660.

An ideal situation on the main road between London and Exeter insured its continued existence. The inn became an important staging post for the Royal Mail in the nineteenth century. And royal reminiscences do not stop there.

George III seems to have started a royal trend when he visited in the eighteenth century. The Prince of Wales, later King

Edward VIII, stayed twice when he came to the area on walking and shooting expeditions. More recently, both Prince Charles and Prince Andrew have lunched at the hotel while on active service at nearby Portland.

The busy High Street in the center of the bustling county town has a number of tourist sights worth noting. A colorful sign on a restaurant marks the former lodgings of the infamous Judge Jeffreys during the Bloody Assize in 1685. Opposite is the fifteenth-century St. Peter's Church. The Dorset County Museum alongside the church houses good collections of local history ranging from pre-Roman and Roman finds to Thomas Hardy memorabilia. High Street shops selling local products such as Dorset knob biscuits tempt the curious, while establishments with names such as the Casterbridge Hotel advertise Hardy's literary contribution. Among the venerable monuments on the High Street, adding variety to literary associations, is the old-fashioned, two-storied coaching inn frequented by Siegfried Sassoon—The King's Arms.

Its name appears in bold letters on the main portico, over which a spacious bow window imbues with romance both the facade and the room behind it. That attractive function room, bright and cheerful and with a splendid brass chandelier, has been named the Casterbridge Lounge, for it may be identified as the dining room associated with the Mayor of Casterbridge. It is also the room into which Boldwood carries Bathsheba after she faints upon hearing the false report of Troy's death by drowning.

The King's Arms is a convenient center for tourists wishing to visit a wide variety of not-to-be-missed places—the Dorset coastline or the exquisite countryside, the prehistoric hill fort of Maiden Castle or the Roman amphitheatre known as Maumbury Rings, the sites associated with Thomas Hardy or with Siegfried Sassoon—all far from the madding London crowd.

THE KING'S ARMS
High East Street
Dorchester
Dorset DT1 1HF

Telephone: (01305) 265353   Fax: (01305) 260269

Thirty-three bedrooms with private bathrooms are supplied with radio and television, direct-dial telephone, and tea/coffee making facilities. The Tutankhamun Suite and the Lawrence of Arabia Suite are equipped with whirlpool baths. The Lawrence of Arabia Suite honors T.E. Lawrence, the author who lived in nearby Clouds Hill, a National Trust cottage now open to the public.

The Casterbridge Lounge is for conferences of up to seventy people. There is also a lounge for residents and a solarium.

The main restaurant offers such traditional fare as venison or lamb and a local cheese known as Dorset Blue Vinney. The Starting Post is an informal bistro serving less traditional fare— pizzas, American hamburgers, chile con carne, moussaka.

Henchards Bar is the place for typical pub food such as steak and kidney pie or Dorset pate, or for the local brew which received Hardy's approval in *The Trumpet Major* as having "the most beautiful colour that the eye of an artist in beer could desire; full in body, yet brisk as a volcano; piquant, yet without a twang."

Large private car park at the rear of the hotel.

WALES

LEWIS CARROLL

at

The Gogarth Abbey Hotel
Llandudno
Gwynedd
Wales

"A knot!" said Alice, already to make
herself useful, and looking anxiously about
her. "Oh, do let me help to undo it!"

--Alice's Adventures in Wonderland

Perhaps the most significant picnic in literary history took place
on 4 July 1862. On that date, the Reverend Charles Lutwidge
Dodgson, a young mathematics lecturer at Christ Church, Oxford,
embarked on a river excursion. With him went his friend Robinson
Duckworth of Trinity College and the three daughters of Dean
Liddell of Christ Church: Lorina, aged thirteen; Alice, ten; and
Edith, eight.

From Folly Bridge, the party set off on their journey up the Isis
to Godstow. As they went along, Dodgson told the story of Alice's
adventures. "Dodgson, is this an extempore romance of yours?"
Duckworth asked. The reply was, "Yes, I'm inventing as we go
along." Three miles up the river the group disembarked to enjoy
tea on the bank at a pretty site with the romantic ruins of Godstow
Nunnery nearby and the Oxford skyline in the distance. The
historic picnic ended with a dessert that the world has been

enjoying ever since, for the heroine fell into a rabbit hole, and the author fell into a whole new literary world in which he was to become better known as Lewis Carroll.

Back at the Deanery, Alice requested, "Oh, Mr. Dodgson, I wish you would write out Alice's adventures for me." To oblige the young lady, he sat up nearly all night. Duckworth, the "Duck" of the story, later persuaded him to publish it, and exactly three years after the famous river expedition, the book with the name *Alice's Adventures Under Ground* appeared.

The beautiful and intelligent Alice Liddell remained his ideal child friend always. They had first met in 1856, just before her fourth birthday. He was twenty-four, an Oxford don, and a shy, stammering bachelor who was also interested in photography. Alice's father was Henry George Liddell, Dean of Christ Church. The Deanery in which the Liddell family lived faced Tom Quad, where Dodgson was one day busily taking photographs of the Christ Church Cathedral. The Liddell children, intrigued by his occupation, engaged him in conversation. A friendship developed. He saw the children constantly, and he photographed them often.

Apparently, he also visited the Liddell family at their holiday house in the Welsh resort town of Llandudno. Then called Pen Morfa, that summer home is now the Gogarth Abbey Hotel. The town of Llandudno has retained its charm despite growing size and popularity. It proudly persists in its Lewis Carroll connections with a statue of the White Rabbit at the end of the Model Yacht Pond, by a street named Carroll Place, and with a marble font, a gift of school children to the memory of Lewis Carroll, in the Church of Our Saviour.

The main beach, North Shore, with a magnificent crescent bay, is enclosed by two headlands—Great Ormes Head and Little Ormes Head. (Did wild rabbits scurrying over Great Ormes Head suggest the rabbit hole with which Alice's adventures begin?) The Gogarth Abbey Hotel is located on the West Shore, which has fine views of Conway Bay and a statue of Lewis Caroll. (Did the long stretch of sand provide a setting for the Gryphon and the Mock

Lewis Carroll (1832-1898). Did he or didn't he visit Alice's family at their holiday home (now the Gogarth Abbey Hotel) in Llandudno?

Turtle?) With a fine location on the seafront and with Lewis Carroll associations, the hotel is an attractive literary shrine.

So far the story is a good one with a great deal of charm, but alas, Dodgson's stay in Llandudno may be as much of a fairy tale as his story of Alice. Lewis Carroll scholars cannot agree, or verify with absolute certainty, that he went to Pen Morfa or indeed whether he ever went to Llandudno at all. What readers choose to believe depends to a very large extent on which authorities they delve into. Such respected sources as *The Oxford Literary Guide to the British Isles* select words carefully: "C.L.Dodgson is believed to have visited Dean Liddell. . . at his summer residence, Pen Morfa, on the West Shore, now part of the Gogarth Abbey Hotel." Tourist guides, with the obvious desire to support local tradition, select words less carefully. One points to "the fact that the author of *Alice in Wonderland* stayed in the town with the Liddells." What are the facts and/or discrepancies?

First of all, it seems reasonably clear that Dodgson was not on good terms with Alice's parents, who simply did not like him. The formidable Mrs. Liddell could be quite abrupt with him, or even rude; so it is not likely that he would have been invited to share their holiday.

If he had stayed at Pen Morfa, surely he would have deemed the event significant enough to record in the diaries he kept regularly, filling thirteen volumes until his death in 1898. There is no such entry. But as the diaries for the years 1858 to 1862 are missing, a visit may have occurred during that period. But the house built for Dean Liddell was not ready for occupation until 1865, says one sceptic. He is corrected by another source who says the Liddell family first occupied it in 1862. Nevertheless, can absent diaries serve as conclusive evidence that he ever—or never—visited Pen Morfa? Curiouser and curiouser, since Alice's marriage to Reginald Hargreaves was not recorded in the Diary, perhaps it is unfair to assume that Dodgson entered every important event.

However, we have the evidence of Alice herself: at the age of eighty, she recalled with great pride his visits to their Llandudno home and their games in the sandhills. Did she remember accurately? Can her memory at that venerable age be trusted?

Further testimony is offered by another first-hand account. Sir William Richmond painted a portrait of the three Liddell daughters ("The Three Graces") which now hangs in the Tate Gallery. He recalls that Lewis Carroll wrote part of *Alice in Wonderland* at Pen Morfa and remembers his reading the story aloud in the evenings to family and guests assembled there.

Sceptics can spoil all sorts of good stories—like the picnic to Godstow, with all the participants confirming that the weather was glorious. An appeal to the Weather Bureau has disclosed adverse conditions for that date—"cool and rather wet" with an inch of rain!

There is no doubt that the house of the Liddells is now part of the Gogarth Abbey Hotel. Dodgson's presence—ghostly, legendary, or otherwise—is real, for the house is certainly associated with Alice. It is still a monument capable of giving pleasure to many. Why spoil a good story? Moreover, it might even be true! The hotel serves as a valuable literary link, even if we apply the logic so succinctly stated by Tweedledee in *Through the Looking Glass*: "Contrariwise," continued Tweedledee, "if it was so, it might be; and if it were so, it would be; but as it isn't, it ain't. That's logic."

GOGARTH ABBEY HOTEL
West Shore
Llandudno
Gwynedd
Wales LL30 2QY

Telephone: (01492) 876211/2   Fax: (01492) 875805

Rooms: 41 modern bedrooms have private facilities, direct dial telephones, mini-bars, television, and tea- and coffee-making facilities.

Amenities: Indoor heated swimming pool, sauna and solarium.

Spacious grounds: Putting green, golf driving net, croquet, French boules.

Public Rooms: Four lounges and Liddell Restaurant with fine views across the sea.

Location: On the quieter shore of Llandudno, minutes from the shopping streets of the town.

THE MIDLANDS

GEORGE ELIOT

at

Griff House Travel Inn
Nuneaton
Warwickshire

There is no sense of ease like the ease we
felt in those scenes where we were born,
where objects became dear to us before we
had known the labour of choice, and where
the outer world seemed only an extension of
our own personality: we accepted and loved
it as we accepted our own sense of existence
and our own limbs.

—The Mill on the Floss

Some thirty miles north of Stratford, in the same county which has
become a mecca for Shakespeare devotees, is the home of one of
the great novelists of all time. Mary Anne Evans was born in
Warwickshire on 22 November 1819. When she died in London
on 22 December 1880, she was well known as the respected and
great author, George Eliot.

Robert Evans, land agent for the Newdigate family of Arbury
Hall, was the head of a family consisting of the two children of his
first marriage and the three children of his second marriage to
Christiana Pearson in 1813, Christiana, Isaac, and Mary Anne.
When Mary Anne was four months old, the Evans family moved
from the house called South Farm in which she was born to another

house on the Arbury estate, the more spacious and attractive Griff House. Griff was to be her home for the next twenty-two years.

Now, well over a century later, Griff House looks much as it did in those early years of George Eliot's life, years that she always recognized as extremely important, as expressed in *Daniel Deronda*: "A human life, I think should be well rooted in some spot of a native land. . .a spot where the definiteness of early memories may be inwrought with affection."

It is with affection that one may visit the red brick house and look for haunting signs of George Eliot's presence. The attic window, above the drawing room with its projecting bow window, is still visible to recall the attic retreat in which Maggie of *The Mill on the Floss* "fretted out all her ill-humours, and talked aloud to the worm-eaten floors and the worm-eaten shelves." A further reminder is inscribed on the plaque built in over the front door announcing, "GEORGE ELIOT lived here March 1820 to March 1841."

The Griff House Inn is an extremely important place because George Eliot had her "childhood in it" and "accepted and loved it as we accepted our own sense of existence and our own limbs."

Located on the Coventry Road just a mile and a half from Nuneaton, Griff House is not situated in the most inspiring or beautiful landscape of England. Nevertheless, its setting delighted children with a pleasant garden for play, a pond and canal, barns filled with cows, and the resultant happy task of butter- and cheese-making. The youngest child enjoyed a tranquil, uneventful, and apparently happy childhood. She was particularly fond of her brother Isaac, who was three years older, and the two were inseparable. A sonnet-sequence called *Brother and Sister* which she wrote from the idealized viewpoint of a middle-aged woman recalls childhood:

> The bunched cowslip's pale transparency
> Carries that sunshine of sweet memories,
> And wild-rose branches take their finest scent
> From those blest hours of infantine content.

George Eliot (1819-1880) and Griff House, near Nuneaton, her home for the first twenty-two years of her life and the background to *The Mill on the Floss*

She returned often to this place of "infantine content" in her writings.

Enjoyable diversions came when Mary Anne accompanied her father on his rounds as he collected rents or attended to business affairs. She took in her native countryside as well as her father's commentary and later recalled those drives in *Middlemarch*:

> ...through a pretty bit of midland landscape.... Little details gave each field a particular physiognomy, dear to the eyes that have looked on them from childhood: the pool in the corner where the grasses were dank and trees leaned whisperingly; the great oak shadowing a bare place in mid- pasture; the high bank where the ash-trees grew; the sudden slope of the old marl-pit....the huddled roofs and ricks of the homestead...the grey gate and fences...the stray hovel, its old, old thatch full of mossy hills and valleys with wondrous modulations of light and shadow....These are the things that make the gamut of joy in landscape to midland-bred souls—the things they toddled among, or perhaps learned by heart standing between their father's knees while he drove leisurely.

The feeling of belonging and vitality associated with the midlands area is summarized in *The Mill on the Floss:*

> We could never have loved the earth so well if we had had no childhood in it—if it were not the earth where the same flowers come up again every spring that we used to gather with our tiny fingers as we sat lisping to ourselves on the grass...What novelty is worth that sweet monotony where everything is known, and *loved* because it is known?

The two children of that novel bear close resemblance to Mary Anne and Isaac Evans; and Dorlecote Mill was based, at least in part, on Griff House. The long attic in which the Tulliver children played has its counterpart in the one which runs from one end of Griff House to the other: "Maggie was already out of hearing, making her way towards the great attic that ran under the old high-pitched roof. . . This attic was Maggie's favourite retreat on a wet day, when the weather was not too cold. . . ."

Other elements of the physical setting appear in other books. The vegetable and flower garden at the rear was probably the Hill Farm garden of *Adam Bede*, and the garden walk was that which led to the summer house at Lowick Manor in *Middlemarch*.

When Isaac was sent away to school, his doting sister took to reading voraciously, and they grew apart. (Her scandalous union with George Lewes many years later was to cause a permanent rift between brother and sister.)

When her mother died in 1836, Mary Anne was made responsible for the running of the house. Five years later Mr. Evans retired; Isaac carried on as land agent and moved with his bride into Griff. Mary Anne continued to care for her father after they both moved to a house known as Bird Grove which still stands at Foleshill at the edge of Coventry.

A stubborn freethinker, Mary Ann—she discarded the "e"— incensed her irate father when she also discarded her religion and refused to accompany him to church. He disowned her. She returned in ignominy to live for a while with Isaac and Sarah at Griff House.

Her father died in 1849. The breach was not entirely healed, and it must have been extremely painful to her to find that he had left the set of Scott's novels, from which she had often read aloud to him, to her half-sister.

Marian (as she now began to call herself) decided to travel on the Continent for a while before settling into a new life in London. She moved into the home of publisher John Chapman, whose *Westminster Review* she helped to edit, and there she met such notables as Charles Dickens, Wilkie Collins, and Florence Nightingale. She also met George Henry Lewes with whom she fell deeply in love; but archaic laws prevented him from securing a divorce from his adulterous wife, once he had acknowledged her child by another. George Eliot daringly consented to live openly with this man in a bond that was to last nearly twenty-five years, until his death in 1878. It was he who encouraged her to write the fiction which she produced under the pen name of George Eliot, a name chosen because "George was Mr. Lewes's Christian name, and Eliot was a good mouth-filling, easily-pronounced word."

She worked hard on translations and reviews but had always wanted to write fiction. Novels, she calculated, would be even more lucrative than the esoteric and intellectual journalism she was producing. Her first story was *Amos Barton*, the first of a series of stories to be called *Scenes of Clerical Life*.

This was followed by the first full-length novel, *Adam Bede*, published in 1859. A journal entry of 16 November 1858 cites Griff House as the source for that novel as she relates an anecdote told by her aunt, which became the germ for the novel: "We were sitting together one afternoon during her visit to me at Griff, probably in 1839 or 1840, when it occurred to her to tell me how she visited a condemned criminal. . . ."

The Mill on the Floss which followed in 1860 had strong autobiographical elements, recalling in particular her closeness to her brother Isaac, now alienated from her because of her shocking and disgraceful union with Lewes. Success was immediate and other novels followed: *Silas Marner* (1861), *Romola* (1862), *Felix Holt* (1866), *Middlemarch* (1871), and *Daniel Deronda* (1876).

A year after the illicit but happy union came to an end with the death of Lewes, her last work, a volume of essays called *The Impressions of Theophrastus Such* (1879), was published.

An infatuated old family friend proposed to her when she was sixty and, after much deliberation, she accepted John Walter Cross, twenty years her junior, as her husband. The marriage was to last just six months. The year was 1880, the year of her death.

Although never considered pretty, George Eliot must have been an extremely lovable person, full of warmth and sincerity. Bret Harte wrote of her, "Her face lights up when she smiles. . ." No, she was not beautiful in the conventional sense of the word, but what an attractive and endearing spirit—what inner beauty—must have been hers! Perhaps the visitor to Griff House can sense some

of her extraordinary qualities in this "spot of native land" that was
once part of George Eliot.

GRIFF HOUSE TRAVEL INN
Coventry Road
Nuneaton
Warwickshire CV10 7PJ

Telephone: (01203) 343584   Fax: (01203) 327156

The middle-priced hotel has thirty-eight bedrooms, most
in a new wing. Most rooms have private baths, and all
have television and tea-making facilities.

The restaurant is the Beefeater Steak House.

Outdoors are a garden, children's play area, and barbecue.

A.E. HOUSMAN

at

Perry Hall Hotel

Bromsgrove

Hereford and Worcester

That is the land of lost content
I see it shining plain,
The happy highways where I went
And cannot come again.

—A Shropshire Lad

When Alfred Edward Housman, the eldest child of Edward and Sarah Jane Housman, was only a few months old, the family moved into Perry Hall in Bromsgrove. Alfred was born in the Valley House in Fockbury, just two miles from Bromsgrove. It was to the Valley House that Edward had brought his bride after their marriage in 1858, and in that house Alfred was born on 26 March 1859. The Housmans lived there for a brief period, just a few hundred yards away from the Fockbury home of Edward's parents, where Edward had spent his boyhood.

At Perry Hall, the Housman family grew. Another child, Robert, was soon born, followed by Clemence and then Katherine. A fifth child, Basil, was followed by a sixth, Laurence. And when Alfred was nine, the last child, George Herbert, was born to the prolific couple. But Sarah Jane's health began to decline, and happy days at Perry Hall were soon to be over. Nevertheless, the house and its surroundings had a shaping influence on the young poet.

The large garden of Perry Hall was the place for childish play where imagination was allowed to run rampant. There was a flowering cherry tree, a vegetable garden, and a secluded rubbish garden filled with fruit trees. Chestnut trees were planted in the garden, one for the birth of each new child. The seven children enjoyed a happy time of sunshine days. They had their own climbing trees and were full of invention and creativity. Alfred's brother Laurence was to become a poet and playwright, the author of the well-known play, *Victoria Regina*. Alfred showed a delight in words and a talent for writing even then. By the time he was fifteen, Alfred was already a published poet; while a pupil at the Bromsgrove School, his *Death of Socrates* won a prize in a school competition and appeared in the *Bromsgrove Messenger* in August 1874.

The tower and spire of Bromsgrove Church could be seen from Perry Hall. Naturally, church attendance was compulsory, and the the sound of church bells became an integral part of their lives. The bell which rang at one o'clock on Sundays (for no known reason) was dubbed "the Yorkshire-pudding bell." The poet was later to use bells quite often in his writing, *Bredon Hill* being perhaps his most popular bell poem:

> In summertime on Bredon
> The bells they sound so clear;
> Round both the shires they ring them
> In steeples far and near,
> A happy noise to hear.

Those happy days lasted until Alfred was about ten. His mother was discovered to have cancer and her health began to fail. Edward was simply unable to cope with her deteriorating state and with financial problems—mortgages and interest payments—and withdrew. He took to drink for escape from his problems. The sensitive Alfred suffered severely and was sent to stay with relatives, where he could avoid the painful scenes. On his twelfth birthday, he received word of the death of his mother.

After Sarah Jane's death, Edward married a cousin, Lucy Housman, who was much loved by all the children. To escape from a house full of memories, Edward took advantage of an opportunity to leave Perry Hall and move two miles away, back to his boyhood home in Fockbury. The Clock House, also known as Fockbury, was the family home where Edward's parents had lived while his father was vicar of the new church in the parish of Catshill.

Fockbury House, the new home of the Housmans, was surrounded by the open countryside and by views of the distant Shropshire hills in contrast with the enclosed garden of Perry Hall. But Laurence Housman wrote in his autobiography, *The Unexpected Years*, that the Fockbury House was "never as intimately our home as Perry Hall had been." The young Alfred habitually walked alone, enjoyed the beautiful landscape, and meditated on the hills which later became a romantic symbol, as expressed in his *Last Poems*:

> From hill and cloud and heaven
>   The hues of evening died;
> Night willed through lane and hollow
>   And hushed the countryside,
>   But I had youth and pride.
>
> And I with earth and nightfall
>   In converse high would stand,
> Late, till the west was ashen
>   And darkness hard at hand,
>   And the eye lost the land.

An unsuccessful lawyer, Edward Housman planned to use Perry Hall as offices, but he had no income to support his life style. Indeed, financial problems plagued him for the rest of his life. When continuing difficulties caused the sale of Fockbury House in 1877, the family returned to Perry Hall. This was also the year when Alfred left Bromsgrove for Oxford, having won a scholarship to St. John's College.

Further financial mishandling of affairs brought the family dangerously close to complete ruin. At one point, in February 1879, Edward's youngest brother, the Reverend Joseph Housman, bought Perry Hall and allowed Edward to stay on, rent free. Edward dealt with the worsening situation by continuing to drink his way into oblivion.

Alfred came home to Perry Hall for several visits, sometimes with Oxford acquaintances. One in particular, A.W. Pollard, was to become a life-long friend. What an enormous strain the old familiar rooms and gardens must have been to him, since the poor family could not even afford now to keep a fire going.

Having done poorly at Oxford, possibly because of emotional problems and involvements, he passed civil service examinations and took a position in the London Patent Office where he worked for ten years. In his spare time, he continued his classical studies reading Greek and Latin in the British Museum Library, and he began to publish articles and papers. Scholarly work and translations paid off. In 1892 he became Professor of Latin at University College, London. He made up for his youthful failure at Oxford by becoming a great and respected scholar in the classics. When an application for a post at Cambridge University was successful, he moved in 1911 to Trinity College for twenty-five years as Professor of Latin.

But during his years in London, when he lived alone in Highgate, he began the writing of much of his serious poetry. Eventually, the volume by which he will always be known, *A Shropshire Lad*, was published in 1896. Originally called *The Poems of Terence Hearsay*, the change of title (suggested by Pollard) helped to ensure its success. Perhaps the Terence of *A Shropshire Lad*, named for the Greek dramatist who was brought to Rome as a slave, parallels Housman's own feeling of exile in London from his childhood home.

Although Alfred had written since childhood, the poems that flowed from his London pen are imbued with the spirit of his boyhood places and with a sense of irretrievable and poignant loss. There is a strong sense of reaching out for remote and idealized places which he once possessed, but which exist now only in his memory. He got geographical facts wrong and later admitted that details of topography were unimportant to him. He mentions actual places such as Ludlow and Wenlock, but Shropshire came to symbolize the unknown, the land of dreams.

As a child, he had walked a great deal and taken in the view to the west of the distant Shropshire hills. But—and this is the astonishing fact—Shropshire was never his home and he spent very little time there. His Shropshire landscape, together with its inhabitants, belongs to the poetic imagination. It does not have the solidity of, for example, Wordsworth's Lake District.

A Shropshire Lad had been rejected by several publishers before it finally appeared at the poet's expense. It got off to a slow start but quickly grew in appeal and reputation. Many of the poems of later volumes were actually written before *A Shropshire Lad* but were withheld from publication until a later date because of their personal nature. By the time *Last Poems* appeared in 1922, Housman was established as the most popular English poet after Kipling.

As for his former home, with the family gone, and with the death of his father in 1894, there was no point in retaining Perry Hall. Alfred came home for his father's funeral, and the sad memories are reflected in a later poem:

> Around the huddling homesteads
> The leafless timber soars,
> And the dead call the dying
> And finger at the doors.
>
> Oh, yonder faltering fingers
> Are hands I used to hold;
> Their false companion drowses
> And leaves them in the cold.

Perry Hall survived, together with its garden and cherry tree and surrounding countryside, in reality as well as in Housman's poems. The seven chestnut trees were transplanted along the graveyard wall of Catshill Church. His ashes were buried in the heart of Shropshire, in Ludlow. There, in the churchyard of St. Laurence, a simple plaque announces: "In memory of Alfred Edward Housman, MA Oxon, Kennedy Professor of Latin and Fellow of Trinity College Cambridge. 1859-1936."

A. E. Housman
(1859-1936) and
his childhood
home, Perry Hall,
Bromsgrove,
now a hotel

But the reference to his poetry is all around—from the purple crocuses in front of the plaque:

> I heard the beechnut rustle down,
> And saw the purple crocus pale

to the cherry tree which still stands in the grounds of Perry Hall:

> Loveliest of trees, the cherry now
> Is hung with bloom along the bough.

Perry Hall was built by John Adams, the great-uncle of Edward Housman, in 1824. He purchased the site for his powder and dye factory and retained the name of the original ruined mansion for the fine new house distinguished by neo-Gothic windows and vast front door. The solid house had a number of pleasantly furnished large rooms, high frescoed ceilings, wide marble fireplaces, huge kitchen, and an altogether elegant and restful atmosphere. It lay at the foot of Adams' Hill (named for the man who also built the sloping path and steps in the hill on which the church stands) in Kidderminster Road (a road which leads northwest to the town of Kidderminster).

Perry Hall remained a private residence until 1952, spent a brief period as a private club, and then became a hotel in April 1956. Although the interior has been greatly altered, it still has the original fireplace (in what is now known as the Clent Room), stained glass, and oak paneling. The rooms now serve as offices, conference rooms, restaurant, reception area, lounge, and bar.

But the exterior has been preserved. Even the oak front door is the original. The Gothic windows and ivy-covered facade make a dignified impression. A plaque proudly commemorates the Housman connection. Outdoors, in fine weather, it is possible to enjoy the enclosed garden with its famous cherry tree which is still thriving. Guests may sit around the small white tables which have been tastefully arranged in the secluded garden, perhaps with refreshments, and contemplate the past. There it becomes appropriate to recall the cyncial words of Terence Hearsay:

Say, for what were hop-yards meant,
Or why was Burton built on Trent?
Oh, many a peer of England brews
Livelier liquor than the Muse,
And malt does more than Milton can
To justify God's ways to man.
Ale, man, ale's the stuff to drink
For fellows whom it hurts to think:
Look into the pewter pot
To see the world as the world's not.

Perry Hall supplies all kinds of memories of a "land of lost content" while its cellars, fuller now than they were for Edward Housman, supply something more tangible.

Edward Housman often indulged at the nearby Golden Cross or Shoulder of Mutton. At the Shoulder of Mutton, just over the road in St. John Street, the burden of supplying him with drink fell on the shoulders of the landlord. Several prominent notices on the front of that public house give the salient facts of the connection. One panel announces, "The poet's father Edward used to hurl a stone on to a tin roof at Perry Hall as a signal for the Landlord to go to him jug in hand." Many visitors repair to this public house, said to be the oldest in town, for its nostalgic offerings.

In the year of the birth of Alfred Edward Housman, Bromsgrove was a small market town with a long history. It is mentioned in the Domesday Book as Bremesgrave and was important enough to be granted a Fair Day by King John. Now it is important enough to be a busy town in the Midlands with light industry and a Market Hall which carries on the tradition. In the center of the pedestrianized main shopping street stands a tall bronze statue of A.E. Housman.

Growth and so-called progress is inevitable, and a fine fifteenth-century merchant's house was among those scheduled for demolition in 1962 to make way for a supermarket. But the dwelling was rescued and re-erected five years later in the nearby Avoncroft Museum of Buildings, where it can be visited along with such other

243

rescued structures as a counting house, barn, granary, cockpit theatre, and windmill. Yet, many fine old buildings still remain in Bromsgrove including the sixteenth-century grammar school, the Church of St. John the Baptist with its fourteenth-century tower and spire, some attractive Georgian houses in the High Street— and Perry Hall.

Bromsgrove is proud of the Housman connection and has set up a Housman Trail with signposts pointing the way to places associated with the poet. A leaflet available from the Tourist Information Center offers a walking guide to the various sites.

For further offerings to Housmania, the pilgrim could imbibe in the non-mythical Shropshire scene, taking in the places which he uses in his poetry: Ludlow (with its eleventh-century castle), Bredon, Shrewsbury, and the ancient market towns of Much Wenlock and Bridgnorth (which he visited when he was staying at Perry Hall after his father's death).

In addition to the Perry Hall Hotel, two other Housman houses in the neighborhood are extant—Fockbury House where Edward and Lucy Housman lived with the children for six years and the Valley House in Fockbury, now known as Housmans, where the poet was born.

> From far, from eve and morning
> And yon twelve-winded sky,
> The stuff of life to knit me
> Blew hither: here am I.

In a very real sense, much remains of various A.E. Housman associations, not only reachable but also well worth reaching.

PERRY HALL HOTEL
Kidderminster Road
Bromsgrove
Hereford and Worcester B61 7JN

Telephone: (01527) 579976   Fax: (01527) 575998

An extension added in 1969 gives the three-star hotel sixty bedrooms, all with bathrooms, television and radio, and a choice of hot beverages.

The unobtrusive new wing is separated from the main house by a corridor.

The Cherry Tree Restaurant offers traditional English dishes.

The approach from the curving driveway and large car park is through the picturesque arched remains of the old stable building.

Located near Bromsgrove town center, the hotel is just 14 miles from Birmingham and 128 miles from London.

Noël Coward

at

Hambleton Hall
Hambleton

Oakham

Rutland

> Mrs. Cooper lived at Hambleton in Rutland,
> about three miles from Oakham in the
> middle of Cottesmore country. The village
> stands on a hill rising abruptly out of
> chequered fields, polite and green and
> neatly hedged.
> — *Present Indicative*

When he was fifteen, Noël Coward accepted an invitation to stay at Hambleton Hall, the home of Mrs. Astley-Cooper. The invitation came at the instigation of Philip Streatfield, an artist with a studio in Chelsea, whom Noël had met the previous year when he was fourteen and Philip was about thirty. They became good friends.

Philip could not have imagined the effect that the country air of Hambleton and the wisdom of Mrs. Cooper would have on the lad. The visit, which took place in June 1915, was to have a profound influence on Noël Coward's future life and career. Hambleton was Noël's introduction to comfortable country-house life, complete with fox-hunting. He thoroughly enjoyed and profited from Mrs. Cooper's style and wit, and the visits to her taught him to be completely at ease with the upper classes, whether socializing with them or writing about them.

Mrs. Cooper was a delightfully eccentric hostess given to spouting words of wisdom from a supine position before the fire. She became a long-time friend, and Noël saw her at many other times and venues. On a later visit to Hambleton Hall, he entertained

246

soldiers when it was being run by Mrs. Cooper as a convalescent hospital during the war. In the spring of 1919, he performed at village concerts, impressing the local audience with his professional London status. Sometimes he sang with Mrs. Cooper's daughter, Phyllis. He recalls the treasured experience in his autobiography, *Present Indicative*:

> Small memories are the most insistent, and I like to catch again, for a moment, the feel of the sharp spring air as we drove home at night after a concert, the smell of the wood fire in the library where we discussed, over hot soup and sandwiches, the triumphs of the evening. All the warm, comfortable ingredients of country-house life were there, the very unfamiliarity of the atmosphere enhancing its charm for me.... This, I reflected, quite wrongly, was my rightful sphere, and I would go upstairs to bed, undress, and brush my teeth, still, until sleep closed down upon me, accurate in my performance of a country gentleman.

On later holidays, he joined Mrs. Cooper in Italy at Alassio, and he stayed with her at Cap Ferrat on the Riviera.

At Hambleton he found and read a volume by Saki which further helped to mold in his own mind the technique to use in writing about Edwardian country-house affairs—how to express its atmosphere and charm by use of wit. Without question, his friendship with Mrs. Cooper and his visits to Hambleton Hall helped to shape his career, a career which could only have been with the stage.

His destiny began to form not many years after his birth on 16 December 1899. He was taken regularly to the theatre from the age of five. At seven, he performed in amateur productions and made his professional debut as a child actor in *The Goldfish* in January 1911. Engagements continued throughout life, and acting became a means of advancing theatrical and literary ambitions.

He learned every aspect of the theatre. After the opening of *The Young Idea*, in February 1923, he was noticed as a brilliant young playwright. A writer of great promise, he had promised himself while still in his teens that he would become famous and rich and this he proceeded to do. By 1925 he had completed three plays which secured his reputation as a dramatist: *The Vortex, Fallen Angels,* and *Hay Fever.* A first-rate playwright, he was also an actor, director, and composer of merit who freely incorporated song, music, and dance into his plays. International fame was his by 1926.

In the golden years from 1928 to 1934 came his great successes as a writer: *This Year of Grace, Bitter Sweet, Private Lives, Cavalcade, Words and Music,* and *Design for Living.* Virginia Woolf wrote in a letter to Noël of *This Year of Grace,* "Some of the numbers struck me on the forehead like a bullet. And what's more I remember them and see them enveloped in atmosphere— works of art in short."

His writing tends to lash out at hypocritical society and denounce smug Victorian attitudes. He saw into the absurdity of the human condition. Often in his plays, one character represents integrity and clarity and thus Coward's own attitude. He can be flippant and laugh away cares, but he can also be serious and see into the heart of things. Enjoyment of life runs through his writing. In *Private Lives,* Elyot expresses to Amanda his zest for living: "Let's blow trumpets and squeakers, and enjoy the party as much as we can, like very small, quite idiotic school children. Let's savour the delight of the moment. Come and kiss me, darling, before your body rots, and worms pop in and out of your eye sockets."

Behind the frivolous dialogue of the characters is a sadder, wiser, and more serious theme. Elyot and Amanda cannot live together because of clashes of ego, and they cannot live apart because of their love for each other. They are honest and intelligent and aware of their situation, which is after all the absurdity of the human condition.

The plays of the 40's include the superbly entertaining *Present Laughter,* in which a group of people fall in and out of love with one another, and *Blithe Spirit,* which again uses a romantic triangle to get at the reality of such human emotions as jealousy.

Nöel Coward
(1899-1973) first
stayed at Hambleton
Hall, Oakham,
former home of
Mrs. Astley-Cooper,
at the age of fifteen
and made frequent
visits later

His plays in the mellowed phase of later life include *Relative Values*, *Quadrille*, and *Nude with Violin*. *Look after Lulu* is an adaptation of a Feydeau farce. *Waiting in the Wings*, the last of his full-length plays, takes place in a home for old and retired actresses. His plays range from farce to serious drama. He revived the comedy of manners, as sophisticated people are caught in comic situations. With techniques of satire, irony, and wit, bad behavior is held up to ridicule, and the loss of chivalrous values is deplored. But behind the fun, there is always the assertion of life, not a cynical denial of it. Even the patriotic *Cavalcade* leaves one with the feeling that, despite tragedy, life is worth living.

Some of his plays have been relegated to literary oblivion, but he remains a popular writer with a prolific and varied output. He also wrote a novel (*Pomp and Circumstance*), several volumes of short stories, travel books, and a book of verse. *In Which We Serve* is a fine film and a good piece of wartime propaganda. He followed up his first autobiography, *Present Indicative*, with another, *Future Indefinite*.

He was knighted in 1969 and awarded an Honorary Doctorate of Letters from the University of Sussex in 1972. When he died suddenly at his Jamaican home on 26 March 1973, he left behind a vast number of plays with enduring and endearing qualities which will keep him in the forefront as one of the wittiest English playwrights ever.

As long as mad dogs and Englishmen go out in the midday sun, as long as the Mrs. Worthingtons of the world try to put their daughters on the stage, Noël Coward's praises will be sung. Good fortune makes it possible for us to return to the site of the early inspiration and expression of his prodigious talent.

Located on a peninsula in a large reservoir called Rutland Water, Hambleton Hall is set in an enchanting position. It is a large Victorian mansion surrounded by acres of gardens and sheer beauty in the county which clings to the name of Rutland.

The present owners are Tim and Stefa Hart, who have converted it into a small hotel. Bedrooms are furnished in traditional style. The drawing room is luxurious and the bar so pleasant and cozy that the visitor may neglect the gorgeous outdoor scene.

Noël "grandly descended the polished oak staircase," and guests who emulate that proud action are in for a particular treat as they too descend for dinner. The hotel restaurant boasts of a young English chef who trained at Maxim's in Paris and creates inspired dishes at Hambleton. Cared for with such love and dedication, Hambleton Hall offers guests the high standards of country-house living so adored by Noël Coward. Above the door of the house is the Rabelaisian motto: *Fay ce que voudras* or "Do as you please." The owners promise a warm and friendly welcome. They do not guarantee that fame and fortune will follow, but with such a precedent already established, anything is possible.

HAMBLETON HALL
Hambleton
Oakham
Rutland LE15 8TH

Telephone: (01572) 756991   Fax: (01572) 724721

Of the fifteen bedrooms, individually decorated and furnished with antiques, nine have views over Rutland Water. All have en suite bathrooms, television, trouser press, and room service.

The Victorian country house provides a luxurious stay with an elegant dining room with meals to match, drawing room with open fire and beautiful views of the outdoors, and bar with inglenook fireplace.

Also outdoors are gardens, tennis courts, and swimming pool. Open all year.

J. B. PRIESTLEY

at

The White Hart Hotel
Lincoln
Lincolnshire

My hotel was near the cathedral. This
hotel was a surprise. It was comfortable and
civilised.

—*English Journey* (1934)

When J. B. Priestley took a tour of England in the autumn of 1933,
he wrote about his travels in a volume with the simple title of
English Journey. His travels took him from Southampton to Bristol
and Swindon, through the Cotswolds, into the industrial cities of
Coventry and Birmingham, and on to Leicester and Nottingham.
He stopped in the Yorkshire city of Bradford, where he was born
in 1894, then continued his journey with the Potteries, Lancashire,
Liverpool, Manchester, Durham. He stayed in Lincoln, another
highlight, before going through Norfolk on the return journey to
London.

The itinerary had the purpose of showing the great variety of
the country he loved. But Priestley felt obliged to disclose the faults
of England as well. His insights and observations continue to earn
him critical respect.

A prolific writer, Priestley had already produced books of essays
and criticism as well as novels. His first book, a collection of
essays, was published in 1922, the year after taking a degree in
history and political science from Cambridge University. Determined to make a living as a full-time freelance writer, Priestley left
for London in 1922 with his young wife to write essays, reviews,
and critical articles for a variety of journals. In the particularly

productive year of 1927, he published five books including his first two novels.

It was his third novel, *The Good Companions*, a colossal success which appeared in 1929, that gave him a name at home and abroad. The long picaresque novel tells the appealing story of three central characters who escape for a while from their dull or unhappy lives and go through a series of encounters in the more glamorous world of show business.

The Good Companions always remained a symbol of his work, but other volumes of fiction indicate his remarkable variety. *Angel Pavement* (1931) evokes the grim mood of London in the depression years. The newspaper world of *Wonder Hero* (1933) deals with economic pressures placed on people. *The Doomsday Men* (1938) is set in the Arizona desert and tells a story of intrigue and scientific fantasy in a surprisingly optimistic tone as three madmen plot to destroy the world. The five novels which followed were concerned with England at war.

Bright Day (1946), his most admired novel and Priestley's own favorite, recounts the life of a script writer who, bored with films and wanting to strike out in another direction, is suddenly able to recall his early years and reach back to piece together a forgotten world. *Lost Empires* (1965) uses English music hall for its backward look within a symbolic structure, and his two-volume *The Image Men* (1968) satirizes the contemporary need for "the right image" (sought mainly by actors and politicians) in a world which deserves to be commercially exploited by the two academics of the title.

But after attaining worldwide fame with *The Good Companions*, Priestley turned to the stage; and his success in the theatre overshadowed the success of his novels. Altogether, he wrote over forty plays with such familiar titles as *Dangerous Corner, Time and the Conways, When We are Married, Johnson Over Jordan*, and *An Inspector Calls*—plays which are still being performed.

He also produced collections of short stories. And during the war years, he made enormously effective radio broadcasts for the BBC. The texts of his wartime transmissions, published in *Britain*

Speaks and *Postscripts*, read as evocatively today as when they were first heard. His technique was to introduce topics that seemed remote from the war—a meat pie in a Bradford window, a visit to Margate, Hardy and Dickens—then give it a twist that enhanced the theme and relevance. The variety of his vast output was unending.

Like the wandering troop of players in the perennially popular *The Good Companions*, he wanted to wander through England and record his impressions. The subtitle of the volume he produced is fully explanatory: "A rambling but truthful account of what one man saw and heard and felt and thought during a journey through England."

But the thoughts of the journey which he began in the autumn of 1933 do not ramble. Nor is his account dated. Certainly, his complimentary words on the White Hart Hotel in Lincoln are still applicable over fifty years later.

Priestly arrived at the White Hart in the darkness and thereby missed a chance to see a distant view of "that splendid apparition of the cathedral on the hill." His taxi from the train station climbed the steep hill to the top, where his hotel was located, and he soon found himself comfortably ensconced: "After settling in and indulging in that preliminary prowl familiar to all travellers, I enquired for the proprietor to congratulate him on his hotel."

Priestley noted a historical coincidence in the fact that the current proprietor was a Jew and that Jewish history was an integral part of medieval Lincoln. He pondered over the connection that brought local history full circle for him and lamented his own lack of knowledge on that segment of the history of Lincoln.

It is a very interesting history indeed and one which is still greatly in evidence. The steep hill to which Priestley refers, appropriately named Steep Hill, exhibits many wealthy twelfth-century houses which attest to the riches of medieval Lincoln, based on the wool industry. A few houses on the hill reveal that early occupants were Jewish.

The Jew's House, a stone building of the late twelfth century with the original Norman doorway and with rooms on the upper floor, is located next door to the Jew's Court, believed to have been the Jewish Synagogue. The Norman House, sometimes mistakenly known as Aaron's House, is another fine example of early domestic architecture. A Jewess who later lived here was accused of debasing coin and hanged in 1290, the year when Jews were expelled from England. Interspersed with the many houses on the hill, or located in them, is an endless array of antique and gift shops, as well as tea shops and restaurants.

An excellent starting point for seeking out the noteworthy historical buildings is the Tourist Information Centre. From this sixteenth-century, timber-framed, merchant's house situated opposite the White Hart, visitors may arm themselves with brochures or maps before meandering down the hill, perhaps digressing to examine the inevitable souvenirs, perhaps stopping for a pot of tea with scones. With the Usher Gallery serving as a worthwhile detour, the tourist may never make it at all to the city below.

Below, in the main shopping area, more ancient sights await. The Stonebow, spanning the High Street, is a sixteenth-century gateway with the Guildhall situated above. High Bridge on the High Street is a medieval bridge lined with shops and with steps leading down to "Glory Hole" where original Norman stonework of the bridge can be seen. Along the High Street are three medieval churches—St. Benedict's with its eleventh century tower, St. Mary-le-Wigford with a part-Norman and part-Saxon tower, and St. Peter-at-Gowts, located close to the Gowts (the Saxon word for channels or watercourses, as in *gut* .

The railway station and a variety of large commercial establishments are located in the lower part, giving Lincoln its share of chimneys, factories, labor, heavy traffic, and rows of dull dwellings—the accoutrements of industrial society. The manufacturing Lincoln still lies in its twentieth-century setting "smoking and spluttering," as Priestley noted when he seems to have devoted as much time on the investigation of a firm manufacturing giant excavators as on the cathedral. Priestley decries the heavy industry which is changing the economy, objects to the manufacture and exportation of dangerous war implements, and reflects on the snobbery which grants high social status only to those who live high up, by the cathedral, in the twelfth century. With the ancient city at the top of the hill, Priestley finds no faults. His love of England comes through in his description of the wondrous sights which confront the visitor, sights which continue to reward the visitor with the pleasures of travel.

Completed in about the year 1235, the cathedral dominates the city and is a spectacular sight from far or near. "A poem in architecture," it has been called. And Ruskin says that it is the best piece of architecture in the British Isles. The facade is richly decorated with a sculptured frieze over three elaborate Norman arches. A central tower of 271 feet is surpassed in height in England by the spires of Salisbury and Norwich. But in sheer beauty, many would agree, it is surpassed by none.

The pride of its interior is the Angel Choir, built toward the end of the thirteenth century at the east end and so dubbed because of the thirty carved angelic figures involved in a variety of activites: reading a scroll, holding up sun and moon, playing instruments. And on one corbel sits the famous Lincoln Imp. Cross-legged, wide-mouthed, elfin-eared, a reminder of the less angelic aspects of life, he is a major attraction.

Other attractions of the cathedral are the dark Purbeck marble columns of the nave, the twelfth-century font embellished with figures of grotesque animals, the stained-glass windows of the transept, one of the four surviving copies of the Magna Carta in the Cathedral Treasury, a library designed by Sir Christopher Wren, and a graceful, thirteenth-century polygonal Chapter House with flying buttresses and single central pillar.

Also situated on the hilltop, in the area opposite the cathedral, is the Lincoln Castle, which William the Conqueror ordered to be built in 1068. The Normans understood the strategic advantage of this site overlooking town activities and the River Witham. So too will anyone who enjoys the excellent view from the top of its Observatory Tower, built on a forty-foot mound.

Of primary importance for the traveler, among the buildings so magnificently set on the summit, and one which gave Priestley much joy, is the White Hart Hotel.

Bust of J. B. Priestley (1894-1984) by Maurice Lambert and the White Hart Hotel, Lincoln, a stop Priestley made when gathering material for his *English Journey*

An inn believed to have been on the site since 1460 was named for King Richard II, who visited the cathedral with his Queen in 1387. King Richard adopted as his emblem the white hart, a beautiful and sturdy animal that could be captured, according to medieval legend, only by one who was able to conquer the world. It is a tribute to King Richard that White Harts are ubiquitous in England as the names of pubs, inns, and hotels.

The fine Georgian building, with its entrance in Bailgate, has a lovely white facade dating to the 1840s with bold, classic pediments over the first floor windows. Window boxes with red and purple flowers are a cheerful addition. The feature of the front is a sculptured, three-dimensional white hart over the portico that displays the letters of the hotel name.

Nearby, just down Exchequer Street, is the entrance to the cathedral and its precincts. In the opposite direction is the castle. At the corner, where Steep Hill begins its decent, a signpost points to the various attractions downhill and to Roman sites in another direction. And it amusingly points to Neustadt an der Weinstrasse, Lincoln's twin city, at a distance of 740 kilometers. A central location in this exciting city is just one of many attributes of the superb White Hart Hotel. Other niceties await indoors.

The entry area is filled with such individual pieces as an oak coffer, a long case clock, a settle, and a cabinet containing gift items and small antiques for sale. When Katherine and Harry Leven owned the hotel from 1913 until it was sold after Mr. Leven's death in 1951, they brought in a collection of fine furniture, china, and antiques, which are still part of the decor. Acquired by Trusthouse Forte in 1981, the hotel is singled out as one of the small group of exclusive inns belonging to the Trusthouse family and retaining an elegant and traditional appeal.

A coin on display in the front hall links the hotel to Roman times; emanating from the reign of the Emperor Nero during the years 54 to 68, it was found during excavations for a new wing in 1975. A further bit of hotel history is related in a framed statement on the left wall very near the entrance.

Sounds and sights are serendipitous aspects of a stay at the White Hart. Hotel guests awaken in the morning to the sound of cathedral bells. And guests do not even have to leave the hotel for magnificent views of the honey-colored stone cathedral. The ever-changing colors vary with the changing time of day and with the seasons. At night, floodlights illuminate the cathedral and give it a magical appearance. So magnetic was one wintry evening view of it from the hotel, with light snow gently falling, that the possibility of missing dinner was a very real threat.

Snow must have fallen on the Roman city of Lindus Colonia, which existed in the first century as a *colonia* for retired veterans of the legions. Newport Arch, a surviving fragment of the north gate of the Roman walls, is unique in Britain, for traffic leaving the city via the main road to the north still goes through this Roman gateway.

Before leaving, the tourist would do well to turn back and take in the view, recalling the poetic tribute paid by Priestley:

> Few things in this island are so breathlessly impressive as Lincoln Cathedral, nobly crowning its hill, seen from below. It offers one of the Pisgah sights of England. There, it seems, gleaming in the sun, are the very ramparts of Heaven.

THE WHITE HART HOTEL
Bailgate
Lincoln
Lincolnshire LN1 3AR

Telephone: (01522) 526222   Fax: (01522) 531798

A Trusthouse Forte Hotel.

A variety of fifty bedrooms and suites, all with private bathrooms, include many rear bedrooms with fine views of the cathedral. Each is tastefully designed and equipped with television, radio, telephone, tea and coffee making facilities. Suites have refrigerated private bars.

The Club Bar, often crowded and smoke-filled, is located near the entrance.

The lounge is a pleasant area with comfortable chairs for enjoying a cup of afternoon tea or whatever. In the fireplace, where once Priestley spoke of a log fire, electric coals now glow.

In the oldest part of the hotel, dating to 1722, the King Richard Restaurant offers good English food.

The place for lighter meals is the Orangery, with an entrance also from the street. The bright, domed room makes a fine setting for tea with cream cakes (which temptingly fill a glass cabinet). Masses of greenery, with one tree reaching up into the opaque glass dome, convey a light and natural aspect, while a grand piano in the corner suggests a musical one.

Car Park opposite the hotel entrance.

WILLA CATHER

at

The Feathers

Ludlow

Shropshire

The Feathers Hotel at which we stopped
was named for the Prince of Wales' crest,
was a flourishing inn before Elizabeth came
to the throne, and was used as a sort of
overflow house for such guests as the castle
could not accommodate. . . .My sleeping-
room overhangs the street, and I walk up an
inclined plane from the dresser to my bed,
but for all that, I never expect to sleep again
in a place so beautiful.

—"Shropshire and A.E. Housman"

When Willa Cather first crossed the Atlantic in 1902 and landed in
Liverpool, she was twenty-eight and a teacher and journalist. On
summer holiday from her high school teaching job in Pittsburgh,
she produced a series of fourteen travel articles for the weekly
columns of the *Nebraska State Journal*, a newspaper for which she
had been writing since 1893, when she was a student at the State
University in Lincoln, Nebraska.

Born on 7 December 1873 in Virginia, Willa Cather nevertheless belongs to Nebraska. When she was ten, the Cather family left
the state which had been their home for six generations to make
a new home in the undeveloped West. They settled in Red Cloud,
the town with which the writer is associated. As a novelist, she
captured the pioneering spirit which she knew from a childhood
spent on the frontier.

The adolescent Willa Cather was known for her tomboy dress and behavior as well as for her voracious reading habits. With interests in biology and medicine, she left Red Cloud to pursue those subjects at the State University in Lincoln. But her remarkable ability with the pen changed the direction of her studies to English. She took up writing and literature and became editor of the college paper, contributing stories, plays, and editorials. After graduation, she accepted a position in Pittsburgh as an editor for a new magazine, *The Home Monthly*, leaving after a year to join the Pittsburgh *Leader*. Although she was to live the rest of her life away from home, she remained a Nebraskan.

In addition to the editorial work which occupied her for several years, she produced articles for a variety of periodicals and newspapers on a diversity of subjects including literary and drama criticism. When the opportunity came, she gave up journalism for teaching.

It was as a high school teacher in Pittsburgh that Cather made her first trip abroad. She was living in the household of her friend Isabelle McClung when the pair embarked on a trip to Europe in 1902. The young schoolteacher had not yet written the books for which she would become famous.

Neither had A.E. Housman yet acquired his reputation as a poet. But Cather, familiar with *A Shropshire Lad*, journeyed from Liverpool to Chester, then through Shropshire to Ludlow, in order to follow the haunts of the poet she so fervently admired. She made it clear in her article on the subject that his lyrics and the source of his poetry were responsible for her visit to Shropshire:

> Anyone who has ever read Housman's verse at all must certainly wish to live awhile among the hillside fields, the brookland and villages, which moved a modern singer to lyric expression of a simplicity, spontaneity, and grace the like of which we have scarcely had in the last hundred years.

Clearly, the Shropshire experience had a lasting influence on Cather. She felt the "time-defying stillness" of that magical land

The Feathers, the Shropshire hotel named for the ostrich feathers from the Prince of Wales' crest, where Willa Cather (1873-1947) stayed while on a literary pilgrimage

and mused in the travel letter sent to the Nebraska newspaper that it "is surely the country for the making of poets if ever one was." It surely contributed at least in some small way toward making Cather a poet. Her first published book of the following year was a volume of poetry called *April Twilights* which included a poem entitled "Poppies on Ludlow Castle."

Ludlow, located in the part of Shropshire she called real Housman country, had special appeal. Always intrigued with old places and associations with the past, Cather was particularly impressed with the town's importance in Elizabethan times. She makes an easy transition in her poem to Sir Philip Sidney, paying tribute to the Elizabethan poet-statesman who spent much of his youth at Ludlow Castle with its "halls of vanished pleasure" of a golden age, long gone.

Cather must have thought of the idyllic landscape while in London, especially when, with characteristic independence of spirit, she elected to stay in an unfashionable hotel near St. Paul's, expecting the district to be convenient for sightseeing. But the sights she reported on from her seedy neighborhood included the filth, the derelicts and deprivation, the homeless women, and the endless crowds of liquor-craving laborers.

She might again have recalled Shropshsire when she made her way to North London to meet the poet in his shabby lodgings far from the romantic setting with which she associated him. In Shropshire, she had found no trace of Housman himself, despite investigations and inquiries. Few people had ever even heard of him, she discovered. Determined to uncover the mystery, she managed to secure his address from his publisher and, before crossing the English Channel to France, called on the poet at his home in Highgate—a convenient location for Housman, who was then teaching Latin at University College in London.

The visit was a great disappointment. Housman had been await-ing the arrival of Canadian cousins when Cather turned up with two friends, Isabelle McClung and Dorothy Canfield. He raced down the stairs to greet his expected guests only to find unexpected strangers. In the awkward situation, Housman tried to be cordial, but he was a reticent and withdrawn academic who would not discuss Ludlow or the countryside but adhered to the safe subject of Latin scholarship in a dialogue with Dorothy Canfield. The magic that Cather had found in the poetry was absent in the poet, and she left the interview bitterly disenchanted. But her travels abroad had an impact, and back in her own country she was well on the way to establishing a solid reputation as a novelist.

Her work reached the attention of the publisher S.S. McClure, and in 1906 he offered her an associate editorship on the staff of his New York magazine. She gave up teaching for the new position, which lasted six years. With publication in 1912 of her first novel, *Alexander's Bridge*, her long apprenticeship was over. She left her successful career at *McClure's Magazine* to devote her time entirely to writing. At thirty-nine, the novelist was off with a late start. But she was soon to achieve the fame and recognition she so well deserves.

When Willa Cather died on 24 April 1947, she left behind a legacy of great novels including *My Antonia* (1918), the Pulitzer prize-winning *One of Ours* (1922), *A Lost Lady* (1923), *The Professor's House* (1925), *My Mortal Enemy (1926)*, and *Death Comes for the Archbishop* (1927). When he was awarded the Nobel Prize, Sinclair Lewis stated that she should have had the coveted honor and that he would give nine Nobel prizes to have written *Death Comes for the Archbishop.*

A modern literary pilgrim might give anything to stay for a while at the inn which gave Cather the thrill of actually dwelling in a place of such great age and charm. She derived enormous pleasure from surroundings enriched by associations with the distant past.

The Feathers, which was a private residence in 1603, is a structural delight. The architectural critic Nicolaus Pevsner calls it "the climax of urban black-and-white houses in the county of Shropshire." The three-story, three-gable building leans over the street known as the Bull Ring, a reference to the medieval cattle market which once occupied the site. Its white facade is covered with timber framing and a fantasy of richly-carved designs with scrolls, heads, animals, or geometric patterns.

Of the three bay windows, the left projects further out than the others, giving the whole an artistic assymetry. The total effect is a feast for the beholder's eye. "Here everything of motifs that was available has been lavished on the facade," writes Pevsner of what he sums up as "that prodigy of timber-framed houses."
The entrance door is the original one, nearly four hundred years old. Initials on the lockplate of the massive door are those of Rees Jones, who took over the property in 1619. It remained a private residence until about 1669, when it was converted to an inn and named in honor of the Prince of Wales whose traditional badge, three ostrich feathers, gives the building its picturesque name. The Feathers is now in the hands of the Edwards family who continue to maintain it as an inn and to cherish its traditions and history.

The venerable door did not escape the attention of Cather, who waxes lyrical over it: "The knocker on the spike-studded outer door alone would make a house desirable." But today no knocker graces the impressive oak door, and no apparent space amidst the studs suggests where a knocker might have been placed. Nor can evidence of its existence be extracted from old records of the Feathers. Although there is always the possibility that the absent knocker was indeed once tacked on during the span of time when she was a guest, it is more likely that Cather was being fanciful, unleashing her imagination as she was to do later in creating her great works of fiction.

Cather imbued a few other statements with great enthusiasm if not with complete accuracy. She reported to her readers in Nebraska that the Feathers was "a flourishing inn before Elizabeth came to the throne." But the building was not converted from a private residence until around 1669. Her hastily-written account goes on with a misleading description of a room which does not exactly accord with any room in the hotel but is undoubtedly meant to portray the James I Lounge, which for many years served as a dining room:

The entire ceiling of the dining-room is carved
with the arms of various lords of the western border,
and about the great fireplace is a mass of intricate

wood-carving, culminating in the work above the mantel, where the star of the Order of the Garter and its creditable motto are cut the size of a tea-table top.

Nevertheless, the inside is as pleasing as the exterior, and Cather's glowing description of its general appearance still applies: "Almost the entire interior is of black oak, with huge beams across the ceiling, and all the windows are of tiny diamond panes." Shiny copper and brass objects and enviable pieces of antique furniture enhance the basic structure throughout—in the reception area, in the maze of corridors, in various rooms.

The large reception area, with comfortable chairs around a log-burning brick fireplace, offers an irresistible invitation to relax with tea or sherry while studying antique coffers, tables, settles, and long-case clocks. Even the wooden bellows, carved with the three feathers symbol, makes its small contribution to the pleasing total design.

The area gives access to public rooms and is a nest of activity, particularly as people begin to arrive prior to dinner. Next to the front entry door, the Tanner's Room (named for the Tanner family who owned the inn from 1909 to 1947) is furnished with oak chairs and tables, two settles, a rack displaying pewter plates, and a grandfather clock; but its main feature is a carved oak overmantel with the coat of arms of King William III. Just opposite, the King Charles II Room or Cocktail Bar offers additional respite and refreshment. The Comus Bar honors an event which occured at the castle in 1634 when John Milton was present for the first performance of his masque, *Comus*. Finally, the Richard III Restaurant, once the kitchen of the establishment, retains its original inglenook fireplace. Other main rooms are upstairs.

Famous for its carved Jacobean mantelpiece and elaborately-carved plaster ceiling, both showing the arms of James I, is the aptly-named James I Lounge. The oak-paneled room, warm and friendly, its windows with small panes of glass overlooking the street, with blazing fire and comfortable chairs, and richly furnished with a seventeenth-century court cupboard among its antique pieces, is an ideal place for after-dinner coffee.

Adjoining it is the handsomely-paneled Edward IV Writing Room with carved Jacobean mantelpiece containing amusing faces, fine Flemish fireback, and arms of two local families of the sixteenth century over the entrance door. The Prince Charles Banqueting Suite (the old Assembly Room in Georgian times), refurbished in the style of a baronial hall and named for the present prince, is used for meetings and conferences, as is the Prince William Suite.

Even without imbibing in each of the many public rooms, maneuvering the corridors to get to bedrooms—turning corners or going down a few steps in order to go up a few steps a bit further along, then perhaps down again—is a challenge. But the effort is certainly worthwhile. Sloping floors lend additional charm to the beamed rooms, and those in front provide the satisfying opportunity to write a letter home echoing Cather's own words: "My sleeping-room overhangs the street."

The Feathers is an architectural gem in the center of a town which is itself an architectural museum. With a population of about eight thousand, the small but lively market town encourages aimless wandering after visiting its principle attractions, the castle and the church.

Cather extols the castle: "On the top of a cliff over a hundred feet high, rise the magnificent remains of Ludlow Castle." Built as a fortress in the eleventh century, it was continuously enlarged until it was abandoned in the eighteenth. The impressive ruin carries two towers on its ramparts. Beyond the outer bailey and the stone bridge over the former moat, in the inner bailey, a circular Norman chapel stands by itself on the greenery, open and roofless.

Empty rooms of the Great Hall call out for the imagination to supply scenes of an ancient past when the castle was peopled with a succession of historical figures—Edward IV and his two princes, who were later taken to the Tower of London and murdered; Prince Arthur who came here with his bride, Catherine of Aragon, only to die in Ludlow a few months later; his younger brother who succeeded him as Henry VIII; his ill-fated daughter who lived in the castle as a girl and in later years earned herself the title "Bloody" Mary; Sir Henry Sidney who, as governor of the castle, had it remodelled during his tenure; his poet-son Sir Philip Sidney; and John Milton, the great poet whose masque was performed in the Great Hall. Rising high above Ludlow and dominating the town is the huge Gothic tower of the Parish Church of St. Laurence. With the size and grandeur of a cathedral, the fourteenth-century church is notable for its misericords with exceptional carvings in high relief on the underside of these choir stalls and for its stained-glass windows. The large east window illustrates the life of St. Laurence, Ludlow's patron saint.

Ludlow is simply a wanderer's delight. All around the central Castle Square, which is particularly bustling on market days, are gems of black-and-white buildings which beckon the visitor, as do alleys and narrow streets with evocative names—Mill Street, Fish Street, Pepper Lane, Harp Lane, The Narrows, Quality Square.

It is sensible to stroll, giving way to diversions which inevitably come from enticing galleries and shops, many purveying antiques, some offering the weary wanderer a welcome break in the form of English tea. Just one such tea oasis adjacent to the castle in Castle Square is the Dinham House Craft Studios which also sells a variety of appealing items while providing the visitor with a good look at the inside of a fine Georgian house.

Broad Street in particular must be singled out for its architectural treasures. It is lined with rows of fourteenth- and fifteenth-century half-timbered houses as well as elegant Georgian buildings which recall another prosperous period in the history of the town. At the top end is the Butter Cross, a classical stone building of the eighteenth century, which leads to a museum of local geology and history. At the lower end is Broad Gate, the only surviving one of the seven gates of the medieval walled city. Buildings along the street reveal such fine details as fan lights over doors or lead waterpipes engraved with dates or faces. Distractions and impediments to a concentrated study arise from intriguing shops along the way. One little antique shop is even tucked into the Gate House on the other side of Broad Gate, where there is also a good view of the original drum tower. Lower Broad Street leads to the fifteenth-century Ludford Bridge over the River Teme. From the bridge are fine views of the countryside all around as well as of the vast church tower high above the town.

The town of Ludlow, 162 miles from the capital city, remains a haven of escape from the crowded London scene in one of the most beautiful towns in England.

THE FEATHERS
The Bull Ring
Ludlow
Shropshire SY8 1AA

Telephone: (01584) 875261   Fax: (01584) 876030

Forty bedrooms, all with private bathrooms, include some four-posters and some suites.

Public rooms are the Tanner's Room, the King Charles II Room, the Comus Bar, and the Richard III Restaurant.

Reachable by car with an easy motorway drive from London or from Heathrow Airport via the M4 or by train from London's Paddington Station (via Newport).

THOMAS DE QUINCEY

at

The Lion Hotel
Shrewsbury
Shropshire

I stepped into the sumptuous room
allotted to me. It was a ball-room of noble
proportions—lighted, if I chose to issue
orders, by three gorgeous chandeliers. . .
And, upon the whole, one thing only was
wanting—viz., a throne—for the completion
of my *apotheosis*.
I, in this Shrewsbury hotel, naturally
contemplated a group of objects tending to
far different results.

—*The Confessions of an English Opium-Eater*

The Confessions of an English Opium-Eater, the most celebrated
work of Thomas De Quincey, is one of only four books he
published. Written in 1821 to alleviate financial pressure, the
book was a complete financial as well as literary success. Six
editions were printed before he revised and enlarged it in 1856.

De Quincey gives an account of his early years in *The
Confessions* without repenting his use of opium. Nor does he
proselytize against the horrific effects of the drug which was then
an accepted and standard form of medical treatment. He believed
in the efficacious effects of the drug, particularly in staving off
tuberculosis, the disease of which his father died when Thomas was
a child of seven. De Quincey began to take opium in 1804 for
palliation of pain from rheumatic toothache. But by about 1813 he
was addicted.

In *The Confessions*, De Quincey attributes the material for his dream prose to opium and describes incidents of his youth which became the basis for his opium dreams. One such incident occurred at the Lion Inn in Shrewsbury at the end of his journey through Wales, a journey undertaken when he ran away from school. Born in Manchester in 1785, young Thomas was sent to the Manchester Grammar School at fifteen. He detested the school and deeply resented the decision made by his mother and guardians to place him there against his own wishes. He craved freedom from its stale atmosphere and, after a year and a half, escaped from the school that imprisoned him. Remembering the magnificent scenery of the Welsh countryside which he had crossed on an earlier trip to Ireland, he now embarked on travels through that pleasurable landscape.

In Wales, he walked ten to fifteen miles a day. He traveled all over—Llangollen, Llanrwst, Conway, Bangor, Caernarvon—making friends, sometimes sleeping in the open to save the price of an inn, sometimes staying at simple cottages. *The Confessions* recounts his adventures, which culminate with a sudden resolve to leave for London. His intention was to seek out certain money lenders and borrow enough to live on until he reached his patrimony at twenty-one. He left Wales in late November 1802.

At his first stopping place in England, he met one of his good Welsh friends who happened to live in the border town of Oswestry. Managing to overcome the temptation to stay on and enjoy his friend's library and hospitality, he walked the eighteen miles from Oswestry to Shrewsbury to pick up the mail coach to London. He reached his destination at seven o'clock and made for the place where coaches from Holyhead to London stopped—the Lion Inn. Itinerant foot passengers without firm travel plans might be viewed suspiciously, but his friend had arranged a seat reservation for him on the coach; consequently, De Quincey was courteously received and well treated at the inn.

It was the practice for coach passengers to wait in a private room. But the inn was being refurbished, and he was given the only room available, the ballroom. Servants lit his way up a broad staircase to the first floor and into the lofty ballroom at the back of the building.

272

Thomas De Quincey
(1785-1859) and the
Lion Hotel, Shrewsbury,
where he had a terrifying
dream as he slept in the
ballroom

It was while he was in that room of the Lion Inn in Shrewsbury that he made the agonizing decision to follow through to London, as related in one powerful episode of the autobiography:

Mindful of the impending journey with its reckless purpose to borrow money, he spends the night awaiting the arrival of the Holyhead Mail in a highly nervous state. Filled with anxiety and apprehension, he experiences "heart-shaking reflections" as if he "stood upon the brink of a precipice." His immediate surroundings in a room of unusual height exacerbate the feelings of terror and foreboding that pervade his mind with dreadful images of what awaits him. As he watches a storm raging outside, he conjures up a vision of dancers and music inside. Anxiety mounts. He sees the "unfathomed abyss in London into which I was now so wilfilly precipitating myself." But he finally reasons that although he may be swallowed up by the spectre that awaits, his path towards it is inexorable and irrevocable. The Holyhead Mail arrives at last, and he is off to London.

In London, he suffered hunger and deprivation and left the inhospitable metropolis the following March. By mid-December of 1803, he entered Oxford. Here began his addiction to opium, originally taken for relief of pain. But De Quincey admits his delight in the pleasurable sensations which the drug imparted, and he willingly experimented. In 1808, he mysteriously left Oxford without completing his examinations or taking a degree.

A year later, he moved to the Lake District to be near the poets he so admired, Coleridge and Wordsworth. His addiction, no longer a secret now, brought about the demise of the deep friendship which he had developed with the Wordsworths. He moved with his wife to London in 1821 and became a regular contributor to *The London Magazine,* which initially published his *Confessions of an English Opium-Eater.*

For the last thirty years of his life—he died in 1859 at the age of seventy-four—he lived almost entirely in Edinburgh and struggled with poverty while continuing to write articles to assuage his financial condition. After his wife died in 1837, he was left, at fifty-two, with a family of six to support. His poverty was so acute at times that his children went hungry. He was forced to hide from

274

creditors and was arrested for debt. But he remained productive, and the output of his later years include some of his greatest volumes—*Suspiria de Profundis*, revisions for a collected edition, and the 1856 revised and extended version of his masterpiece, *The Confessions of an English Opium-Eater.*

The Confessions offers basically authentic accounts of crucial events in the life of the author from schoolboy days to addiction and deep narcosis. It recounts those climactic moments when critical decisions were made or deep insights acquired. The Lion Inn plays an essential role, for the Shrewsbury inn episode indicates how his life began to take on a dream-like character.

Shrewsbury, the county seat of Shropshire, is a picturesque black-and-white town where timber-framed Elizabethan buildings dominate. A strategic location only twelve miles from the Welsh border has influenced its history and architecture. Offa's Dyke, built by King Offa in the eighth century to mark the boundary between England and Wales, is still visible. The thirteenth- century castle, rebuilt by Edward I during campaigns against Wales, now contains a regimental museum. All around the central square, with its old Market House of 1596, narrow medieval streets filled with half-timbered houses make a splendid background for envisioning the Shakespearean dramatization of an episode of the bloody Battle of Shrewsbury of 1403 when Falstaff tells the future King Henry V that he himself killed Percy Hotspur after fighting "a long hour by Shrewsbury clock."

The town center is small, no more than half a mile by half a mile, making perambulation pleasurable in this museum of architecture with its timbered Tudor houses, elegant Queen Anne and Georgian buildings, and fine Victorian structures such as the railway station. Curving streets, curious alleyways called "shuts," and mysterious street names such as Wyle Cop add appeal for the meanderer.

Situated in the town center, within a horseshoe bend of the River Severn, is the early seventeenth-century Lion Inn at the top of Wyle Cop, one of the oldest streets of medieval Shrewsbury. The long and attractive hotel front is made up of a late eighteenth century section of three stories, a white timber-framed part dating to the fifteenth century, and the main four-storied part with stuccoed ground floor and red brick above. A large golden lion made in 1777 stands on the portico of the main entrance to the old coaching inn.

Beyond the front door, a series of open rooms includes one to the right furnished with comfortable red leather chairs and one to the left with a bar and chairs surrounding small tables. Ahead is an extremely attractive room with a dominant huge stone fireplace capable of burning many logs and bringing welcome warmth in cold winter months. A tapestry on the wall above the fireplace and upholstered arm chairs add additional warmth. A timbered design on the upper half of the walls and wood paneling on the lower half complete the effect. The old traditional feeling is enhanced by portraits and by the leaded lights of three large windows with three smaller ones above.

Off the reception area is an enclosed bar and lounge with beamed wooden ceiling, half-paneled walls, and red leather chairs around tables. To the right of the reception desk a lift ascends to upper floors, where tortuous passages, a frequent feature of old English inns, wind their way to guest bedrooms.

Also off the reception area is the Georgian staircase leading to the grand ballroom in which Thomas De Quincey slept and dreamt. The ballroom was built in the 1770s in Robert Adam style under the direction of the proprietor John Richards, who was also responsible for extensive rebuilding of the entire hotel. A minstrels gallery on Adam-like columns is opposite the apsed end of the room. On one side, two oval mirrors between the windows face the wall with two carved fireplaces. Delicate plasterwork on light green walls, a saucer dome in the center of the ceiling, and three crystal chandeliers complete the bright and pleasing composition in which it is difficult to envision the dark night of "eerie splendour" experienced by De Quincey in this very room.

It was in the late eighteenth century that the Lion became a major stop for coaches. Richard Lawrence, the proprietor when De Quincey arrived in 1802, had developed a fast coach service for people as well as for direct mail between Shrewsbury and London. His coach route made the town an important center and the Lion a prosperous hotel, ready to welcome many distinguished and even royal visitors. Prince William of Gloucester, later King William IV, stayed in 1803. Paganini gave concerts in the ballroom in 1831, and Jenny Lind sang here on two occasions. Benjamin Disraeli stayed in 1841 and returned with his wife two years later to attend a ball. Charles Dickens, possibly the most famous guest, lodged at the Lion in 1858 and wrote about its unique charm:

> We have the strangest little rooms, the ceilings of which I can touch with my hands. The windows bulge out over the street as if they were little stern windows in a ship and a door opens out of the sitting room onto a little open gallery with plants in it where one leans over a queer old rail and looks all down hill and slantwise at the crookedest old black and yellow houses.

The Lion retains its role as a major inn, and the list grows of distinguished visitors and tourists who continue to turn up for a worthwhile visit to the lovely old town of Shrewsbury.

THE LION
Wyle Cop
Shrewsbury
Shropshire SY1 1UY

Telephone: (01743) 353107   Fax: (01743) 352744

59 rooms, including some beamed bedrooms, each with private bathroom, television, and tea and coffee making facilities.

The Dickens Suite, consisting of Rooms 1 and 2, has been redecorated and is preserved in Dickensian style by Trusthouse Forte, which owns the hotel.

Public rooms are the Truffles Restaurant, Tudor Bar, and Tapestry Lounge.

There are also three conference rooms—the Adam Room suite (for up to 200 people), the Lion Room (for 80), and the Pickwick Room (for 25).

GEORGE FARQUHAR

at

The George Inn

Lichfield

Staffordshire

"Come, Captain, you'll stay to Night, I
suppose, I'll shew you a Chamber..."

—The Beaux' Stratagem

The author of two masterful Restoration comedies, *The Recruiting
Officer* and *The Beaux' Stratagem*, began his connection with the
theatre as an actor. But he had a weak voice, lacked boldness and
presence, and suffered from stage fright. When he accidentally
wounded a fellow player in a stage duel, he gave up acting
altogether, leaving Dublin (where he was playing at the Smock
Alley Theatre) and Ireland (where he was born in 1678) and set
forth for London.

His first play, *Love and a Bottle*, was successfully produced at
the Drury Lane Theatre in 1698. Next came *The Constant Couple*,
also highly acclaimed, but followed by a series of failures and by
non-dramatic works such as prologues and epilogues, letters and
verse, and an epistolary novel.

It was several years before Farquhar came into his own as a
playwright with a warm style that set him apart from the cynical
and artificial comedy that marked theatre fare of the day. As an
Irishman, he was able to give a detached view of the pretensions
of English social life in comedies that conveyed a strong
and accurate sense of contemporary life in easy and vivacious
colloquial dialogue. Filled with genial good humor, his plays also
broke away from the trend by being set outside fashionable

London, in the provinces. His last play departed from convention still further by tackling a subject entirely new to Restoration drama, the problem of divorce.

But Farquhar was unable to earn a living from writing for the theatre and took a job as a recruiting officer. His army experiences gave him the background for the two major plays on which his reputation rests. *The Recruiting Officer*, successfully performed in 1706, earned for him great acclamation but little remuneration. He was forced deeper into poverty and debt.

The following year saw the production of his last and finest comedy, *The Beaux' Stratagem*. An absolute triumph, the lively comedy continues to delight audiences today. But it was too late for the playwright. After a brief literary life of some eight or nine years, George Farquhar, at the peak of his dramatic power, but miserable and ill with tuberculosis, died in poverty in a back garret in May 1707 at the age of twenty-nine.

Farquhar had first come to Lichfield in 1704, when he temporarily gave up his career as a playwright to sign up recruits for the army. He stayed at the George Inn, returning to it three years later when he used the inn as the setting, and actual townspeople as characters, in *The Beaux' Stratagem*.

The landlord of the George Inn became the prototype for Bonniface the innkeeper, while his daughter became Cherry, the innkeeper's daughter. French officers, prisoners of war, were quartered at the inn, and one of those lodgers was the basis for the character of Count Bellair.

Outside the inn, Farquhar became friendly with Sir Michael and Lady Biddulph (immortalized as Lady Bountiful). He used their country house at Elmhurst as the model for Lady Bountiful's home, and Sir Michael's amusing servant, Thomas Bond, he reproduced as Sullen's servant.

Even without Farquhar's characters and allusions, Lichfield warrants a visit. Worthy of exploration are the Gothic cathedral with its three spires, the Tudor St. John's Hospital, and the Roman site of Letocetum at Wall. But Lichfield is distinguished by the

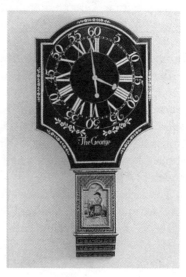

The George Inn, Lichfield, where George Farquhar (1678-1707) stayed while signing up recruits for the army and establishing the setting used in his two major plays, *The Recruiting Officer* and *The Beaux' Stratagem*

significant number of varied literary links which dominate and enliven the city.

Lichfield is first of all the birthplace of Samuel Johnson, in 1709, in a house now open to the public and known as the Samuel Johnson Birthplace Museum. His connection has been the source of a continual influx of pilgrims. James Boswell and Hester Thrale were among the first of a long line of admirers to journey to the shrine. In 1855 it inspired a visit from Nathaniel Hawthorne. The American author expressed rapture at being able to place his hand on the balustrade and his foot on the steps "where Johnson's hand and foot must many a time have been."

When Johnson lived in Lichfield, he was himself inspired by Joseph Addison's presence in the town. Born in 1652, Addison— poet, essayist, critic, and founder of *The Spectator*—lived in a house near the cathedral when his father was Dean of Lichfield. To augment the illustrious list of writers with the name of George Farquhar is to further enhance Lichfield's literary reputation.

With a location in the English Midlands, 123 miles from London, Lichfield also makes a convenient geographical center for additional literary pilgrimages. It is a relatively easy matter to travel from George Farquhar's Lichfield to George Eliot's Nuneaton, for example. Or to indulge in exploration of Arnold Bennett's Five Towns around Stoke-on-Trent. Or Housman's Shropshire. Or . . . the possibilities are endless.

But why go far afield? All can be savored from the George Hotel, which has of course been refurbished since the opening years of the eighteenth century when George Farquhar frequented it and when it was a staging post for coaches linking Lichfield with London, York, Bristol, and Chester. (Perhaps Farquhar first stopped here in 1697 when he left Ireland at the age of twenty and landed in Chester.)

The former hostelry retains its cobbled courtyard, making it easy to imagine the landlord in *The Beaux' Stratagem* being awakened by the arrival of unexpected guests:

282

"Coming, coming—A Coach and six foaming Horses at this Time o'Night! Some great Man, as the saying is, for he scorns to travel with other People."

It also boasts of good food and local draught bitters. Again, the landlord attributes his state of well being to the local ale, which Farquhar describes as "smooth as oil, sweet as milk, clear as amber, and strong as brandy." One final and appropriate tribute may be offered in words expressed by a newly-arrived guest in *The Beaux' Stratagem*:

> I have heard your Town of Lichfield much fam'd for ale, I think I'll taste that.

The two beaux, who devise a stratagem to obtain rich wives by posing as lord and footman, speak of leaving Lichfield for other places if their fortune-hunting scheme fails. It does not fail. They find beauty and wealth, and the amiable Aimwell stays on to enjoy his newfound happiness.

It might be construed as an invitation to the tourist to follow the example and stay on. The descendants of the affable hero might yield promising new material for a novel or a twelve-part television serial. The inspiration is there. To Lichfield and its hospitality we already owe one of the finest plays in English literature.

THE GEORGE INN
Bird Street
Lichfield
Staffordshire WS13 6PR

Telephone: (01543) 414822   Fax: (01543) 415817

38 bedrooms, all with private bathrooms, television, telephone, and tea- and coffee-making facilities.

JOHN GALSWORTHY

at

The Shakespeare
Stratford-upon-Avon
Warwickshire

And to each of us there will be some ingle-
nook where the spirit of our country most
inhabits, where the fire of hearth and home
glows best, and draws us with its warmth
from wanderings bodily or spiritual.

—"The Islands of the Blessed" in *A Sheaf* (1916)

Although he was obsessed with the idea of writing, John Galsworthy had trained for a career in law. Born in 1867, he was educated at Harrow and Oxford and qualified as a barrister; but he remained singularly unenthusiastic about the legal profession. The vocation he wanted was not the one his lawyer-father had pressed on him.

After being admitted to the bar, Galsworthy embarked on a series of voyages in 1892. The extensive travels around the world were motivated somewhat by his father's desire for him to acquire a background of maritime and international law. On the return journey to England, he met the first mate, who was to have an enormous influence on him—Joseph Conrad. Conrad had with him the unfinished manuscript of his first novel, *Almayer's Folly*. They became lifelong friends, and both were destined to embark on literary seas. Back in England, any notion of a career in law was totally abandoned.

Ada Galsworthy, the woman who was to become his wife, was a further influence. When Galsworthy expressed to her his inner-most desire to be a writer if only he had the gift, she made the sensitive and inspiring remark, "But you are just the person to write. Why don't you?"

Ada's marriage to John's first cousin was a dismal failure, and she was extremely unhappy. She and John met frequently, and she continued to encourage him in his new task. John became committed to both Ada and his writing. His art flourished, as did their relationship. By September 1895, they were lovers. By 1897, his cherished wish to become an author was realized with publication of his first piece of fiction, *From the Four Winds*. But not until the death in December 1904 of his father, the model for old Jolyon of *The Forsyte Saga*, did Ada feel able to face the scandal of divorce. On the very day on which the divorce decree was issued, 23 September 1905, they were married.

The year 1906 marked a double success for John Galsworthy. He was at the peak of his writing career, having published his most famous novel, *The Man of Property*, and produced his highly successful first play, *The Silver Box*. He continued to write in both genres to high acclaim, describing the world he knew and exposing social evils. Altogether, he produced twenty-seven plays, twenty novels, and nearly twenty volumes of collected pieces including poems.

His most important work was the series of novels concerning the Forsyte family. *The Man of Property* together with *In Chancery* (1920) and *To Let* (1921) came out in 1922 as a trilogy entitled *The Forsyte Saga* and made him world famous at fifty-five. His last six novels formed the second and third of the vast trilogies, as he continued the history of the Forsyte family.

The BBC created a resurgence of interest in Galsworthy by producing a lengthy television serialization of *The Forsyte Chronicles* for the centenary of his birth in 1967. The twenty-six episode dramatization, enjoyed by millions the world over, was repeated by popular demand the following year.

Galsworthy's plays dramatized the world of ideas and made effective comments on social issues. *The Silver Box*, dealing with class justice, illustrated the different treatments meted out by the law to a rich man and a poor man. *Strife* (1909) depicted the effects and agonies of a strike at a Cornish tin mine. *Justice* (1910) was instrumental in reforming the prison system when it led Home Secretary Winston Churchill to end the practice of solitary confinement as punishment for all prisoners in the first part of their prison sentences.

It was his strong social conscience that brought him to the Shakespeare Hotel in Stratford-on-Avon. A frequent traveler who often escaped on holidays in England or abroad, Galsworthy also did much traveling to various English cities to attend performances of his plays. But when he came to Stratford in 1916 he was there to read a paper at a conference on how to plan for eventual peace.

Galsworthy was made despondent by the war, its casualities, and the endless debates about the amount of commitment needed to win the war. The paper he read for the National Life of the Allied Countries, "The Islands of the Blessed," invoked patriotism, moral standards, and ideals needed for a better future. It was published in *A Sheaf,* a volume of essays dealing with a variety of topics from the treatment of animals to prisons and punishment and ending with "The Islands of the Blessed."

Galsworthy recorded in his diary that the paper presented on 5 August 1916 to an audience of about two hundred forty was well received. After lunch at the hotel, he toured Stratford visiting Hall's Croft, which he described as a "beautiful old house, once Susanna Hall's, Shakespeare's sister." Susanna Hall was actually the Bard's daughter, who lived there with her husband, Dr. John Hall.

On this first visit to Stratford, on the 4th and 5th of August, the Galsworthys lodged in The Winter's Tale bedroom of the Shakespeare Hotel. The hotel remains a convenient location for visiting the Stratford sights associated with Shakespeare as well as the Royal Shakespeare Theatre, a modern edifice of 1932 in a prominent setting on the riverside. And Stratford itself remains a picturesque town filled with timber-framed buildings. The poet was born on 23 April 1564 in one such timbered house, now preserved as a museum by the Shakespeare Birthplace Trust. Only the foundations remain of New Place, the house in which he lived after becoming a successful playwright, but an Elizabethan knot garden makes it a delightful site. Shakespeare died in 1616 and lies

John Galsworthy (1867-1933) and the Shakespeare Hotel, Stratford-on-Avon, where he read a paper at a conference

buried in Holy Trinity Church, under the chancel, with Susanna and John Hall.

Among the plethora of charming buildings contributing to the enormous character of Stratford-upon-Avon is the Shakespeare Hotel. Originally three separate buildings, it was gradually expanded to become one of the largest hotels in town. With an exterior of nine gables and a timbered facade, the hotel dates back to at least 1637. In Galsworthy's time, it was owned by Annie Justins, the town's first mayor. Now owned as a Forte Heritage hotel, it proudly maintains history and tradition. Antique furnishings and open fireplaces may even recall the words Galsworthy spoke in Stratford as he looked toward "some ingle-nook where the spirit of our country most inhabits, where the fire of hearth and home glows best. . ."

Galsworthy refused a knighthood because of his conviction that men of letters who write criticism of life and philosophy should not accept titles or rewards but should remain independent. Other awards and honors piled up. He may have refused a knighthood, but he accepted the Order of Merit. He was awarded honorary degrees from over half a dozen universities. And near the end of his life, he received the Nobel Prize for Literature. However, he was too seriously ill to attend the ceremonies in Stockholm on 10 December and died the following month, on 31 January 1933.

THE SHAKESPEARE
Chapel Street
Stratford-upon-Avon
Warwickshire CV37 6ER

Telephone: (01789) 294771   Fax: (01789) 415411

Seventy bedrooms all have tiled and well-lit bathrooms with tubs and good showers; each room bears the name of a Shakespearean play or character; and 23 rooms are designated non-smoking.

The David Garrick Restaurant, with Elizabethan decor, offers a pre-theatre menu.

Public rooms have open fireplaces, antique furnishings, low-beamed ceilings, flagstone floors, and old-world charm.

EAST ANGLIA

CHARLES DICKENS

at

The Great White Horse Hotel
Ipswich
Suffolk

In the main street of Ipswich. . .stands an
inn known far and wide by the appellation
of The Great White Horse, rendered the
more conspicuous by a stone statue of some
rampacious animal with flowing mane and
tail, distantly resembling an insane cart-
horse, which is elevated above the principal
door. The Great White Horse is famous in
the neighbourhood, in the same degree as a
prize ox, or county paper-chronicled turnip,
or unwieldy pig—for its enormous size.

—*Pickwick Papers*

Charles Dickens is associated with more geographical locations
than almost any other author and slept in more places than George
Washington. In Broadstairs alone, where he wrote *Nicholas
Nickleby* and *Bleak House* among others, so many plaques abound
attesting to his residence within, that one plaque facetiously points
out that Dickens did *not* live there. His job as a journalist gave him
many opportunities to visit a variety of places.

Although born in Portsmouth on 7 February 1812, in a house which is now the Charles Dickens Birthplace Museum, his happy childhood years were spent in Kent. The family moved to Chatham when Charles was five, and he explored thoroughly the Kentish area all around, including nearby Rochester. He roamed through town and dockyard, watched ships sailing down the Medway out to sea, and examined Rochester's Norman cathedral and its ruined castle. He sometimes took long walks with his father in which they climbed the long hill to ramble through Cobham woods, ending up by Gad's Hill, scene of Falstaff's revels. There they admired the rose-brick country house known as Gad's Hill Place.

He wrote about all these places in his books, thereby immortalizing them. In later life he returned rich and famous and able to purchase the very house he had coveted, Gad's Hill Place, where he lived for the last twelve years of his life until his death on 8 June 1870.

But for the young boy, his years in London meant misery. In the winter of 1822 the family moved to the city where the struggle with poverty was unremitting. When his father was arrested for debt and thrust into the Marshalsea debtors' prison in Southwark in February 1824, Charles was thrust into manhood. He was not allowed to continue his schooling and bitterly resented the work he did at Warren's Blacking Factory (later described in *David Copperfield*) pasting labels onto bottles of the factory's product in a rat-infested warehouse by the river for a few shillings a week. He felt betrayed and humiliated and abandoned. Eventually, through a small and lucky legacy, the debt was paid, and John Dickens took on work as a political reporter while his son resumed schooling.

With a strong need now for success and security, Charles became a clerk in a firm of solicitors and at the same time emulated his father by learning shorthand. He mastered the system in less than a year, and the skill enabled him to do freelance legal reporting in courts known as Doctors' Commons, no longer in existence. He took down every word in the cases assigned to him, transcribing his symbols into reports and sometimes using even the most trivial incidents in his own writings.

After two years he became a newspaper reporter for the *True Sun*, then for the *Mirror of Parliament*. He recorded speeches made in the House of Commons and reproduced them verbatim. His speed and accuracy led to his appointment within two years as political reporter for the prestigious *Morning Chronicle*. Meanwhile, he wrote short pieces for the *Monthly Magazine* and the *Morning Chronicle* to which he appended the pseudonym Boz. One of the sketches contains a description of Doctors' Commons, "where they grant marriage-licences to love-sick couples and divorces to unfaithful ones, register the wills of people who have any property to leave, and punish hasty gentlemen who call ladies by unpleasant names." The collection was published in volume form as the *Sketches of Boz*. Years later, references to Doctors' Commons appeared in *Pickwick Papers, Oliver Twist, David Copperfield*, and *Master Humphrey's Clock*.

With his first attempt at authorship, he was well on the way to becoming a great writer. The year was 1836, the year also of his marriage to Catherine Hogarth. Charles Dickens himself took out a marriage licence at Doctors' Commons.

He was to become a brilliant literary artist as well as a concerned and compassionate human being. Exploration of London's slums and of England's factory towns made him work and write to help victims of industrial civilization by calling attention to their plight. The marriage was to be an unhappy one which filled his life with domestic misery, although he remained attached to his children. But his rise to the highest literary position in the land was meteoric, and by 1848 he was an international celebrity.

As a young journalist on the staff of the *Chronicle*, he was sent out into the provinces to report on elections and political speeches. Fortunately, he loved travel. Coaches and coaching inns became part of his way of life, a life which shows up as pretty little scenes on tin biscuit boxes or on greeting cards but which is actually not so romantic as those scenes would have the onlooker believe. But the young reporter did find excitement and invigoration in the change of vistas, and he found an opportunity for adapting his experiences to his writing purposes.

Charles Dickens
(1812-1870) used
The Great White
Horse Hotel,
Ipswich, in
Pickwick Papers

His impressions, full of accurate observations and originality, ultimately found an outlet as he wrote a stage coach traveler's view of the country starring Mr. Pickwick. Printed in monthly parts, this revolutionary practice in publishing engaged a large reading public attracted to the often hilarious experiences of his amusing characters, especially Sam Weller. The episodic *Pickwick Papers* of 1837 launched his immensely successful career as a novelist. Shortly thereafter came *Oliver Twist, Nicholas Nickleby, The Old Curiosity Shop*, and *Barnaby Rudge*—five books in five years.

As a traveler, Dickens seems to have relished in particular the welcome produced by a good inn for the guest who, after the hardships of a wearying or cold coach ride, is in great need of the comforts of a blazing log fire and good food and wine in a friendly atmosphere. He knew a variety of inns and appreciated the character and individuality of each. From the decrepit public houses to the smart hotels—he wrote about them all in his diary, in his letters, and in his books. And because he mentioned them, they became famous.

He described his travels and the inns he frequented with his reporter's discriminating eye for detail and with honesty, both for the comforts and the discomforts. He describes the George in Grantham, where he went to gather material for *Nicholas Nickleby*, as "the very best inn I have ever put up at." But he was rather unkind to the Great White Horse in Ipswich, where he went in 1835 to report on the Suffolk elections at Ipswich and Sudbury. The opportunity supplied him with his Eatanswill of *Pickwick Papers* and gave him the material for his novel.

Travelers receive their first impressions of an inn and judge it initially by outer appearance, and Dickens introduces the readers of *Pickwick Papers* to the Great White Horse by citing its location "in the main street of Ipswich. . ." followed by an impression of the exterior. Today's visitor might view the stone statue of his "rampacious animal" as a gentle horse who acts as a jolly signboard to indicate the name of the haven to be found within.

After maligning the facade, Dickens goes on to castigate the menu and the service which greeted the new arrivals: "After the lapse of an hour, a bit of fish and a steak were served up to the travellers, and when the dinner was cleared away, [they]... ordered a bottle of the worst possible port wine, at the highest possible price...."

Dickens must have known the interior of the inn well for he wrote in *Pickwick Papers*: "Never were such labyrinths of uncarpeted passages, such clusters of mouldy, ill-lighted rooms, such huge numbers of small dens for eating or sleeping in, beneath any one roof, as are collected together between the four walls of the Great White Horse Inn." His Mr. Pickwick gets into difficulty because of the rambling geography of the inn which thoroughly confused him when he tried to retrieve the watch he had left downstairs: "The more stairs Mr. Pickwick went down, the more stairs there seemed to be to ascend, and again and again, when Mr. Pickwick got into some narrow passage, and began to congratulate himself on having gained the ground-floor, did another flight of stairs appear before his astonished eyes.... Passage after passage did he explore; room after room did he peep into...."

He recovered his watch but not his way back and entered the wrong bedchamber where he found himself sharing the bedroom of a strange lady with curl-papers in her hair: "Mr. Pickwick almost fainted with horror and dismay. Standing before the dressing-glass was a middle-aged lady, in yellow curl-papers, busily engaged in brushing what ladies call their 'back-hair.' "

Dickens stayed at the Great White Horse for several weeks, and the experience of being in the wrong bedroom may well have been his own. That might explain his prejudice and his criticisms. Since the white horse which highsteps over the portico is tamer than the animal he describes, perhaps his derogatory comments in general could be tamed down as well.

Dickens' comments notwithstanding, the hotel is alive and well and thriving in Ipswich, a town located some seventy miles from London and worth a visit in its own right.

Situated on the River Orwell Estuary, it has always been a flourishing seaport. Chaucer refers to it in the Prologue to the *Canterbury Tales* when he describes the pompous Merchant of Ipswich:

He wolde the see were kept for anythyng
Bitwixe Middleburgh and Orewelle.

Appropriately, Dickens loved the sea and sea towns. But the heart of Ipswich today has largely lost its seafaring atmosphere. The narrow, congested streets arranged in a medieval pattern contain interesting old buildings everywhere. One particularly fine architectural example is the Ancient House in the Buttermarket, a gorgeous specimen of an ornate plasterwork decoration characteristic of East Anglia and known as "pargeting." Amidst the distinctive old buildings is the centrally-located hotel which makes the most of the Dickens association.

The inn, well over four hundred years old, has the charm of age. Thanks to the efforts of the Dickens Fellowship, this galleried inn has been preserved with the remains of the timber-framed courtyard inside. And carpets instead of cobblestones contribute to the comfort of the feet and to the inviting, pleasant atmosphere.

The Great White Horse Hotel treasures a connection which would be envied by the grandest of hotels. It proudly capitalizes on the faults Dickens attributed to it and uses them for advertising, showing off Mr. Pickwick's bedroom where the famous adventure is supposed to have occurred. Actually, it is a fine room and even Dickens relents: "It was a tolerably large double-bedded room, with a fire; upon the whole, a more comfortable-looking apartment than Mr. Pickwick's short experience of the accommodations of the Great White Horse had led him to expect."

Everywhere are Pickwick pictures and the Pickwick spirit. Yes, the hotel does have tortuous passages, no doubt more noticeable because of Mr. Pickwick's experience. Furthermore, meandering corridors and staircases are typical of any English hotel with a history.

Such notables are supposed to have stayed here as King George II and Admiral Nelson and Lady Hamilton, but the words written by Dickens give him the dominant association and give the hotel immortality. With such a background, the hotel will no doubt continue to thrive without ever losing the modifier of its title—"Great"!

THE GREAT WHITE HORSE HOTEL
Tavern Street
Ipswich
Suffolk IP1 3AH

Telephone: (01473) 256558   Fax: (01473) 253396

62 bedrooms, all with en-suite facilities, include single and double rooms and three suites.

The Pickwick Room maintains a Dickens style with its antique furnishings and a four-poster bed.

The foyer or reception area, formerly the open courtyard of this coaching inn, is a pleasant venue for snacks or drinks.

The Tavern Bar is adjacent.

Nickleby's Restaurant offers a wide selection of food from table d'hote or a la carte menus.

Just a ten-minute walk from Railway Station.

LORD BYRON

at

Swynford Paddocks

Six Mile Bottom

Cambridgeshire

For thee, my own sweet sister, in thy heart
I know myself secure, as thou in mine;
We were and are—I am, even as thou art—
Beings who ne'er each other can resign. . .

—*Epistle to Augusta*

"Try everything once," said Sir Thomas Beecham, "except incest and folk dancing." It is not known whether Byron ever tried folk dancing.

When Byron and Augusta met in 1813 in London, the attraction was strong and mutual. The graceful couple quickly became steady companions and shared a busy social life. To an outsider, the situation might have seemed to contain all of the elements of a perfect romance. Never mind that she was twenty-nine and five years older than he. Never mind that she was married. Or that she had three children. The problem was that they were brother and sister.

Her mother died shortly after Augusta was born, and the infant was brought up in the care of her maternal grandmother, Lady Holderness. In 1785 her father remarried, and her half-brother George Gordon Byron, born on 22 January 1788, was the son of that second marriage. "Mad Jack," as their father was known, died when Byron was three.

Brother and sister grew up apart and shared none of the ordinary experiences of siblings. They had met earlier, but his mother discouraged contact with Augusta. They had corresponded, but exchanges became infrequent from 1807 when she married her cousin, Colonel George Leigh, and ceased in 1809 when Byron left on his grand tour—his Childe Harold's Pilgrimage.

Back in England after his two-year sojourn, communication between Augusta and Byron resumed with her letter of sympathy on the death of his mother. He was a sensational overnight success with the publication of the first two cantos of *Childe Harold* and became the lion of London society. Augusta was full of curiosity about her "baby Byron." They arranged to meet.

Hers was not a happy marriage. Her wandering and worthless husband was a selfish egotist, a spendthrift and a gambler, who was always in financial difficulty. Appointed equerry, Colonel Leigh managed race horses at Newmarket for the Prince of Wales, who gave him the conveniently-located house in the hamlet of Six Mile Bottom. He was usually busy at the races and away from home. Left alone with her three small children, Augusta felt neglected and bored. On a visit to a friend in London, she and Byron met and found that they shared not only the same father but a deep affection, which was to grow into a permanent and passionate love.

They spent most of the summer of 1813 together, and Byron made several visits to her Cambridgeshire home. He followed her to Six Mile Bottom within a few days of her departure from London. After his second visit, he persuaded her to come back with him to London. That summer they decided to remain together always and planned to flee to the continent. Lady Melbourne, his confidante, who was privy to the escape plan, helped to dissuade him by arguing that it was a "crime for which there was no salvation in this world, whatever there might be in the next."

Byron's regular visits to Six Mile Bottom continued. He often wrote outside in the summer garden under a huge tree which came to be known as "Byron's tree" but, alas, not destined for the kind of immortality alloted to Milton's mulberry in Cambridge. Byron's beech was felled some twenty years ago and only the rise in the ground from the huge roots remains to mark the spot where he worked on *The Corsair.* His tale of incestuous love features Medora, a name later chosen for Augusta's fourth child, as one of the characters. The hero, a "man of loneliness and mystery," was identified by many as the author:

> He left a Corsair's name to other times,
> Linked with one virtue, and a thousand crimes.

Their love continued unabated, and in January of the following year, Byron took Augusta to his ancestral Newstead Abbey home, just as any loving husband might give a pregnant wife a holiday break. There they were alone and extremely happy—and snowbound for ten days. They carved their names on a tree. There is no doubt that they adored each other. The blissful holiday over, she returned to Six Mile Bottom; he, to London. He visited her again in March, then returned the following April when Elizabeth Medora Leigh was born. The Colonel was away in Yorkshire, but Byron came to Six Mile Bottom to be with her.

They both agreed that he should take the expedient step of securing a wife. Marriage would deflect gossip. After proposing to Annabella Milbanke, he was again at Six Mile Bottom. His impending marriage seemed doomed before it took place. He hesitated about going to see his future wife, and he hesitated about the marriage. But the wedding finally took place on 2 January 1815, a date that enabled him to spend the preceding Christmas with Augusta.

The honeymoon was dreadful and the aftermath was worse. The newlyweds were Augusta's guests at Six Mile Bottom for some two weeks in March. His behavior towards his wife was cruel from the beginning. He humiliated the young bride by sending her to bed early, indicating that he preferred his sister's company. He hinted strongly at his incestuous affair. He once pointed to Medora and announced that she was his own child.

Augusta returned the visit to the Byrons in April and stayed at their fashionable London address, which was filled with domestic strife. Annabella left him after their child Augusta Ada was born in December. She tried to have her husband certified insane. Augusta was dragged into the scandalous proceedings, which ended in a deed of separation in April 1816. On the 23rd of that

Lord Byron (1788-1824)
and Swynford Paddocks,
where he lived with his
half-sister Augusta Leigh

month, he left England, having said good-bye to Augusta a week earlier. Abroad, "the wandering outlaw of his own dark mind" turned to his poetry. Augusta continued to occupy his thoughts, and his poems include the *Epistle to Augusta:*

> My sister! my sweet sister! if a name
> Dearer and purer were, it should be thine;
> Mountains and seas divide us, but I claim
> No tears, but tenderness to answer mine:
> Go where I will, to me thou art the same—
> A loved regret which I would not resign,
> There yet are two things in my destiny,—
> A world to roam through, and a home with thee.

But he was destined never to see his beloved Augusta—or England—again. He traveled to Switzerland and Italy, where he produced among other works, the third and fourth cantos of *Childe Harold, Don Juan, Beppo, Manfred,* and *Mazeppa.* He set out in 1823 to join the Greek insurgents in their fight for freedom and died of fever in Missolonghi, Greece, on 19 April 1824.

Byron's biography contains many unsolved problems. While it may never be known with absolute certainty that Byron slept with Augusta, it is certainly known that he slept in Augusta's home in Six Mile Bottom.

The Byron spirit still lives in that house, formerly known simply as the Lodge. Renamed and remodelled, it is now a country-house hotel called Swynford Paddocks. It sits at the end of a long drive amidst large trees in pleasant grounds. With gabled roof and prominent chimneys, and with attractive greenery which partly covers the white exterior, it still gives the impression of a large private home. The interior is tastefully decorated throughout, and the lounge is furnished with antique pieces.

The present proprietor admits that his purpose in purchasing the property with some forty acres of paddocks was to make it a profitable stud. The hotel aspect came as something of an after-thought. But what started as a comfortable home for the owner with a few rooms for guests has become a comfortable house for guests, with the owner residing in a smaller house elsewhere in the grounds.

The approach to Swynford Paddocks from London, fifty-eight miles to the south, passes through the hamlet with the suggestive name of Six Mile Bottom. Actually, the name derives from the fact that it stands in a hollow six miles from Newmarket.

This area of England, famous for horses and horse-racing since the time of Charles II who loved the sport, offers a variety of activities. If walking around the stud results in boredom, there is the possibility of visiting the Newmarket racecourse. There is always the lovely countryside to be enjoyed by taking drives, as did Augusta, across the Devil's Dyke to the town of Newmarket or over the Gog Magog Hills with their prehistoric Iron Age hill-fort of Wandlebury Ring. Cambridge is just nine miles away, and stately homes such as Anglesey Abbey are open to the public. But one can just as easily stay indoors and imbibe the Byron atmosphere of Swynford Paddocks.

The management displays great awareness of the scandalous scenes played out in its premises well over a century and a half ago. Huge, dominating portraits of Byron, Augusta, and Medora hang on the staircase wall. The extremely comfortable bedrooms are supplied with such amenities as fresh flowers and books, among which is a biography of Medora Leigh, *Byron's Daughter*; the guest may choose between sin or sanctity, biography or Bible, for bedtime reading.

Swynford Paddocks dispels dark and gloomy accusations of dreaded incest in its bright, cheerful, and elegant atmosphere. Those able to create their own canto for a private pilgrimage are in for a treat. Byron traveled in style. It is fitting that those who follow his travels can do so stylishly at Swynford Paddocks.

SWYNFORD PADDOCKS
Six Mile Bottom
Cambridgeshire CB8 0UE

Telephone: (01638) 570234   Fax: (01638) 570283

Fifteen bedrooms—all with bathroom, television, trouser press, mini-bar, and room service—are individually decorated, giving each a character of its own.

The restaurant offers culinary excellence with a liaison of English and French dishes, changing its menu regularly to take advantage of seasonal fare. Wines too are distinguished, and a few are unique, including some pleasant English wines.

The Medora Room, with a large boardroom table and comfortable armchairs, is the venue for business meetings of up to twenty delegates.

Garden, tennis, putting, croquet.

THE NORTH OF ENGLAND

AGATHA CHRISTIE

at

The Old Swan Hotel
Harrogate
North Yorkshire

This next little fact—no! Ah, that is
curious! There is something missing—a
link in the chain that is not there.

—*The Mysterious Affair at Styles*

How Agatha Christie came to write is no mystery, for she tells it in
her autobiography. A challenge from her older sister ("I bet you
can't write a good detective story"), together with her love for story
telling, produced in 1915 what has been called "one of the finest
firsts ever written," *The Mysterious Affair at Styles*. From the time
it was published in 1920, the prolific Agatha produced at least a
book a year. "A sausage machine, a perfect sausage machine," she
has called herself.

A great deal of mystery surrounds a particular episode in the life
of Agatha Christie when the lady vanished, only to be discovered
eventually at a Harrogate hotel. One essential clue to her disappearance, which reveals something of her nature, might be that, with a
penchant for titles that intrigue, she chooses for the story of her life
a title that could hardly be simpler— *An Autobiography*—and
she omits any mention of her stay in Harrogate. The silence is
deafening, the mystery deep. Why the use of the indefinite article?
Why the omission? It is as if she shuns calling attention to herself

as anyone very special. Yet, the case does not call for the uncanny abilities of a Hercule Poirot to solve the riddle and uncover the facts which make up the account of her disappearance.

Agatha Miller and Archibald Christie were married in 1914 and divorced in 1928. In 1926 she was under considerable strain brought about by the death of her mother, the pressures of constant work, and the impending breakup of her marriage. That year, on the evening of 4 December, she left her London house in a highly emotional state, after learning that her husband had left for the home of his mistress, and she drove off; her abandoned car was found in Surrey with absolutely no trace of the driver.

A search for the missing Agatha ensued. As if dealing with one of her own bizarre plots in which the author became the unlucky victim, the public suspected foul play. Headlines screamed. One newspaper offered a reward. Policemen and amateurs scoured the countryside for clues. A nationwide search ended with the tip that she was at the Swan Hydro (as the Old Swan was then known) in Harrogate. It was revealed that she had in fact been staying there for nine days under an assumed name, the name of the woman who was later to become Colonel Christie's second wife. The disclosure made sensational news. The press capitalized on it. The public, perhaps feeling resentful and cheated by a non-tragic, anticlimactic outcome, claimed it was all a publicity stunt. Most likely, it was an actual case of amnesia.

Agatha Christie was a shy and modest person who always valued her privacy. When the disappearance of her happiness proved more than she could cope with, her mind ordered her own disappearance.

Why Harrogate? Why not! The author once said that the best way of getting down to work is in a very bad hotel where there is nothing else to do but write, for there are no distracting comforts to indulge in, no good meals or interesting guests. But she was not there to write when she sought refuge at a very good hotel in Harrogate. In fact, she was an entertaining and charming guest whose engaging personality was enjoyed by those present. She even played the piano with the orchestra and seemed to be having quite a happy holiday in Harrogate.

Agatha Christie
(1890-1976) and
The Old Swan,
Harrogate, formerly
the Swan Hydro,
where the lady who
vanished in 1926
was discovered

The possibility for a happy and healthy holiday is the reason for the existence of Harrogate in the first place. The history of the elegant spa town begins when the insignificant hamlets of High and Low Haregate were destined to become a new and important town after a chalybeate (iron) spring, called Tewit Well was discovered there in 1571. Discoveries of other mineral springs followed. With the publication in 1626 of a book by Dr. Edmund Deane extolling the virtues of the mineral spirits, crowds began to pour in to pour out the recommended waters of the Old Sulphur Well. Daniel Defoe visited in 1724 and wrote of a pleasant time in this "desolate out-of-the-World Place." But the place became more and more worldly.

Accommodation had to be provided for the enthusiastic hordes who followed the enthusiastic reports of many physicians, and the historic and elegant Old Swan Hotel was built in the beginning of the eighteenth century to provide for the fashionable clientele.

Constructed of Yorkshire stone, the Old Swan retains its dignity in a town which has become a center for tourism and conferences now that the fashion for taking the waters has declined. Nevertheless, the elements of the spa town are still there to be seen and enjoyed—the Royal Baths Assembly Rooms, the prettily-domed Tewit Well, the many gardens, the long glass-covered walk known as the Sun Colonnade, the Royal Hall, and the Royal Pump Room, which now serves as a museum and supplies samples of the smelly sulphur water which started a social trend.

The grand hotel offers excellent service, good food, and over a hundred attractive rooms. It offers also the atmosphere of a stately home as it pays tribute to the past and honors one famous literary guest by its naming of the Agatha Christie Library Restaurant.

The hotel's situation near the Yorkshire Dales presents an endless array of attractions to explore. But when Agatha Christie was found there in 1926, she was exploring inner needs, and she was afterwards able to return to a normal and productive existence.

In 1930, Agatha Christie married the archeologist Max Mallowan, after which she began a happy life which included her appointment in 1971 as Dame of the British Empire. She died in 1976 at the age of eighty-six.

During her hard-working life, she produced over eighty titles, contriving to have her eightieth title appear on her eightieth birthday. Her books are enormously popular and are outsold only by the Bible and Shakespeare. Her films and plays are equally successful with *The Mousetrap* (which opened in 1952) setting a record as the longest running stage play ever. Her books, translated into over a hundred foreign languages, are known around the world.

The detective story may be considered an ephemeral literary form, and critics may ponder the reasons for her vast success and permanence. But it does not require the skill of Hercule Poirot muttering about his little grey cells to solve this mystery: Dame Agatha creates a puzzle full of suspense and supplies a satisfying solution which restores order to a chaotic world. Simply, she offers a good read.

THE OLD SWAN HOTEL
Swan Road
Harrogate
North Yorkshire HG1 2SR

Telephone: (01423) 500055   Fax: (01423) 501154

The four-star hotel has 135 bedrooms and suites, many with garden views; all have private bathrooms, television with in-house films, and a welcome tray for coffee or tea.

The Garden Room suite and the Red Lounge, with its baronial fireplace, contribute to a stately home atmosphere. The Wedgwood Room is for banquets for up to 400 guests, while the Garden Room Ballroom Suite is ideal for gala celebrations.

Four Super Sleuth Weekends per year continue the mystery tradition. The hotel is located in peaceful gardens near city center, 208 miles from London.

WILKIE COLLINS

at

The Royal Hotel
Whitby
North Yorkshire

Eastward was the grey majesty of the sea,
hushed in breathless calm; the horizon line
invisibly melting into the monotonously
misty sky; the idle ships shadowy and still
on the idle water.

—No Name

A born storyteller, William Wilkie Collins was born in London on 8 January 1824. He was apprenticed to a firm of tea importers at the age of seventeen, later studied law, and even appeared on stage as an actor. But he was always interested in writing, and his sketch called *The Last Stage Coachman* was published when he was nineteen and still in the tea business. He eventually made the decision to devote himself to writing as a profession.

The writing career of Wilkie Collins spans forty years and shows a yield of over twenty novels as well as novelettes, short stories, essays, and plays. But the large output of this popular Victorian novelist contained only two novels which have achieved status as classics, *The Woman in White* and *The Moonstone*.

His first book was a debt to his father, a successful landscape painter who died in 1847 leaving his son with the obligation of producing a biography. His journal contained words construed as a command: "I think it quite possible that my dear son, William Wilkie Collins, may be tempted, should it please God to spare his life beyond that of his father, to furnish the world with a memoir of my life. . . ." *Memoirs of the Life of William Collins, Esq., RA* was published in two volumes in 1848. The biography is disappointing to today's readers because so little is revealed about the author, who kept himself out of his father's picture.

In 1851 Wilkie Collins met Charles Dickens, who became a great friend. Dickens was then forty years old, and the friendship lasted until the death of the older man some twenty years later. Completely overshadowed by his friend, Collins wrote for *Household Words*, the periodical which Dickens had founded in 1850. They collaborated on stories which appeared in that publication as well as in *All the Year Round* which succeeded it. They went on holidays together on the Continent and in Britain. A walking tour in Cumberland made by the two in 1857 became a joint writing venture for *Household Words* in which it appeared as *The Lazy Tour of Two Idle Apprentices*.

Antomina was Wilkie Collins' first novel. Its reception at the time of publication in 1850 was full of critical and popular praise. There followed a series of novels and short stories in the 1850s, largely unknown today. But *Basil, Hide and Seek*, and *The Dead Secret* are a few of the commendable titles. *The Frozen Deep*, a drama of 1857, gave Dickens the idea for *A Tale of Two Cities*. Then *The Woman in White* began to appear in serial form in November 1859 and appeared in book form in 1860. It made Collins a celebrity. One envious rival publisher called it "the most popular novel of the century."

No Name, which followed in December 1860, tells an exciting story and deserves a better fate than the state of neglect to which it has been relegated. *Armadale* (1866) is another adventurous novel which T. S. Eliot commended for having "every merit that melodrama can have" and for "being never dull."

Of his works of the 1860s, *The Moonstone* (1868), an immediate and perennial success, has been singled out as the first English detective novel, and Dorothy L. Sayers has called it "probably the very finest detective story ever written." Charles Dickens paid the ultimate compliment by emulating it in *The Mystery of Edwin Drood*. Trollope was also influenced by it in his *The Eustace Diamonds*.

After 1870 Wilkie Collins' health, as well as the quality of his writing, declined. He was tortured by an illness diagnosed as rheumatic gout and became addicted to opium taken as a palliative for pain. The "all-powerful and all-merciful drug" had been discussed by Dr. Ezra Jennings of *The Moonstone*.

Despite his agony, Collins continued to write and remained a popular novelist, no doubt always aware of the single work which had established and maintained his reputation and popularity throughout his lifetime. After his death on 23 September 1889, these words were inscribed, according to his own directions, on his tombstone in the Kensal Green Cemetery: "Author of *The Woman in White* and other works of fiction."

Such are the basic facts of the literary life of Wilkie Collins. The facts of his private life are more difficult to ascertain. Collins was reluctant to allow his private life to become public knowledge. His close friends respected his wishes and remained silent. Many letters were destroyed, and certain biographical details were omitted from contemporary accounts. His life style was unconventional, indeed shocking, and could only be condemned by Victorian standards of morality.

In 1859 Collins met Caroline Elizabeth Graves with whom he lived for about eight years. He also formed a liaison with Martha Rudd, the mother of his three children. Caroline left and married Joseph Clow in October 1868 but returned to live with Collins in the early 1870s and remained with him until his death. She was the prototype for *The Woman in White*. The story of their meeting and how it inspired his great work is as melodramatic as anything he wrote.

Wilkie Collins and his brother Charles were accompanying their friend Millais home after a dinner given by Mrs. Collins, when a piercing female shriek from a nearby villa broke the peace of the summer evening. Then the iron garden gate opened and a beautiful young woman in white flowing drapery materialized. She paused briefly where the three men stood before running off to disappear into the moonlit night. Wilkie dashed out after the white luminescent figure and did not return to his waiting friends.

Wilkie Collins
(1824-1889) and the
Royal Hotel, Whitby,
where he went to stay
with Caroline Graves,
the original
'Woman in White'

The next day, Wilkie related to his friends her story: she had been imprisoned in the Regent's Park house which the threesome happened to be passing at the time of the scream. A man, perhaps her husband, used threats, restraints, or mesmerism to keep her captive. But that night, she managed to escape from the fortress and fled, pursued by Collins who reported her to be in a suicidal condition. Collins, entranced and haunted by the mysterious figure, followed her about all night to prevent harm.

Forty years after the fateful meeting, and ten years after the death of Wilkie Collins, *The Life of John Everett Millais* (1899) by J. G. Millais was published—another son fulfilling an obligation to a father. The account of the fantastic meeting with the woman in white is contained in that biography.

Further testimony is offered by the wife of Charles Collins who asserted in her old age that the distressed damsel of the Millais account was the same woman who came to live with Collins. She was Caroline, wife or widow of George Robert Graves. She was in her early twenties at the time of the meeting and had a daughter less than a year old. Caroline was to play an influential role in the life of Wilkie Collins.

Whether the incident is a product of the imagination or not, the novel of sensation which resulted was a sensational success. Collins became the celebrated author of a bestseller which was so popular that fashionable articles of clothing, perfumes and toilet accessories, and musical compositions were named Woman in White.

In great demand, Wilkie Collins had already begun his next novel, *No Name*, when he decided to leave the oppressive heat of London for a pleasant seaside location. In August 1861, he took a month's holiday with Caroline Graves, staying at the Royal Hotel in Whitby. That hotel did not, however, succumb to the fad of the day by renaming itself the Woman in White Hotel.

Whitby is on the northeast coast of England about twenty miles north of the more famous Scarborough. The Royal Hotel stands on the West Cliff overlooking the harbor of this fascinating old fishing port, once known for whaling. The view from the hotel takes in the East Cliff on which stands the ruined thirteenth-century

Whitby Abbey. A statue of Captain Cook, who lived in a cottage in Grape Lane near the abbey, looks out to the sea from the West Cliff which fronts on to a fine, sandy beach.

Built by the railway king George Hudson, the hotel developed a reputation for good service. It is described in *Reed's Illustrated Guide to Whitby* of 1854 as a "splendid establishment" in which "every attention is paid to the comfort and requirements of the visitor" and as a hotel which is "replete with accommodations for visitors."

Today, with six bars (including the Captain Cook Bar which pays tribute to the eighteenth-century explorer), with 135 rooms, and with ballrooms and conference facilities, the hotel can offer a coastal resort holiday to multitudes. In August 1861 it offered a holiday to Wilkie Collins and the woman in white.

From his pleasant room overlooking the harbor and the boats, Collins worked on his novel. . . From her window overlooking the harbor, the heroine of *No Name* watches ships glide slowly by, her hand clutching a bottle of laudanum. In a state of remorse and despair, she considers suicide and determines to leave the decision to chance. If an even number of ships pass by within a half hour, she will live; if an odd number, she will take the poison. It is a highly dramatic scene as she counts passing ships against passing time:

> . . .Twenty-five, twenty-six, twenty-seven, twenty-eight; and the next uneven number—the fatal Seven—glided into view. Two minutes to the end of the half-hour. And seven ships.
>
> Twenty-nine; and nothing followed in the wake of the seventh ship. The minute-hand of the watch moved on half-way to thirty—and still the white heaving sea was a misty blank. Without moving her head from the window, she took the poison in one hand, and raised the watch in the other. As the quick seconds counted each other out, her eyes, as quick as they, looked from the watch to the sea, from the sea to the watch— looked for the last time at the sea—

Collins continued to write—that is, when he was not distracted by the noise of dozens of children including the *"fourteen* young ones" of an English matron to whom he referred as a rabbit. He was further disturbed by a "brass band hired by the proprietor to play four hours a day." After spending most of the month at the hotel, he made the pronouncement that "working against noise is the hardest work of all" and returned to London. In fact, he became increasingly intolerant to noise and left his Harley Street home a few years later in search of quieter quarters.

One of his later novels, *The Haunted Hotel*, might have sufficed as a new name for the Royal Hotel which is haunted by the presence there of an important Victorian writer. The great exponent of the melodramatic tale has left us the mysteries of his stories and of his life. But there is relatively little mystery about Wilkie at Whitby.

Nor is there any mystery about his place in literary history if we take the word of T. S. Eliot who described him as a master of his genre: "There is no contemporary novelist who could not learn something from Collins in the art of interesting and exciting the reader. So long as novels are written, the possibilities of melodrama must from time to time be re-explored. The contemporary 'thriller' is in danger of becoming stereotyped. . .The resources of Wilkie Collins are, in comparison, inexhaustible."

THE ROYAL HOTEL
West Cliff
Whitby
North Yorkshire YO21 3HT

Telephone: (01947) 602234   Fax: (01947) 820355

Rooms: 135, most with private facilities, all with tea/coffee making facilities.

Amenities: Restaurant, six bars, cabaret nightly during summer season, television in lounges.

BEATRIX POTTER

at

Hardcragg Hall
Grange-over-Sands
Cumbria

The sun rose while they were crossing the
moor, a dazzle of light over the tops of the
hills. The sunshine crept down the slopes
into the peaceful green valleys, where little
white cottages nestled in gardens and
orchards.

—The Tale of Pigling Bland

Among the large and impressive group of famous poets and writers
associated with the English Lake District is Beatrix Potter. Her
Hill Top home in Near Sawrey is now a National Trust property
and is visited and enjoyed as a central symbol of her beloved Lake
District and the source of her delightful stories.

But Beatrix Potter also knew the seaside resort of Grange-over-
Sands on the southern shore of the Lake District. A journal entry
made as early as 1887 mentions a visit with her itinerant
parents to "Grange-over-Sands on Morecambe Bay." The Townley
family, who became good friends, lived there in a house known as
Hardcragg.

The sixteenth-century manor house then stood in open countryside and functioned as a farm. Now the road to Hardcragg Hall
Hotel goes gently uphill from the Main Street, through a built-up
area, and the view from the small white house overlooks slate
rooftops towards Morecambe Bay.

The cozy interior of the hotel, particularly when the crackling
log fire gives off warmth, still has original oak flooring and

paneled rooms. The paneled dining room was the original dining room. Upstairs are eight, prettily-furnished bedrooms. But how Beatrix Potter came to Hardcragg, or indeed to the Lake District, is another story.

Born in a genteel district of London on 28 July 1866 (in a house that was destroyed by bombing in 1940), Beatrix Potter learned to appreciate and love non-city life. She traveled a great deal from early childhood, as her wealthy parents were always off on holidays, always visiting or making the rounds of hotels. In the journal that she kept from the age of fifteen to thirty, Beatrix Potter made sensitive observations on such places as Exeter ("I am very fond of Exeter. . .it retains its primitive self-contained air of importance."); Weymouth ("Much surprised by the extent and dreariness of the New Forest"); and Stonehenge ("The first view of Stonehenge is disappointing, not because it is small, but because the place whereon it stands is so immense. The stones are large enough to satisfy anybody.").

Her ability to observe and record fine detail extended to the nature studies in which she immersed herself from childhood. Together with her brother Bertram, who was five years younger, she collected fossils, skeletons, and animals—dead or alive. Committed to the study of nature, she drew and painted pictures of animals and flowers and made regular visits to the South Kensington Museum to further her learning. She was in fact an amateur naturalist. Her knowledge and skill were put to good use many years later when she came to write and to illustrate her stories.

Beatrix developed a special love for the north country and responded fully to its way of life. The rental of the turreted Victorian Wray Castle on the western shore of Lake Windermere near Hawkshead provided the opportunity for her to explore and learn about the lakes and fells of those poetic parts.

The Potters stayed in one rented property after another in their frequent summer holidays in the Lake District and were in and around Near Sawrey several times. Lakefield, now the handsome Ees-Wyke Country House Hotel, was a favorite place; and the village of Sawry was to become the source

Beatrix Potter
(1866-1943) and
Hardcragg Hall,
Grange-over-Sands,
which inspired
*The Tale of Pigling
Bland*

of her greatest fulfillment and happiness. Situated near Esthwaite Water, which she considered "the most beauful of the Lakes," Sawrey must have had a salubrious effect on her, for she wrote in the journal on her birthday, "I feel much younger at thirty than I did at twenty." It was from the Lake District that she was encouraged to write and publish her first little book for children. The story of that book is a charming one, reminiscent of Lewis Carroll's *Alice in Wonderland,* which also began as a tale for a special child. Beatrix Potter had remained attached to her former governess even after Miss Annie Carter became Mrs. Moore and the mother of a large family. When five-year-old Noël Moore fell ill and was confined to bed for months, Beatrix Potter wrote a letter to him on 4 September 1893 which contained a story of her rabbit Peter, enhanced by her own little pictures: "Dear Noël, I don't know what to write to you, so I shall tell you a story about four little rabbits, whose names are Flopsy, Mopsy, Cottontail and Peter. . . ."

Fortunately, Noël had kept that letter and was able to relinquish it when she decided, eight years later, to copy it, revise and enlarge it, and send it to the publishers, Frederick Warne & Company—who promptly rejected it. Undaunted, she brought out a privately-printed edition of 250 copies of Peter Rabbit in December 1901. The following year, she resubmitted the story—and her writing career was inaugurated.

Other tales followed, and the earnings went toward the purchase of Hill Top Farm in Near Sawrey, that much loved place. Another career, in farming, was launched at Hill Top with the tenant farmer staying on to act as manager. The next eight years were the period of her greatest creativity. She produced thirteen books, of which six are concerned with the setting, activities, and people of Hill Top and Sawrey, in which she so delighted. Her children's fantasy world became extremely popular, and the financial success enabled her to buy more land.

But perhaps Hardcragg should be credited with giving Beatrix Potter the inspiration for her *Tale of Pigling Bland,* for she could look down at the piggery from a window of an upper bedroom in

320

which she stayed. Although she had her own prize-winning pigs, one of which became the prototype for the Pigling Bland character, another charming story attaches itself to Hardcragg:

The manager who ran the farm for Beatrix Potter often bought pedigree baby pigs from Farmer Townley. On one occasion he found himself too busy to fetch the baby pigs he had ordered. Beatrix offered to go there herself to visit the Townley farm and return with the pigs. While there, she took a liking to a tiny black female pig; but Townley refused to allow her to include it in the purchase, for it was non-pedigree. She pleaded and insisted that she would keep it apart and care for it herself. Townley had to give in. Obviously, Beatrix saw a story in it. She saw the baby pig as a companion for Pigling Bland. So Hardcragg Hall is intimately connected with the famous author. When the tale was published in 1913, it was to the two Townley children that it was dedicated: "For Cecily and Charlie, A Tale of the Christmas Pig."

That was the year for a major change in her life. She had purchased in 1909 Castle Farm, which could be seen from Hill Top and which had a field adjoining Hill Top property. The transaction was handled by the solicitor William Heelis, and she became Mrs. William Heelis in October 1913. She was forty-seven, and it was time for a change. Mrs. Heelis of Sawrey was a wife, farmer, conservationist, and happy resident of the Lake District for the next thirty years—until her death on 22 December 1943 at the age of seventy-seven.

HARDCRAGG HALL
Grange Fell Road
Grange-over-Sands
Cumbria LA11 6BJ

Telephone/Fax: (015395) 33353

All rooms have en suite bathrooms, television, and tea and coffee facilities.

The Dining Room seats 40 and offers an a la carte menu with local specialties such as Morecambe Bay shrimps.

Gardens have views over Morecambe Bay.

Lake Windermere is just a fifteen-minute drive to the north.

LADY MARY WORTLEY MONTAGU

at

Middlethorpe Hall

York

North Yorkshire

> I will be at M[iddlethorpe] with my family
> Tuesday next. . . . I will conclude you have
> taken M[iddlethorpe] and set out Monday if
> you don't say any thing to the Contrary
> between this and then.

—Letter to Wortley, 28 August 1713

Literary fame came to Lady Mary Wortley Montagu a year after her death, when her Turkish Embassy letters were published. Private letters, mostly to her daughter, Lady Bute, appeared still later, further enhancing her reputation as a writer of great wit and insight. Her reputation today rests primarily on her letters, and anthologies generally include examples of her art.

Her long and fascinating life shows many aspects of an intelligent, varied, and somewhat enigmatic existence. She accompanied her husband on his embassy to Turkey, popularized smallpox inoculation in England, was a patron of writers, and produced witty verse and lively essays on feminist topics. After her friendship with Alexander Pope deteriorated for reasons which remain unknown, she was attacked by the great poet of the day in his caustic verse. Finally, inexplicably, although still married, she left England at the age of fifty to live abroad until the year of her death in 1762, at the age of seventy-three.

Born on 26 May 1689, the infant assumed the title Lady Mary Pierrepont when her father inherited an earldom at the death of his older brother in 1690. An avid reader and learner, she began writing in her teens. During the London winter season of 1707, she met Edward Wortley Montagu, a rising Member of Parliament. Other meetings at other winter seasons followed. Despite a disapproving father and an unsmooth courtship, marriage came in 1712, and she became Lady Wortley Montagu.

During the summer of 1713, Wortley's political activities required his presence in the Yorkshire town of Boroughbridge. Lady Mary found a house in the village of Middlethorpe near York where the family, which now had an infant son, could be together. They all moved in in September. But her husband lost the election and returned to London. She followed him for a brief visit in the summer of 1714.

Back in Middlethorpe in mid-July, she complained bitterly in letters to her husband of his neglect: "You have forgot, I suppose, that you have a little Boy. . .I think you use me very unkindly. . . You write seldom. . . I complain of ill health and you only say, you hope tis not so bad as I make it. . . You never enquire after your Child. . . ."

Despite races at Hambledon Down near York, despite visits to Castle Howard some fourteen miles north of York, she felt lonely in the country and resented missing the coronation of King George I. Finally, she was able to return to the capital city. It must have been with great relief that she wrote to her husband on 5 January 1715, "I set out to Day from Middlethorpe. . . and hope to see you in London on Sunday or Monday next."

In London, the Montagus were active in social and literary circles. She attended court. Greatly admired for her intellect, wit, and beauty, she was a central and shining figure of the Augustan age. An aristocratic lady with much more than a room of her own, she applied herself to the writing of essays and verse. Her ecologues, noted for the satire aimed at particular people, were widely circulated. *Town Ecolgues* and *Court Poems by a Lady of Quality*, vibrant pictures of contemporary society, were first published in 1716.

In later years, she became herself the object of strong satiric barbs when the friendship with Alexander Pope turned to bitter enmity and Pope turned from compliments to castigation. From a

Portrait of Lady Mary Wortley Montagu (1689-1762) over oak staircase of the house in which she lived, Middlethorpe Hall, near York

beauty whose eyes "other Beauties envy," she became a "battered jade" who had given a French lover venereal disease. She survives in his verse, vilified by his vicious and insulting attacks.

Her husband became English ambassador to Constantinople in 1716, and the Montagus lived in Turkey. No mere appendage, she learned the Turkish language in order to gain valuable insights into that exotic country. Her fascinating letters include accounts of the feminine aspect of Turkish life. She saved the letters and edited them, having written them with the intention of achieving literary fame and recognition. Her success as a writer has secured a firm literary link for Middlethorpe.

Middlethorpe Hall measures up to the courtly circles in which the Montagus associated. The handsome home of the eminent lady of letters and writer of distinction was magnificently restored in 1984 and converted into a luxurious hotel under the aegis of Historic House Hotels. More like an elegant country house than a hotel, it offers pleasurable experiences to the literary pilgrim.

Originally built around 1699 for Thomas Barlow, a master cutler from Sheffield who wanted to achieve status as a country gentleman, Middlethorpe Hall makes an impressive appearance in its gardens and parkland setting. The red brick facade, with three full stories plus basement and raised stone parapet, is crowned by an eagle, the Barlow family crest. Flanking wings added in the mid-eighteenth century complete the striking picture.

Outbuildings include a restored seventeenth-century dovecote and a stable block converted to provide additional accommodation. The grounds have been improved with the construction of a lake and ha-ha (sunken fence to preserve the view), with planting of trees and replanting of the kitchen garden.

Good taste is carried into the interior where one particularly attractive feature is the oak staircase with carved balustrade leading to the twelve bedrooms on upper floors. A large portrait of Lady Mary Wortley Montague looks down from among the many paintings on the walls above the cantilevered staircase. There is also the paneled dining room, library, drawing rooms, and conference center.

Middlethorpe's convenient location allows for easy touring of the historic city of York with its medieval walls, the Minster, the Shambles, the Castle, the Jorvik Center with its Viking exposition, and countless other attractions. Add to these the attractions to be found in the countryside all around—Fountains Abbey, Castle Howard, Newby Hall, the Yorkshire dales—and the literary-pilgrim-turned-tourist could no doubt be persuaded to remain in this most pleasing of environments for a longer and happier time than the erstwhile lady of letters.

MIDDLETHORPE HALL
Bishopthorpe Road
York
North Yorkshire YO2 1QB

Telephone: (01904) 641241   Fax: (01904) 620176

Historic House Hotels Limited

A total of 31 bedrooms, some in the restored eighteenth-century courtyard, are individually decorated, each with Edwardian-style bathroom as well as television, radio, telephone, trouser press.

Public Rooms include dining room, library, drawing rooms, and a conference center known as the Barlow Room.

Gardens and parkland include a walled garden and small lake.

The hotel, overlooking the York racecourse, is situated a mile and a half from York city center and the railway station. The train journey from London, 209 miles away, takes one hour and fifty minutes.

ROBERT BURNS

at

Murray Arms Hotel
Gatehouse-of-Fleet
Dumfries and Galloway
Scotland

Scots, wha hae wi' Wallace bled,
Scots, wham Bruce has aften led,
Welcome to your gory bed,
    Or to victorie.

—March to Bannockburn

At the Murray Arms Hotel in Gatehouse-of-Fleet, they proudly point out the room—the Burns Room—in which Robert Burns composed the song that ranks with his "Auld Lang Syne" as one of the two most popular in Scotland. "Scots, wha hae wi' Wallace bled" would be the Scottish national anthem, if Scotland had a national anthem. "Patronised by Robert Burns" is the claim of this small, charming, and friendly hotel in a white-washed village about eight miles from the ancient town of Kirkcudbright.

Places associated with Burns are legion, thanks to his itinerant lifestyle. Particularly in his corner of Scotland, the southwest, Burns is celebrated everywhere. There is the Land o'Burns Motoring School, the Burns Emporium, garages, bakeries, restaurants, and innumerable, inevitable gift shops. Some adapt his poetic phrases for their names, as in "The Giftie Gie Us."

Robert Burns
(1759-1796)
and Murray
Arms Hotel,
Scotland, where
the poet penned
"Scots, wha hae
wi' Wallace
bled"

The cult of Burns has something of the seriousness of a religion with a pilgrimage route known as the Burns Heritage Trail. But in addition to places on the trail, the Murray Arms at Gatehouse-of-Fleet represents a stop that Burns made on a tour through Galloway.

Despite hard times, Burns managed the luxury of a week's holiday with John Syme. The two men first met in 1788 and became very close friends. Indeed, it was Syme who arranged the funeral when Burns died at the age of thirty-seven after long suffering from a heart ailment. On their tour through Galloway, the two friends made their first stop at Kenmore, where they stayed for three days before moving on to Gatehouse. They were caught in a storm and arrived at the inn wet through and railing at the elements. Burns comforted himself with drink. In the morning, his anger returned, for his boots had been badly dried and did not fit. He tore them trying in vain to pull them on and left bootless and feeling ill. Off they rode, and his good humor returned when they reached St. Mary's Isle as the guests of the Earl of Selkirk.

The trip took six days and took in very little territory but produced one very important work. Syme gives this account of the tour: "I told you that in the midst of the storm on the wilds of Kenmore, Burns was rapt in meditation. What do you think he was about? He was charging the English army, along with Bruce, at Bannockburn. He was engaged in the same manner on our ride from St. Mary's Isle, and I did not disturb him. . ."

Burns was immersed in political thoughts on the ride back to Dumfries but had apparently already sketched out the words which would express the defiant fight for liberty in "Scots, wha hae wi' Wallace bled." The idea must have been with him for a while, for his own account is expressed in a letter of 30 August 1793 to his Edinburgh music publisher, George Thomson. He wrote that "the old air, *Hey, Tutti Taitie*. . .has often filled my eyes with tears.— There is a tradition, which I have met with in many places of Scotland, that it was Robert Bruce's March at the battle of Bannockburn.—This thought, in my yesternight's evening walk, warmed me to a pitch of enthusiasm on the theme of Liberty & Independence, which I threw into a kind of Scots Ode, fitted to the

Air, that one might suppose to be the gallant ROYAL SCOT'S address to his heroic followers on that eventful morning."

Varying accounts describing the creation of the song are further complicated by the publisher's arbitrary decision to alter the tune and modify the words to make them fit. But he wisely relented and in a later edition allowed the words to revert to their original form. The history may remain unclear, but the song which was eventually produced is unquestionably inspired. It referred to the Battle of Bannockburn of 1314—except for the last two verses which clearly referred to the present:

> By Oppression's woes and pains!
> By your Sons in servile chains!
> We will drain our dearest vains,
> But they *shall* be free!

> Lay the proud Usurpers low!
> Tyrants fall in every foe!
> LIBERTY's in every blow!
> Let us DO—OR DIE!!!

The Murray Arms takes the credit for housing the poet when he felt inspired to create this rousing anthem. Perhaps they can do a better job now of drying wet boots. After all, they've been at it for a long time. In 1642 the part of the building that is now the coffee room housed the gatekeeper of the ford across the river, from which the town's name emanates. In 1760, James Murray enlarged the house and built the coaching inn that bears his name. The Murray Arms at Gatehouse-of-Fleet ought to be a worthwhile stop near the end of a Burns pilgrimage.

Chronologically, the Burns Heritage Trail begins at Alloway in Ayrshire where Burns was born on 25 January 1759. Alloway might have remained unnoticed were it not for Burns. The cottage in which he was born has been restored to admit throngs to one of the most visited houses in Scotland. Nearby is the Alloway Kirk ruin and the picturesque old Brig o'Doon over the River Doon.

Years later, he wrote the largely autobiographical *Cotter's Saturday Night* which relates to his early family life in this area:

> The toil-worn Cotter frae his labour goes,
> This night his weekly moil is at an end,
> Collects his spades, his mattocks and his hoes,
> Hoping the morn in ease and rest to spend,
> And weary, o'er the muir, his course does hameward bend.

The trail continues. His father, in the struggle to obtain a living as a farmer, left Alloway for the more remote Mount Oliphant farm, a few miles off, where Robert lived until his twelfth year. He was sent to Kirkoswald to learn "mensuration, surveying and dialling" in the hope that he could be spared the hardships of a farming life. In Kirkoswald, he bragged, he learned to drink (an activity for which he is famous). He also met and fell in love with a young lady (another of his famous activities) who distracted him from trigonometry. His studies were unsuccessful, but he did meet many colorful Kirkoswald people, on whom he later based the characters who appear in his well-known *Tam O'Shanter*. Also on the pilgrim's trail is the thatched cottage of Souter Johnnie, Tam's drinking companion in the poem. The Tam O'Shanter Inn, a favorite alehouse of Burns on his frequent visits to Ayr, appears in that famous work of his and exists today as a museum.

Unremitting poverty followed the family, and another move was made in 1777 to Lochlie, two miles from the village of Tarbolton. To enliven village life, Burns and his friends founded a debating society in 1780, the Bachelors' Club, in a thatched cottage which now serves as a museum.

When his father, worn out by work and worry, died in 1784, the family moved to the neighboring Mossgiel farm. It still stands, but the best remembrance of the Burns connection there is the poem he was inspired to write while ploughing, *To a Mountain-Daisy*:

> Wee, modest, crimson-tipped flow'r,
> Thou's met me in an evil hour;
> For I maun crush amang the stours

Thy slender stem:
To spare thee now is past my pow'r,
Thou bonnie gem.

In the nearby village of Mauchline (with its memorial tower that contains yet another museum), he met and fell in love with Jean Armour. The young couple began married life in 1788 in a house in Castle Street, now a museum known, inevitably, as the Burns House. Another Mauchline landmark is Poosie Nansie's Tavern, not much changed from the poet's time and immortalized in *The Jolly Beggars*.

After a final unproductive and unprofitable attempt at farming in Ellisland, Burns became an excise officer and went with his family to Dumfries in 1791. There he spent his final years. At the Globe Inn in Dumfries, the visitor may still imbibe refreshment as Burns did. The family lived in a three-room flat in Wee Vennel (now Bank Street) before moving to a house in Mill Vennell (now Burns Street) where he died on 21 July 1796. That fine sandstone house of two stories completes the cycle—as you might have guessed—as a museum of Burns relics.

The tourist interested in seeing Scotland would probably unavoidably come upon taverns and sights related to Burns. With luck, a visitor might even chance upon the Murray Arms Hotel. But why take the risk of missing this attractive, old, former coaching inn? It is a place full of character, a friendly place for enjoying a pint with the locals in one of the two cozy bars or for relaxing in one of the four comfortable lounges. Even in fiction, in *The Five Red Herrings* by Dorothy L. Sayers, a character has a "drink at the Murray Arms in Gatehouse . . . ."

The Murray Arms is an ideal location for investigating the historically rich and beautiful countryside. "A very popular base from which to explore Galloway," states the hotel brochure. There would seem to be no escape from Burns, for that is exactly what Burns was doing when he stopped at the Murray Arms in Gatehouse-of-Fleet—exploring Galloway. Properly fortified, like Burns, the guest might, like Burns, find poetic inspiration.

THE MURRAY ARMS HOTEL
Gatehouse-of-Fleet
Dumfries and Galloway
Scotland DG7 2HY

Telephone: (01557) 814207   Fax: (01557) 814370

Rooms: Twelve bedrooms with private bathrooms, plus a self-contained garden suite.

Restaurants: One of the three dining rooms of this Scottish coaching inn, the Lunky Hole, is open all day and serves a wide range of hot and cold snacks and meals.

DOROTHY L. SAYERS

at

The Anwoth Hotel
Gatehouse-of-Fleet
Dumfries and Galloway
Scotland

Passing over the bridge at Gatehouse,
with these intentions, he was arrested by
the sight of a tall man standing outside the
Anwoth Hotel in conference with the local
constable.

—*Five Red Herrings*

A writer of detective novels, poetry, religious dramas, articles on
the Christian faith, translator of Dante, and lecturer, Dorothy Leigh
Sayers was born in Oxford on 13 June 1893. But when she was
four, her father, headmaster of the Christ Church Cathedral Choir
School transferred to the country rectory of Bluntisham in the fens
of East Anglia. Some years later, her unworldly father moved again
to the even more remote, smaller parish of Christchurch deeper in
the Cambridgeshire fens.

Educated at the rectory until she was fifteen, the awkward
teenager was sent to the Godolphin School in Salisbury where she
was a lonely misfit. A severe case of measles caused baldness, and
she suffered a nervous breakdown. It was Oxford at last when she
received a scholarship for Somerville College. She completed her
studies in modern languages as an honors graduate, but a degree
was not granted until 1920, when Oxford changed its rules about
awarding degrees to women.

Uncertain what to do with her life, she worked for a while in Oxford, learning the publishing trade at Blackwell's. Then she went to a boys' school in France as administrative assistant to Eric Whelpton, the first great but unreciprocated love of her life. When that position came to an end after a year, she decided to live in London and found a residence in Bloomsbury which she retained until the end of her life. She also found a job as a copywriter at an advertising agency which she retained for ten years.

While happily employed at Benson's Advertising Agency in the production of such projects as the great mustard campaign, she reasoned that writing detective fiction could be the best means for earning the most money and created her famous detective-hero, Lord Peter Wimsey. The second son of the late Duke of Denver shared her own tastes for scholarship, languages, good music, and fine wine. Blessed with elegant manners, wit, and talent, he could play piano and harpsichord, punt a boat, swim, dance, or play cricket. He materialized with apparent ease, she explained, for he simply "walked in, complete with spats, and applied in an airy don't-care-if-I-get-it way for the job of hero."

A slightly arrogant figure who sported a monocle, Lord Peter was also a lovable and intriguing personality who did indeed bring her fame and fortune. He was engaged for fifteen years, going from an initial appearance in *Whose Body?* in 1923 to appearances in eleven other novels, three volumes of short stories, a play, and numerous articles.

That year, she took a six months' leave of absence from her job as copywriter, ostensibly to write another novel. It was a good reason. The real reason was that she was pregnant. She went to Bournemouth where her son was born on 3 January 1924. Maintaining total secrecy, she placed him in the care of Ivy Shrimpton, an eccentric cousin who was making a living by caring for orphaned children. Having provided for his upkeep, she returned to her work at Benson's and to the writing of her second novel, *Clouds of Witness*. She had managed to cover her tracks and to conceal all the misery she was feeling by putting on an untroubled facade. But her physical appearance was changing, for she began during this period to put on weight.

Dorothy L. Sayers (1893-1957) and the Anwoth Hotel in Gatehouse-of-Fleet, Scotland, the setting for *Five Red Herrings*

Quite wretched and quite unable to find a Peter Wimsey in her own life, that special and permanent partner who could offer love and happiness, she was becoming plump and ungainly, with thin hair and thick glasses. Then she met Oswald Arthur Fleming, whom she married in 1926.

Fleming, a divorced man with two daughters, was a journalist who, it turned out, embellished his credentials and his talents. His involvement in a myriad of interests and subjects was part of the appeal of this attractive and personable man. She shared his love of good food, and his interest in gourmet cooking resulted in production of a cookery book, dedicated to his wife "who can make an Omelette." As an amateur painter, he was able to supply the facts his wife needed for *Five Red Herrings*. But he was basically a second-rate writer, a braggart and pretender, and it was not long before the marriage went wrong.

Happiness continued to elude her; a rich or rewarding love relationship never developed between them. The charm he had at first exhibited waned as he became unwell, unemployed, and resentful. He never allowed her son to live with them, although the boy took on his name. His dependence on drink intensified, and the marriage became increasingly uncomfortable. She decided to stick it out with him despite the strangeness, illness, and excessive drinking which made him an ever-present problem. (He died in 1950 at the age of sixty-nine.)

Her writing progressed. The third Wimsey novel, *Unnatural Death*, appeared in 1927. The following year saw publication of *The Unpleasantness at the Bellona Club* and a volume of short stories, *Lord Peter Views the Body*. She revealed her troubles in *The Documents in the Case* (1930), her only crime novel in which Wimsey does not appear and in which the victim Harrison— jealous, nagging, demanding—is based on Fleming.

That year, in *Strong Poison*, she introduced the character of Harriet Vane, a tall, dark-haired, plain person, who is based on Sayers herself. Harriet, like the author, is a detective-story writer who came from a small village and went to Oxford. She is totally oblivious to fashionable dress, enjoys smoking, and loves her work. Having tired of Wimsey, Sayers created Harriet as a means of dispensing with him by marrying him off to her alter ego. However, she needed the income her hero generated, and he was allowed to live.

Wimsey next appeared in a book which emanated from regular summer holidays in southern Scotland taken to help Fleming recuperate from deteriorating health. *Five Red Herrings* (1931), set in the landscape around Galloway, was a tribute to the place and the people she liked so well. They stayed at the Anwoth Hotel in Gatehouse-of-Fleet, an artistic colony with a temperate climate, where Fleming painted while she wrote.

With her strong sense of place, Sayers was often inspired by the settings she knew from life. *Murder Must Advertise* (1933), written a few years after she left Benson's, emanated from the advertising world in which she worked. The countryside of her childhood, the fens of East Anglia, she used in *The Nine Tailors* (1934). The drama she found in Oxford was incorporated into *Gaudy Night* (1935), the Oxford novel in which Harriet and Peter finally come together. It was quite natural for the Galloway landscape of her pleasurable summer holiday excursions to become the background for *Five Red Herrings*. She assured her readers that the landscape was authentic, although the characters were not.

With *Busman's Honeymoon* (1937), the last Wimsey novel, the acknowledged master of the detective story form turned to the theatre. She now had enough steady income from royalties to feel free to choose her own path, and her path led from theatre to theology and Dante scholarship.

After *Busman's Honeymoon* was produced in the West End, she was asked to write a play for the Canterbury Festival, and *The Zeal of Thy House* was performed in the cathedral in June 1937. Other religious plays followed, particularly for the BBC, as well as articles and books on the Christian faith. *The Mind of the Maker*, generally singled out as the best of her theological works, examined the Trinity in terms of human creativity.

She found fulfillment with devotion to Dante—translation and interpretation of an interest that was always there. Her very first novel began with Wimsey going to a book auction to bid on a medieval folio Dante. Now, some twenty-five years later, she wanted to write a translation suitable for ordinary readers, not scholars. *Hell* was completed in 1949 and *Purgatory* in 1953. But only twenty cantos of *Paradise* were completed before she died suddenly in December 1957.

Dorothy L. Sayers was an exceptional writer in a wide variety of forms. She was also a speaker who enthralled her audiences. For her Dante scholarship, she received an honorary Doctorate in Letters. But of all her works—poetical, historical, scholarly— it is surely the detective novels that will last the longest. They continue to be printed, read, dramatized, and enjoyed. It is satisfying to consider that in one of those enduring detective mysteries, the pleasant hotel in Gatehouse-of-Fleet has been immortalized.

The Anwoth Hotel appears in *Five Red Herrings* as a hub of activity. Not only is the suspect Jock Graham staying there, but a bicycle belonging to the landlord's son has been stolen from the Anwoth; it must be retrieved as a prime exhibit for the murder inquiry.

In a foreward to the novel, the author addresses Joe Dignam as the "kindliest of landlords." She gives her assurance that "all the landscapes are correct" and that "we shall come back next summer to eat some more potato-scones at the Anwoth."

The landlords at the Anwoth Hotel are still kindly as they maintain a small and friendly family-run hotel. It has a pretty setting with gardens backing up to the River Fleet. A good view can be had from the first-floor hotel dining room, which offers traditional Scottish fare from a menu that presumably includes potato scones. Also on the first floor is a function room, often used for large parties.

A total of nine bedrooms are on the upper two floors. When Dorothy L. Sayers stayed with her husband, the proprietor informs, they occupied what is now Room Number 6, a twin-bedded room at the back, overlooking the river.

In addition to the present landlord's testimony, older inhabitants of Gatehouse recall her residency at the hotel. A few are happy to recount such reminiscences as that of an intoxicated Fleming driving home at night and crashing into a wall, fortunately with no one hurt. The accident occurred on the very stretch of road described in *Five Red Herrings* as "about half-way between Gatehouse and Kirkudbright, at a point where the road makes a very sharp and dangerous S-bend"; it is the spot where the spanner, the murder weapon, was found.

The presence of Dorothy L. Sayers at the Anwoth Hotel is unmistakable. She stayed there, dined there, and knew the people who ran it. Her existence is permanently impressed in the little hotel which she made the center of the area used as the background of her book.

The exceptionally beautiful landscape of the Dumfries and Galloway area is dotted with castles. A fifteenth-century tower house on the edge of town, Cardoness Castle, finds its way into *Five Red Herrings* when Wimsey drives his Daimler down the highway that is now the A75. "He passed through Gatehouse, waving a cheerful hand to the proprietor of the Anwoth Hotel, climbed up beneath the grim blackness of Cardoness Castle. . . . then Newton-Stewart."

Although he went to view the body at Newton-Stewart, one might go to view the woolen mills in this lovely little Galloway town on the River Cree, spanned by a granite bridge which links it to Minnigaff and its ruined church on the other side. One might also take in all the sights viewed by the fictional hero—"the Italian loveliness of Kirkdale, with its fringe of thin and twisted trees and the blue Wigtownshire coast gleaming across the bay. . . .the old Border keep of Barholm. . . salmon-nets and the wide semi- circular sweep of the bay. . . the huge hump of Cairnsmuir rising darkly over Creetown. . . . the cottages with their roses and asters clustered against white and yellow walls. . . then Newton-Stewart, all grey roofs huddling down to the stony bed of the Cree. . . .Over the bridge and away to the right by the kirkyard. . . ."

Or one could remain at the Anwoth Hotel in Gatehouse pondering the mystery of good detective fiction at a place that gave pleasure to one who wrote it.

THE ANWOTH HOTEL
Gatehouse-of-Fleet
Dumfries and Galloway
Scotland DG7 2JT

Telephone: (01557) 814217

Nine bedrooms, seven with private bathrooms, are simply furnished with fitted wardrobes and dressing tables. Two on the top story are family rooms, and four have river views.

Dinner and lunch menus offer a choice of traditional Scottish fare as well as Continental dishes.

The Ship Cocktail Bar also serves meals throughout the day, and pub food is availabe in the Public Bar.

ROBERT LOUIS STEVENSON

at

The Hawes Inn
South Queensferry
Lothian
Scotland

The old Hawes Inn at the Queen's Ferry
makes a similar call upon my fancy. There it
stands, apart from the town, beside the pier,
in a climate of its own, half inland, half
marine—in front, the ferry bubbling with
the tide. . .behind, the old garden with the
trees.

—A Gossip on Romance

Eight miles from Stevenson's birthplace of Edinburgh, on the
Firth of Forth where the long suspension bridge was completed in
1964, is Queensferry. For some eight hundred years before the
gigantic bridge was built, travelers were taken across the Firth of
Forth by ferry. In the late eleventh century, Queen Margaret was a
regular passenger, thereby giving the town its name.

Just south of the Forth Bridge, an ancient and inconspicuous
little inn which has managed to retain its character for some
three hundred years, makes itself known because of its literary
connections—the Hawes Inn. Sir Walter Scott used the Hawes Inn
in *The Antiquary*, and Robert Louis Stevenson took himself and
the hero of *Kidnapped* to the inn. Apart from the imposing steel
railway bridge which overhangs the inn today, the scene is very
much as it was when Stevenson described it. The ancient-looking
grey town straggles westward from the Hawes along a single street,
melancholy and sleepy. David Balfour says in Chapter XXVII of

Kidnapped: "I was in the long street of Queensferry before the sun was up. It was a fairly built burgh, the houses of good stone, many slated; the town-hall not so fine, I thought, as that of Peebles, nor yet the street so noble; but, take it altogether, it put me to shame for my foul tatters."

The Hawes Inn today, with its old oak beams, is full of charm and is fully capable of transporting the visitor to the past and to the pages of Stevenson's adventure story.

At the Hawes Inn they may kindly point out the room in which the author wrote *Kidnapped*, but he actually wrote it many years later while living at Bournemouth. Stevenson is associated with a wide variety of geographical names throughout the world. Because of poor health, and the concomitant need to reside in more salubrious climes than Edinburgh, he developed an early love for travel.

From the time of his birth on 13 November 1850, Robert Louis Stevenson was always frail and sickly. Even as a child, he went to Scottish health resorts or left the cold North altogether for recuperative holidays. His precarious state of health instilled in him a restlessness and made him an incurable wanderer who always collected the memories of places he had been to and enjoyed. Those scenes he stored away to be selected and used as needed in his later writing, making them come alive for future generations.

He had always been a great story-teller with an active imagination. Alison Cunningham, the nurse who looked after him through illnesses and helped to guard his feeble strength, maintained that he was only three when he told her a story he had made up and asked her to write it down. Even if her testimony lacks real evidence, he did dictate to his mother, when he was six, an essay which still exists. And he had written many stories by the time he was thirteen.

He was expected to follow in his father's footsteps and become an engineer. But he desperately wanted to be a writer. He and his father reached an impasse when he found engineering unsuitable as a profession, and his father found writing unacceptable as a career. A compromise was reached when he was allowed to read for the bar. Although he passed the examination and became a

Robert Louis
Stevenson
(1850-1894) and
Hawes Inn, where
both the author
and the hero of
Kidnapped stayed

lawyer in Edinburgh, he never gave up the idea of authorship. Added to the constant struggle with ill health was the struggle for recognition as a writer.

Fortunately, the places he visited made keen impressions on his mind and gave him sources for his writing. His first book, *An Inland Voyage,* was an account of a canoe trip taken in 1876 in Belgium and France. In it he wrote: "On my tomb, if ever I have one, I mean to get these words inscribed: 'He clung to his paddle'." He did cling to his paddle—that is, to his pen. Two years later he set out on a donkey and described that journey in *Travels with a Donkey in the Cévennes.*

While traveling in France he met Fanny van de Grift Osbourne and made what would seem a most unsuitable match. She was an American, estranged from her husband, with two children (her youngest had recently died), and ten years older than he. Naturally, his parents disapproved and cut off financial support. Fanny returned to California in 1878, and he joined her the following year when he learned that she was suffering from inflammation of the brain. The journey, made in dire circumstances, across the ocean on an emigrant ship and then across the country by train, made him critically ill. On arrival, it was he, not Fanny, who was close to death. She nursed him back to health and, her divorce granted, they were married in May 1880.

The strange honeymoon, which included Fanny's twelve-year-old son Lloyd, produced *The Silverado Squatters.* It describes the time spent in a deserted mining camp fifty miles north of San Francisco and makes Silverado sound exotic with depictions of adventure, freedom, excitement. But the author also describes accurately the filth, squalor, discomforts, hardships, and dangers of their derelict living quarters in a place infested with rattlesnakes.

On a reconciliation visit to his forgiving and affectionate parents in Edinburgh, Fanny captivated her in-laws and was completely accepted by them. But Stevenson was prevented from living in Scotland by the severe winters which were detrimental to his health.

For amusement on one rainy holiday morning in Scotland, young Lloyd drew a map of an imaginary island. His stepfather

346

elaborated on the map, labelled it "Treasure Island," and improvised an accompanying story; thus began Stevenson's first novel, a spontaneous work of fiction with a magic that continues to enchant readers. When it was published as a book in November 1884, *Treasure Island* established his literary reputation.

It was while abroad, during a winter in Davos, that he wrote *A Gossip on Romance* to define his aims in the writing of fiction. After more traveling in the south of France and more serious illness, the Stevensons settled in Bournemouth in a house called Skerryvore. There, as part of his prolific output and proof of versatility, he finished *A Child's Garden of Verses*. He wrote the hugely successful *Dr. Jekyll and Mr. Hyde,* and he produced, in 1886, *Kidnapped,* the book considered his best by many, including Henry James who came often to Skerryvore to visit his friend. Now, at the age of thirty-six, his financial independence was achieved.

Letters from Bournemouth to his father and to a cousin show how meticulous he was about getting the geography and topography of *Kidnapped* right. He knew the island of Earraid on which the ship is wrecked, and he knew the country in which the young hero wanders and meets Alan Breck. And he certainly knew the Hawes Inn and the neighborhood of the inn. From the Hawes Inn, David Balfour sets out at the beginning of *Kidnapped.* To it he returns after his dangerous wanderings through the wilderness of Scotland.

So the visitor to Queensferry and the Hawes Inn may actually *feel* the presence there of Robert Louis Stevenson. Identification with the author's words is made complete by looking at the Firth of Forth setting and recalling the scene:

> . . .backed against a pretty garden of holly-trees and hawthorne, I could see the building which they called the Hawes Inn.
> The town of Queensferry lies farther west, and the neighbourhood of the inn looked pretty lonely at that time of day, for the boat had just gone north with passengers.

A year after *Kidnapped* was published, Stevenson, who had remained an invalid during the three-year period spent in Bournemouth, decided to return to America, having been advised to live in Colorado for his health. But the idea of a yacht voyage took hold of him, and from San Francisco he undertook a cruise of the South Pacific.

His wanderings came to an end in Samoa, where he settled in December 1889 and lived for the rest of his life. In Samoa, he wrote *Catriona*, a sequel to *Kidnapped*. He found health and a high literary position in his Utopia.

His sudden death occurred on 3 December 1894, when he was forty-four. He was buried in Samoa, and his own lines are engraved on the tombstone:

> Under the wide and starry sky,
> Dig the grave and let me lie.
> Glad did I live and gladly die,
> And I laid me down with a will.

> This be the verse you grave for me:
> *Here he lies where he longed to be;*
> *Home is the sailor, home from the sea,*
> *And the hunter home from the hill.*

HAWES INN
Newhalls Road
South Queensferry
Lothian
Scotland EH30 9TA

Telephone: (0131) 331 1990   Fax: (0131) 319 1120

Eight bedrooms, all with tea/coffee making facilities and full Scottish breakfast, invite the guest to emulate Stevenson who "lived at the Hawes in a perpetual flutter on the heels. . . of some adventure." Available and overlooking the Firth of Forth is room number 13, the bedroom in which Stevenson wrote.

Other facilities of this traditional Scottish coaching inn: the Hawes Inn Restaurant, the Turret Room (for private parties of up to thirty-five people), the Grill Room (for up to seventy- eight people), a bar with a family room, and a large garden.

The location is ten miles from Edinburgh city center, five miles from Edinburgh airport, and just one mile from Dalmeny railway station.

INDEX